ROSECRANS MEETS PRICE

The Battle of Iuka, Mississippi

By Ben Earl Kitchens

Thornwood Book Publishers
Florence, Alabama

Dedicated to Kakijane, Laura, and Kecia.

Library of Congress Cataloging in Publication Data

Kitchens, Ben Earl, 1942–
  Rosecrans meets Price, the Battle of Iuka.

  Bibliography: p.
  Includes index.
1. Iuka (Miss.) --History, Siege, 1862. I. Title.
E474.42.K57 1987   973.7'33   87-18089
ISBN 0-943054-42-7   (pbk. : alk. paper)

Manufactured in the United States of America

Published by Thornwood Book Publishers
P. O. Box 1442
Florence,   AL 35631

CONTENTS

PREFACE

While encamped in the woods near Jacinto, Mississippi and half expecting to be attacked, Union Major S. H. M. Byers obtained notice that General Sterling Price's great Southern Army was in Iuka, some eighteen miles away. Eagerly his excited regiment, the 5th Iowa Infantry, led the march of Rosecran's army over the narrow country roads toward the Confederates. The fall foliage was showy and Byers later commented that it seemed too lovely a day for war and bloodshed. How wrong he was! Within only a few hours, almost half of the Iowans would be dying among the colorful autumn leaves a mile south of Iuka.

During the War Between the States, Major Byers met the Confederates at Corinth, Missionary Ridge, and in other battles but it was the Battle of Iuka that he said was the "fiercest little conflict of the war . . .Antietam, Gettysburg, the Wilderness, could show nothing like it," he later wrote. "Only the setting sun put an end to what part of the time was a hand to hand conflict," he said. "For hours the blue and the gray stood within forty yards of each other and poured in sheets of musketry."

Many other participants in the Battle of Iuka commented, in later writings, on the ferociousness of the contest and upon how uninterrupted was the musket fire. According to Captain Albert Smith of the 8th Wisconsin Infantry the musketry was the "heaviest and most continuous that I have ever heard, entirely drowning the sound of a section of artillery" which was stationed on his right.

It is the story of this intensively savage but brief and indecisive engagement that occured one mile south of the village of Iuka, Mississippi on the afternoon of September 19, 1862, that I have attempted to tell in this writing. Events leading up to the battle, including Colonel Robert C. Murphy's brief occupation of Iuka prior to the battle and General Price's rapid retreat thereafter, are described. Considerable space is given to the death and burial of General Price's beloved division commander, General Henry Little. His passing was of such importance, especially as to its effect on General Price, that had he lived, the outcome of the contest might have been greatly altered.

With the exception of Dudley's <u>Battle of Iuka</u>, there have been no other books published that have dealt exclusively with the overall Iuka battle. Dudley was editor of the Iuka <u>Vidette</u> and quite a history buff. When he published his work in 1896 he had the advantage of being able to consult with participants in the battle who were still living at that time. A copy of his book is in the Mississippi Archives and Lyla McDonald preserved most of his account in her <u>Iuka's History</u> published in 1923, reprints of which are available at the Iuka Public Library. I found Dudley's work helpful and generally accurate.

For students of history interested in pursuing the Battle of Iuka in more detail, there are many informative and delightful works listed in the bibliography. Anderson's history of the First Missouri Confederate Brigade, Barron's <u>Lone Star Defenders,</u> and Tunnard's story of the 3rd Louisiana Infantry are classic works available in reprint with informative chapters on Iuka. Volume II of <u>Battles</u> and <u>Leaders of the Civil War</u> has descriptions of the battle by General Price's Adjutant Snead and Union General Hamilton. <u>The Official Records of the War of the Rebellion</u> contains a wealth of information, particularly as regards battle reports and correspondence. Bearss, in <u>Decision in Mississippi</u>, reorganized much of the scattered information in the <u>Official Records</u> to provide a lengthy and factual account.

Although I never found General Henry Little's original leather-backed diaries, the U. S. Army Military History Institute provided a copy of the original transcriptions and William Winter of Des Peres, Missouri led me to Castel's edited version which was published in "Civil War Times Illustrated" in 1972. The latter was very descriptive and helpful.

Albert Castel's book on General Price, <u>General Sterling Price and the Civil War in the West</u>, Hartje's biography of Van Dorn, Cresap's book about General Ord, and Grant's <u>Personal Memoirs</u> were all useful. Lamer's biography of Rosecrans, <u>The Edge of Glory, A Biography of General William S. Rosecrans</u>, was the best I found, although a bit one sided. General Grant and Rosecrans feuded for years after the Battle of Iuka, partially as the result of disagreements regarding troop development there. Grant apparently never completely forgave Rosecrans for leaving the Fulton Road open, allowing General Price's army to escape.

A first-hand account of the decimation of the 11th Ohio Battery is aptly and handsomely given in Neil's <u>A Battery at Close Quarters</u>. Another account, remarkably done, is Brown's <u>History of the Fourth Regiment of Minnesota Infantry Volunteers During the Great Rebellion.</u> Brown makes the assertion, after descriptions of several instances of Unionist firing into their own men due to smoke, darkness, and carelessness, that he believed that there were more Union men killed as the result of men firing into their own lines, than by the Confederates!!

Besides those already mentioned, there are many others to whom I owe much thanks. Dr. Gerald Golden of Martinsburg, West Virginia contributed a lot of unpublished information about the 37th Alabama

Regiment. Mike Vanderboegh of Pinson, Alabama helped tremendously with sources of information. Lamar Fly of Cuero, Texas graciously loaned his grandfather's unpublished account, Major George Washington Lafayette Fly's "Before, During, and After the Battle of Iuka." Finally, my search for information was much facilitated by interlibrary loans. To the excellent staffs of the Iuka Public Library and the Northeast Mississippi Regional Library System, I am much indebted.

Ben Earl Kitchens
September 1987

"OLE PAP" AND "ROSY"
CHAPTER ONE

The early summer of 1862 was oppressively hot and daytime mid-June temperatures hovered around 100 degrees in the hills and valleys of Old Tishomingo County. Thick layers of dust settled over yards, roadbeds and fields and rose in dense clouds from the parched ground whenever it was disturbed by men or animals. "Terrible weather for marching," General Sherman wrote, "dust and heat insufferable." [1] It was a very unpleasant time for General Beauregard's Confederates, who were encamped in the region of Tupelo, Mississippi, and for the huge army of Federal troops commanded by General Halleck that was spread along the Memphis and Charleston Railroad with headquarters in Corinth, Mississippi. Most of the Confederates had no tents but had become accustomed to camping without them. They had built huts of green branches that shielded them from the hot sun [2] Creeks and small streams were shriveled and usually dependable wells had dried up. Even the Iuka Springs, where tourists had flocked each summer before the war began, went dry for the third time in a century. The huge concentration of soldiers and their mules, horses, and other animals had polluted the drinking water around Corinth, rendering it unsafe. Both the Federals, heavily garrisoned in Corinth, and the Rebels in the Tupelo area, relied heavily on wells. [3] One of the Yankee soldiers wrote in his diary, "Hot and dusty; poor water and not much to eat; boys grumbling." [4]

Fleas and body lice tormented Yankees and Rebels alike and diarrhea and dysentery were all-pervasive and had no respect for position or rank. Union General Halleck corresponded with fellow officer General Pope. He told him that he would come to see him but that he had been confined to his tent with the "Evacuation of Corinth." [5] General Pope was also ill and General Sherman was "quite unwell". [6] Confederate General Henry Little, in the Tupelo area, was so sick that he had to be transported around by ambulance. [7] One of the Louisiana Confederate officers later summed up the extent of illness in Tupelo: "Look at our company . . 21 have died of disease, 18 have become so unhealthy as to be discharged, and only 4 have been killed in battle." [8]

One of the Union soldiers wrote from the hospital:

"For weeks the deaths averaged one a day for each of the new regiments, and nearly that for the old regiments counting the same number of men. For a while the dead were buried with customary honors of war; finally the sound of the three volleys became so depressing to the sick that it was by order discontinued. The men moved around with a sort of dogged indifference, apparently careless what befell them . . . . The weather was excessively hot, the water was filthy, the air was poisoned by the exhalations from thousands of sinks and cesspools, as well as from thousands of graves of men and animals, while it was almost impossible to find any open ground within a radius of five miles from Corinth that had not been used as a camp by the troops of one or the other of the armies. Under such circumstances no one can wonder that disease and death had a rich harvest."[9]

When Corinth was evacuated by Confederate General P. G. T. Beauregard on May 30, 1862, he reported about 53,000 effectives under his command. General Halleck's Union forces at the time numbered over 100,000 effectives. As the Confederates moved toward Tupelo, General Halleck garrisoned his army in the Corinth area along the line of the railroad. Then both armies lapsed into a period of inactivity. General Beauregard, who had been in ill health, went on sick leave to Mobile and left General Braxton Bragg in command of the Confederate forces. Apparently awaiting a good chance to dispose Beauregard of his command, President Jefferson Davis appointed General Bragg to the position. [10]

While General Bragg was shaping up his troops in Tupelo, Halleck's giant army dismantled. General John Pope was ordered to the East and his army distributed among other generals: General Don Carlos Buell's Army was turned eastward toward Chattanooga; General George H. Thomas was reassigned to his division in the Army of the Ohio; and Generals S. A. Hurlbut and W. T. Sherman were sent westward. [11] In July, General Halleck was called to Washington to become General-in-Chief and General U. S. Grant was left in command of about 60,000 troops in the vicinity of Corinth and Memphis. [12]

When Union General Buell moved into eastern Tennessee, Chattanooga was placed in danger and Rebel leader Bragg counteracted by moving an army of about 35,000 effectives to that city. All horsedrawn elements were directed to move overland and the infantry was sent by rail by way of Mobile, Montgomery, and Atlanta. The defense of Mississippi was left to Major General Earl Van Dorn who was to hold the line of the Mississippi and Major General Sterling Price who was to operate against the Union troops stationed in Corinth and posted along the Memphis and Charleston Railroad. [13]

General Price assumed his command on July 21, 1862. His district was named the District of the Tennessee, which comprised Northwestern Alabama and all that portion of the State of Mississippi which lay north of the 32nd parallel latitude and east of the Pearl River, and of the line of the Mississippi Central Railroad from Jackson to Grand Junction. His headquarters were to be in Tupelo until further orders were given.[14]

General Price's troops were distributed into two divisions and a cavalry brigade, commanded, respectively, by Brigadier Generals Little and Maury and acting Brigadier General Armstrong. Little's division (which was larger because of the recent addition of six regiments of Mississippi troops) consisted of four brigades, commanded by Brigadier Generals He'bert and Green and Colonels Gates and Martin. Maury's division consisted of three brigades, under the command of Brigadier General Moore and Majors Cabell and Phifer. Colonel Armstrong, who commanded the cavalry brigade, was an acting brigadier general by appointment of General Bragg. His brigade consisted of five regiments and three battalions.[15]

As General Price became so important in the struggle for Iuka, a brief review of his life's history to this point is appropriate:

As measured by the usual standards of military leadership, General Price would probably not be considered an outstanding commander. To the common soldiers of his command, however, he was the "greatest" and they affectionately referred to him as "Old Pap". His men were unwavering in their loyalty to him and followed him with blind devotion in battle after battle.

General Price was over six feet tall, handsome, and genteel. His striking presence on the battlefield or in parade commanded respect from all who saw him. He felt comfortable in the exercise of authority and, with his white hair and sideburns, was a dashing figure as he personally led his men into the heat of battle. Although loved and admired by those in his army, his personal ambition and vanity caused him numerous problems with other leaders of the Confederate command system.

Sterling Price was born in 1809 in Prince Edward County, Virginia, the third son of Pugh and Elizabeth Price. His father was from an established Virginia family. As a young boy, Sterling assisted with the family's tobacco crop as Prince Edward County planters considered it necessary that their sons learn tobacco farming. Upon completion of his primary education, young Price attended a nearby college for one year and later went to Creed Taylor's Law School in Cumberland County. He did not graduate, however, nor receive more than a minimal legal education.

Sterling did not wish to remain in Virginia and, in 1830, moved with his family to Missouri. His father owned about a dozen slaves and these were taken with them on the strenuous overland trip. Upon reaching

Willie Smith of Belmont, Mississippi with a 3 inch fired Hotchkiss shell found near the Iuka battleground.

Missouri, the Price family purchased land for tobacco growing and tried to recreate the old Virginia plantation type lifestlye they had enjoyed in the Old Dominion. Sterling was ambitious as well as able and within two years of his arrival in Missouri, easily moved among the county's leading citizens. [16]

In 1833 Sterling married Martha Head, a judge's daughter who had also been born in Virginia. The union produced five sons and one daughter and several others who died at birth or early infancy. [17] By 1840 Sterling had became prosperous and owned several dozen slaves. He decided that it was time to enter politics and soon was elected to the Missouri legislature. Two years later he became speaker of the House of Representatives. His spectacular political career continued and, in 1844, he was elected to the House of Representatives in Washington. [18]

Price's powerful presence and persuasive skills were well suited to his work in congress and later as a military officer. He was described as pompous by some of his political opponents but he had the ability to elicit loyalty from the voters and he became a leading figure in the state Democratic party. [19]

In August 1846, following the outbreak of the Mexican War, Price resigned from Congress and became a colonel of a regiment of Missourians. He subsequently assumed command of the American occupation of New Mexico. Although he sometimes acted insubordinately, quarreled with other officials, and was lax in discipline, he had many successes. The reinforcement of these types of behavior gave him an overrated opinion of himself and his abilities. [20] He was promoted to brigadier general and returned from the war with a reputation as a military leader, although his military experience had, in fact, been quite minimal. During the Mexican War many of his victories were obtained by dashing after poorly armed Indians and Mexicans without proper regard for logistical support. During that conflict he was able to fight without much support but during the subsequent American Civil War his lack of concern for logistics would be more telling and cause him a lot of problems. [21]

After the Mexican War, Price reentered politics and in 1853 was elected governor of Missouri. It was one of the most trying times in Missouri's history; the railroads and the slavery issues being paramount. His position on slavery was well-defined: He believed the Negro could not exist in freedom without degrading the rest of society. The most revealing expression of his feelings came after the Civil War when he fled to Mexico to live rather than live in a society with free Negroes. He wrote: "I pray to God that my fears for the future of the South may never be realized: but when the right is given to the negro to bring suit, testify before courts, and vote in elections, you had all better be in Mexico."[22]

During the 1860 presidental campaign, Price was for Stephen A. Douglas. Lincoln won the election and Missouri became divided: secessionists against unionists and slaveholders against those holding antislavery views. Price was named president of the Missouri State Convention. He explained to a friend: "It is now inevitable that the general government will attempt the coercion of the southern states. War will ensue. I am a military man, a southern man, and if we have to fight, I will do so on the part of the South."[23]

Price was correct. The War began and the Missouri secessionists organized military companies. General Price was given command of all the Missouri State Troops. He quickly went to work to organize the recruits and with his charming and dashing manner, early won their devotion and admiration. Transforming the mob into an adequate fighting force was a more difficult matter. The men had only a handful of uniforms. The officers could be distinguished from the enlisted men only by bits of red flannel or pieces of cotton cloth fastened to their shoulders or tied around their arms. Many were unarmed - of the force of 7,000, approximately 2,000 were without weapons but went along with the armed troops hoping to acquire a rifle from wounded or dead Union soldiers. Those that were armed carried hunting rifles, shotguns, or old flintlock guns. Few knew anything about military discipline.[24] According to a Confederate Army general sent to assist the Missourians, "I find that (Price's) force or 8,000 or 9,000 men (sic) is badly organized, badly armed, and now almost entirely out of ammunition."[25]

As the Civil War progressed, General Price, having cast his fortune with Missouri, did not wish to abandon his adopted state. His army won many encounters across Missouri and his fame became widespread. Many of his men were mustered into the Confederate service, however, and on April 8, 1862, Price reluctantly resigned as commander of the Missouri troops and formally became a major general in the Confederate Army. Before departing, Price vowed that soon he would "return and reconquer Missouri."[26]

The Missourians arrived in Memphis, Tennessee on April 15, 1862 and traveled by train on the Memphis and Charleston Railroad to Corinth. They arrived in North Mississippi too late for the Battle of Shiloh but reinforced General Beauregard's troops at Corinth. Shortly after arriving in Corinth, General Beauregard was said to have taken Price on a tour of the extensive breastworks he had constructed. After viewing the magnificent engineering project General Price's only comment was :

"Well, these things may be very fine. I never saw anything of the kind but once, and then I took them. [27] This remark received a lot of attention in the press and helped to bolster Price's image.

From Corinth, Price withdrew south with the rest of Beauregard's men and, while the Confederates were safely encamped in the Tupelo, Mississippi area, he decided to go to Richmond to try to persuade President Davis to send him and his Missourians back across the Mississippi. Although he was well received in his native state of Virginia, he did not get much sympathy from the President. His written request was refused but the final decision was apparently left to General Bragg, who wrote on July 12:

"Major-General Price has exhibited to me the authority of the War Department to allow his command, at my direction, to return to the west of the Mississippi River. Were it at all prudent for me to spare them, I do not see how it is practicable to cross such a force over the river." [28]

With some consolation, General Price accepted the command of the District of the Tennessee and began working to bring his men into an effective fighting force. One of his divisions, Little's, consisted of four brigades and contained most of the Missouri troops. The other division was commanded by General Dabney H. Maury and was composed of three brigades of Louisiana, Arkansas, Texas, and Mississippi regiments. In addition, there was the separate cavalry brigade commanded by Brigadier General Frank C. Armstrong. General Price's total strength was about 16,000 men, plus some 40 pieces of artillery. General Little, Price's most able junior commander, devoted himself to improving the drill and discipline of his division in preparation for the projected offensive. [29]

While in Tupelo, an interesting rivalry developed between two of General Price's outstanding regiments, the 3rd Louisiana Regiment of He'bert's Brigade and the 2nd Texas of General Maury's Division. He'bert's drilled the 3rd Louisiana thoroughly and many thought the regiment was unsurpassed in its maneuvering but others had decided that the 2nd Texas was superior. After the Battle of Shiloh, Colonel Moore had been promoted for gallantry and had become a brigadier general and cor .nanded the brigade of which the 2nd Texas was a member. Colonel W. P. Rogers, for the same reason, had been made Colonel of the 2nd Texas. Colonel Rogers and General Moore were extremely proud of the 2nd Texas and utilized great skill in drilling and disciplining the regiment. At the same time, Colonel (later General) He'bert commanded the 3rd Louisiana and General Whitfield the brigade. There was to be a general review of the troops before General Bragg. Colonel

Purvis Cappleman of Iuka, Mississippi with shells fired during the Battle of Iuka. These include a 6 lb. solid shell, a 16 lb. bombshell, a Hotchkiss, and a 10 lb. Reed Parrott shot. These shells were once in the possession of Mr. Wilmer Price and are pictured in his Souvenir History of Iuka, Mississippi.

Rogers and General Whitfield agreed to back their regiments with a bet as to which was the better drilled. Each put up five hundred dollars. Rogers would win if the 2nd Texas took the contest and General Whitfield if the 3rd Louisiana was found to be superior. The judges were to be appointed by General Bragg and the contest was to be held the day after the general review. During the review the 3rd Louisiana was in the lead. After the regiment passed the reviewing officers, the 3rd Louisiana was permitted to break ranks and await the coming of the 2nd Texas. After the review was completed, General Whitfield rode over to Colonel Rogers' tent and called him out. Whitfield asked Rogers if he would agree to withdraw the wager since, after watching them in parade, he realized that the 2nd Texas was superior to the 3rd Louisiana in drill. After some chaffing, the Colonel agreed to call the contest off, provided the General would admit that the 2nd Texas was the better drilled regiment. To this the General agreed, to the delight of the 2nd Texans who, it must be admitted, had little faith in their success as they had seen the 3rd Louisiana maneuvering on several occasions. [30]

He'bert's Brigade contained some of the most efficient and well-trained soldiers in General Price's Army and they would soon demonstrate their abilities and valor on the Iuka battlefield. General He'bert demanded a rigorous training program and strict military discipline. A typical day's duty in one of He'bert's units was as follows: Every day's duty was very much like the duties of every other day except there was some variation for Sunday. The same men did not have the same duties to perform every day, as guard duty and fatigue duty were regulated by details made from the alphabetical rolls of the companies, but the same round of duties came every day of the week. At reveille the soldiers had to promptly rise, dress, and hurry out into line for roll call. Then they would eat breakfast. The meal was followed by guard-mounting for the next twenty-four hours, the guards walking their posts day and night, two hours on and four hours off. Before noon, there were two hours' drill for all men not on guard duty or other special duty. Next the men would have dinner, followed by clean-up camps, gun cleaning and dress parade at sundown. Finally, the men ate supper and had to be in bed at taps. On Sunday there was no drill but the man had to don all their armor and have a review, which with the marching, halting, and waiting, usually lasted until about noon. [31]

Meanwhile, on the Union side, General Rosecrans, with an estimated 35% of his men sick, decided to move his camp from Corinth to a more salubrious area. A region about 5 miles southeast of Corinth known as Clear Creek was selected. Here there was a wide, running stream of excellent water with many springs, but no swamps. One of the Union soldiers described the stream which contrasted so greatly with the muddy, sluggish water of Tuscumbia creek:

"Clear creek is a clear, running brook of excellent water, twenty-five or thirty feet wide, with many springs along the banks, and with no swampy land whatever in the neighborhood. It affords fine water to drink and abundance for bathing purposes. There is no such stream between Tuscumbia Creek and Guntown." [32]

Many of Rosecran's men still remained ill, however, with the diarrheal diseases. Alonzo Brown described his brother's ordeal:

"On several mornings after we went to Camp Clear Creek our men were abused and blackguarded by an officer when they went to sick call. I stood and heard it and my blood fairly boiled with indignation. Several who stated that they had been suffering with chronic diarrhea for quite a length of time were strongly recommended to make use of a red-hot poker for their affliction . . . . but the blackguardism and abuse of our sick and accusing them of playing-off when they went to sick call soon ceased, because the angel of death visited us and almost every evening at sundown the solemn, mournful strains of the dead march and the funeral volley sounded through the camp as our heroes were being laid to rest. My brother, Charles H. Brown of Company B, went there and on his return I asked him if he had received any medicine or advice, and he replied: 'I received nothing but abuse, I was abused like a dog and told that I was not sick but playing-off. All of our boys are abused who go there. I will not go back there again. No! I would rather die than go back to that sick call.' The next morning he was delirious and unconscious. I procured a hospital stretcher and by the help of a comrade belonging to our company carried him into one of the tents used as our regimental hospital, and leaving my duties in the subsistence department spent all of my time nursing him. Dr. Cross soon came into the tent, pronounced the disease typhoid fever, and prescribed. I procured the remedies at the dispensary and remained day and night by his cot until he expired." [33]

With the bulk of his army camped at Clear Creek, with cavalry battalions at Jacinto, Blackland, and Booneville, and a brigade at Rienzi, General Rosecrans guarded the Confederates' southern approaches to Corinth. In early July, Rosecrans reorganized his command. Paine commanded the first division; Stanley, the second; Hamilton, the third; Jefferson C. Davis, the fourth; Asboth, the fifth; and Gordon Granger, the cavalry. General Hamilton, soon to take the most active part in the Battle of Iuka, was more difficult for General Rosecrans to get along with than the rest. [34]

As General William Starke Rosecrans became (along with General Grant), Price's chief antagonist in the struggle for Iuka, a few words about his life and military career to this point are necessary.

William Starke was born on September 6, 1819 in Delaware County, Ohio. As a boy he had little formal education but had inherited his father's strong interest in history and was an avid reader. His self-reliant father was his lifelong ideal and everyone agreed that they talked, looked, and were alike. William went to work at the age of 14 and, in 1838, was given an appointment to the U.S. Military Academy where he graduated in 1842. In his class were James Longstreet, Don Carlos Buell, Earl Van Dorn, and John Pope. It was at the Academy that Rosecrans received his first nickname, "Rosy", or more often, "Old Rosy." 35

William's 10 years career in the Engineer Corps was not exceptional and he resigned from the army in 1854. At the outbreak of the war in 1861 he was in the kerosine business in Cincinnati. In June, 1861, he became a brigadier general in the regular army and fought General Lee in Western Virginia. In May of 1862, Rosecrans directed the left wing of John Pope's Army in the slow movement from Shiloh to Corinth. After Pope was summoned to the Eastern theater of activities, Rosecrans was placed in his position. 36

Having suceeded General Halleck as commander on July 17, by the end of the month General Grant was personally commanding the Army of the Tennessee with 65,000 men, present and absent, in Corinth, Memphis, Jackson, Cairo, and scattered at other places. General Rosecrans commanded the Army of the Mississippi with about 40,000 men, present and absent, at Jacinto and Clear Creek, Mississippi, and Cherokee Station, Alabama. The Union troops had been countered by Hardee's Confederate Army of Mississippi and Price's Army of the West at Tupelo, Mississippi, about 68,000 troops, and Van Dorn's 14,000 at Vicksburg. When General Bragg departed Mississippi on July 24 to move against Union General Buell, however, it left the defense of Mississippi to Price's and Van Dorn's combined force of about 30,000. 37

Before he left Mississippi, General Bragg ordered General Van Dorn to "do all things deemed needful without awaiting instructions." He and "Old Pap" were to operate separately, but to "consult freely" and to co-operate whenever possible. Their prime goal was the defense of the section of the Mississippi River that was still controlled by the Confederacy and the prevention of Grant's and **Rosecrans' troops from** following General Bragg into Tennessee. 38

Finally, General Price's men began to recover from their illnesses and

The Emmett Reed Home. This painting by Mrs. Lila Hamm, belongs to Mr. and Mrs. Robert L. Brown Jr. and presently hangs in Mr. Brown's insurance office. This home was used as a shelter during the Battle of Iuka and was later used by Confederate General Nathan Bedford Forrest. Local tradition has it that General Kelly was resting on a sofa in the hall when a courier brought news of Federal transports on the Tennessee River. He ordered Colonel Kelly with his brigade and one section of Hudson's Battery commanded by Lieutenant Walton, to Eastport where the Rebels successfully ambushed two Federal gunboats and three transports.

Mrs. Reed lived in the house until her death in 1944. It was located on the corner of Main and Quitman and faced east, toward Mineral Springs Park. The house was originally at Eastport and was torn down and moved to Iuka by Mrs. Reed's father Mr. A. T. Matthews. The home of Mr. and Mrs. Robert L. Brown Jr. now occupies the site of the Emmett Reed Home.

12

got their clothes washed and mended. About this time, a large quantity of summer clothing arrived to be distributed among them. These garments did not come from the Confederate quartermaster's department, however, but from the homes and families of the men themselves. This consignment was augmented by "ladies' associations," which had become a powerful factor in the administration of the war. The zeal displayed by the ladies' organizations was incredible and nothing seemed too good for them to sacrifice for the men on the front. Beautiful silk dresses had been cut up and made into tunics and rich shawls and plaids had been sewed together for blankets. Seemingly everything that could be utilized by the soldiers was donated by these unselfish women.[39]

One of the Louisiana regiments received a fair share of these articles and on the following Sunday morning when they turned out for parade inspection they presented a neat and clean but bizarre appearance and were subjected to a lot of ridicule for the "pretty pictures" as they called them, on some of their beautifully-flowered tunics. The appearance of the "dirty, smoke-begrimed, ragged wretches" had certainly changed since their retreat from Pea Ridge.[40]

In the middle of August, 1862, General Rosecrans' Army of the Mississippi was stationed as follows: General Paine's First Division, with an additional cavalry regiment, was at Tuscumbia; General Stanley's Second Division was at Camp Clear Creek; General Hamilton's Third Division was stationed at Jacinto; the Fourth Division of General Davis occupied the line of roads between Tuscumbia and Corinth; and the Fifth Division was at Rienzi. The several regiments of cavalry divisions were distributed at the several stations with the infantry divisions.[41]

As Union General Buell needed reinforcements in Kentucky, General Grant ordered General Rosecrans to detach the First and Fourth Divisions of the Army of the Mississippi and send them toward Decatur, Alabama. Rosecrans' remaining divisions were to be spread thinner to cover the areas held by the divisions that were being removed.[42] Rosecrans replied that he would direct Stanley to occupy Tuscumbia and Iuka. The First Division was to cross at Tuscumbia, Courtland, and Decatur and the Fourth Division at Eastport. Rosecrans' Army of the Mississippi would then extend from Rienzi to Tuscumbia, a distance of 50 miles, while Grant's entire Corps would extend a distance of 30 miles northwestward. Rosecrans commented, "A small army covering a front of 80 miles parallel with the enemy's front . . . . A speedy remedy must be applied or a bad result must be expected."[43]

On August 18 the 2nd Brigade of Stanley's Division left their camp at Clear Creek for Tuscumbia, passing through Iuka. His 1st brigade had not moved, although they were aware of their orders to go to "a little place on the railroad called Iuka."[44] Two days later the men of the 1st Brigade struck their tents and took up the line of march for Iuka, a distance of about 25 miles. They got off about 8 o'clock and marched about 15 miles. It was rather warm but the men withstood the trip relatively well. The next morning they began the march a little after sunrise and arrived in Iuka about 10:00 a.m.[45]

The 39th Ohio Regiment, Colonel Alfred West Gilbert commanding, was assigned a position in the southeastern part of Iuka. The Colonel found Iuka to be a "very pretty village". Almost all of the buildings were new, although some were transplants, having been torn down and moved from Eastport when the Memphis and Charleston Railroad bypassed the Tennessee River port. The residences were almost all painted white with green window shutters. They were noted by the colonel to be "commodious and pleasant dwellings."[46]

Colonel Gilbert was especially fond of the Brinkley Home which was occupied by General Rosecrans for his headquarters. He described the home:

" . . a very airy & pleasant building. One of the most pleasant in the place --- built it is said by a gentlemen of Memphis, a bachelor, as a summer residence, large halls crossing each other in the middle with stairways to the upper story & commodious verandahs."[47]

The Federals residing in Iuka found much to admire about the quiet summer resort. They discovered the landscape to be rolling and picturesque and the seven springs in the park well-kept and proper. One spring of fine cool water of great volume was known as the Alum Spring. Many of the inhabitants of Iuka, although expressing secessionist views, remained in their houses rather than flee from the invading bluecoats.[48]

On August 24, Lieutenant Fletcher Hypes arrived in Iuka with new recruits for the 39th Ohio Regiment from Cincinnati. Colonel Gilbert wrote in his diary that they were "hardy looking men and will make good soldiers."[49]

One of the new soldiers was Private George Cadman, a native of London, England, who had lived in the United States for five years. He was a typical soldier in that he frequently griped about army food and complained that on the long journey from Ohio to Iuka, all that the recruits had to eat were crackers and raw bacon. The day after their tiring journey, one of the Cadman's lieutenants said that he might rest, but that it would be better if he "chose to go out with the picket guard and learn something."[50]

On the evening of August 24 the train from Tuscumbia brought in a

Twin Magnolias. This house on Quitman Street across from the old Tishomingo County Courthouse is presently the home of Mr. & Mrs. C. Neil Davis. Throughout most of its existence it was known as the "Coman House." The cottage served as Brigadier General Henry Little's headquarters before the Battle of Iuka and after his fatal injury his body was buried in an adjoining garden.

15

load of contrabands (Negroes taken into the Union lines). The following day Colonel Gilbert went down to the Iuka Depot with General Stanley where they found the quartermaster registering them and trying to ascertain their names, places of birth, and their masters' names. Colonel Gilbert needed a man to attend his horses and selected a Negro by the name of Walker. The colonel thought that he was "young & spry and I doubt not will be useful."[51]

On August 26 Rosecrans' pickets brought into Iuka a Negro man who desired to be admitted into the Union camp. Upon General Stanley's orders, Colonel Gilbert took down the man's name and that of his master and turned him over to the quartermaster. The Negro lived in a section of the country where the Union troops had been ravaging and burning houses. Two Union men had been killed about 4 or 5 miles south of Iuka on Sunday, August 24 and General Stanley had sent out the Kansas Cavalry to lay the country waste around the place of the killings. The Negro reported that nine dwellings and three mills had been burned by the Yankees.[52]

Another group of contrabands was brought into Iuka on the evening of August 26. Colonel Gilbert reported that the teams were all being driven by Negro drivers and that he expected soon to get this class of drivers for the regimental teams. In doing so, it would allow fifteen more Union soldiers to be utilized in the ranks. If Negro drivers could be placed in the ambulance, 4 more soldiers, or 19 in all, would be released. "This is the right way to employ the contrabands," Colonel Gilbert wrote in his diary on August 27.[53]

General Rosecrans wrote the War Department from Iuka on August 28, requesting additional firearms:

"I have a disciplined cavalry regiment only half filled. We are in the presence of the enemy superior in numbers, having a cloud of irregulars to do their hard riding and messenger work. It is cruel and impolitic to leave us in this condition . . . You can double our force . . add five regiments to our cavalry by giving 2,500 revolving rifles and 2,000 revolvers. Even good rifled carbines would add a full regiment to our strength . . We are receiving infantry recruits, and the army will need 5,000 Springfield or Whitney rifles within four weeks. Two thousand are wanted to-day to arm those who are in front of the enemy. Wants elsewhere may be pressing; these are extreme."[54]

The poverty, destitution, and discontent with the Confederate Government was so great in northwestern Alabama and northeastern Mississippi that General Rosecrans felt that he could raise a large force of Mississippians and Alabamans to fight under the Union flag. He suggested to the mountaineers the possibility of their being organized at once as Tennessee troops. On August 29 he corresponded with the Assistant Adjutant-General asking if he might obtain authority from the War Department to organize Alabama and Mississippi regiments. "Will give these Mississippi and Alabama boys an opportunity to go into the cavalry," he wrote General Grant.55

On August 29 while headquartered in Iuka, Rosecrans proposed to General Grant to stretch the line of the Army of the Mississippi toward Decatur in order to cover all approaches to the Tennessee River. In this position, Rosecrans felt that his troops could hold the line against the Rebels and that "they will be driven into the mountains, where corn is scarce. To attack a force will only give the better chance to retreat or concentrate. "A surprise," he said, "would be no worse there than elsewhere."56

The following day General Rosecrans issued orders assigning General Stanley the duty of occupying the Tennessee Valley. He was to guard the railroad from Iuka to Decatur, the road to Eastport, and the depots at that point.He was to occupy Iuka with one brigade, covering with these troops all ground as far east as Cane Creek. The other brigade was to be posted in Tuscumbia, on the road to Decatur, and at Moulton, Russellville and Frankfort. Stanley was also to erect block-houses at all bridges and trestlework that required guards and, if time sufficed, to build defensive works at Iuka, Eastport, Tuscumbia, Courtland, and Decatur. Cavalry troops were to be posted at Moulton, Russellville, and Frankfort to cooperate with General Stanley's forces.37

The 39th Ohio Regiment was divided, with two companies being sent to Eastport, four companies distributed at different points along the railroad, and four companies stationed near Iuka. August 31 was payday for the soldiers and Colonel Gilbert, having a boil on his leg, sent Lieutenant Colonel Noyes to Eastport to muster the troops there.58

The high prices and poor quality of food offered by private sellers in Tishomingo County were often discouraging to the soldiers. Shortly after Private George Cadman arrived in Iuka, watermelons were selling for 50¢ a piece, peaches at almost 1¢ a piece, butter for 30 cents a pound, a "mouthful of pie" for 15¢, and a loaf of bread, which he could eat at one meal, for 5¢.59

Food containers and utensils were also very expensive in Iuka. Cadman advised new soldiers to bring tin cups, plates, spoons, knives, and forks with them. He was "positive" that they could get as much tinware for 25¢ in Cincinnati as they could buy for $1.50 in Iuka. It seemed ludicrous to him that he could find only two six-quart buckets in that "whole damned" Mississippi town.60

Battle Flag of the Third Texas Cavalry Regiment (note "Iuka" in the center of the flag.) The Third Texas fought with Whitfield's Texas Legion, the Third Louisiana, the Fourteenth and Seventeenth Arkansas, and the Fortieth Mississippi as a part of He'bert's Brigade. This regiment had twenty-two men killed and seventy-four wounded during the Iuka battle and had to leave behind forty-one men when Price's Army retreated south the morning after the battle.

GENERAL PRICE'S DILEMMA
CHAPTER TWO

Official dispatches from General Armstrong and reports of scouts convinced General Price that General Halleck's giant army was breaking up and being rapidly transferred eastward. He did not believe that General Grant would have more than 20,000 troops remaining in the Corinth area and thought that it was the time to move forward and strike. "This will be our opportunity," he wrote General Van Dorn on July 31st, "and I am extremely anxious that we shall avail ourselves of it."[1] General Price felt that if the combined armies advanced rapidly and concurrently toward Grand Junction or some other point on the Tennessee line and blocked the railroads at the same time, they could move irresistibly through Tennessee into Kentucky. "The enemy," he wrote Van Dorn, "can only confront us by weakening the army opposed to General Bragg. The result will be the same in either case -- a victory to the Confederate arms either through our forces or through those under the immediate command of General Bragg . . . . I can put 15,000 effective men in the field. I am getting them in readiness for instant service. I will gladly place them under your command if you will cooperate with me in the proposed movement . . ."[2]

General Van Dorn, however, was having problems of his own. He had sent General John C. Breckinridge against Baton Rouge and had asked General Price for reinforcements to help him. But General Braxton Bragg was Price's commander and had telegraphed him that Grant was reinforcing Union General Buell, leaving the way open for a move into west Tennessee.[3] Price sent another message to General Van Dorn on August 4.

"General: I telegraphed you yesterday that dispatches from General Bragg make it almost impossible for me to re-enforce General Breckinridge. He says very pointedly that West Tennessee is now open to my army, intimating that he expects me to enter it. I do not feel at liberty to disregard such an intimation, especially when I consider the very important relations which this army bears to that in East Tennessee. I cannot get possession of the railroad before Thursday. I will then take at least a week to transport to this point the troops, & c., which must be brought hither preparatory to a forward movement. I regret very much that I have to submit to even this unavoidable delay. I cannot think of protracting it, except under compulsion of the gravest necessity. To attempt to re-enforce General Breckinridge would protract it indefinitely. The success of the campaign depends now upon the promptness and boldness of our movements and the ability which we may manifest to avail ourselves of our present advantages. The enemy are still transferring their troops from Corinth and its vicinity eastward. They will by the end of this week have reduced their force to its minimum. We should be quick to take advantage of this, for they will soon begin to get in re-enforcements under the late call for volunteers. The present obstructed condition of the railroads is another reason for instant action. In fact, every consideration makes it important that I shall move forward without a day's unnecessary delay. I earnestly desire your co-operation in such a movement . . . . "[4]

General Bragg was in agreement with General Price and ordered General Van Dorn on August 11 to "press the enemy closely in West Tennessee. We learn their forces there are being rapidly reduced," Bragg stated, "and when our movements become known it is certain they must throw more forces into Middle Tennessee and Kentucky or lose those regions. If you hold them in check we are sure of success here ."[5]

General Bragg did not give Van Dorn specific instructions because of changing circumstances and military conditions, but offered suggestions that he might move by railroad to Holly Springs and then into West Tennessee in a venture with Price; or alternatively, to move by rail to Tupelo and join Price there. "Of course," Bragg said, "when you join Price your rank gives you the command of the whole force."[6]

The next day Bragg wrote General Price and enclosed a copy of his letters to Van Dorn asking co-operation. "The details of your movements," he wrote, "I must leave to your own judgement and intelligence, relying on your patriotism for a cordial co-operation."[7] He then revealed his own plans. General E. K. Smith was on the move to Cumberland Gap which Union General Morgan held with about 10,000 troops. Bragg was ready to march shortly into Middle Tennessee, where he hoped to take "the enemy's rear, strike Nashville, or perhaps, leaving that to the left, strike for Lexington and Cincinnati, both of which are entirely unprotected."[8] Then he cautioned "Old Pap": "I hope the enemy will so weaken himself as to enable you to do more; but you must be cautious and not allow him to strike you a fatal blow."[9]

General Bragg had received a report that General Rosecrans had crossed the Tennessee to join General Buell. In two reports on August 12, General Price disclosed that Rosecrans was still on the Mississippi side, at Corinth and Rienzi. Rosecrans had sent two divisions of his army to Buell on orders of General Grant but he and the remainder of his troops were still in the vicinity of Corinth.[10] Bragg advised General Price on August 19, " . . do not depend much on Van Dorn; he has his hands

20

full,"[11] and on August 25, " Watch your front and strike whenever it is weakened."[12]

General Price was in a dilemma. To follow General Bragg's orders, he needed the cooperation of Van Dorn, who stubbornly refused to comply. Price and Van Dorn continued their communication about a cooperative action. Both agreed regarding the necessity of a movement into Tennessee, but there was a disagreement about where they should meet. General Van Dorn wanted the two armies to join farther west than General Price felt was safe. Price wrote from Tupelo on August 27:

"(I) am glad that you agree to my proposition to unite our forces for an aggressive campaign. I fully concur in the opinion that we should move our combined armies through Western Tennessee toward Paducah, and thence wherever circumstances may dictate. It seems to me that we should first drive the enemy from his position at and near Corinth, so as to retain control of the railroad. I fear that my own forces are hardly sufficient to accomplish this, as the enemy are equal to them in numbers and strongly entrenched, and I am not willing to risk a doubtful engagement under present circumstances. I therefore think that it is decidedly better that we should concentrate our forces at or near this point for the purpose of attacking the enemy at Corinth. This ought to be done straightway, so as to hinder and delay the re-enforcements of Buell as much as possible, and also to anticipate any re-enforcements which may be on their way to Corinth . . . . Let us meanwhile hasten our preparations to move. I can have my army ready within five days."[13]

On September 1 General Price received another important communication from his superior, General Bragg. Afraid that General Rosecrans would try to move his army into Middle Tennessee to reinforce Union General Buell's Army, Bragg ordered "Old Pap" to do whatever was necessary to observe "Old Rosy" and prevent him from joining Buell. " . . if he escapes you," Bragg ordered, "follow him closely."[14] General Price enclosed this message in a dispatch to Van Dorn in which he said: "I feel that this order requires me to advance immediately, and I shall have my whole command ready to move in three days . . . I hope nothing will prevent you from coming forward without delay with all your disposable troops."[15]

In obeyance to General Bragg's orders, General Price began making immediate plans to move north from Tupelo, in General Rosecrans' direction. Old Pap discussed the military situation with his officers and they assured him that they would be ready to move in three days. He again contacted General Van Dorn at Jackson, Mississippi to try to gain his support in the offensive. General Van Dorn, in disregard of Bragg's wishes, answered on September 3 that he planned to move his troops to Holly Springs on September 12. He advised Price not to follow Rosecrans into Middle Tennessee if he could avoid it. Instead, Van Dorn wanted his and Price's troops to allign and first push the Yankees out of West Tennessee and then possibly later join General Bragg.[16]

Van Dorn hoped that the two armies could unite west of Corinth and maneuver Rosecrans from his strong fortifications there. He asked General Price:

"Do not leave me and go east if you can avoid it; we can do more together west of Tennessee, for awhile at least. We should try and shake them loose from all points in West Tennessee; then march to join Bragg, if necessary. We will have 10,000 more men, too, in a short time; these would join by way of Grand Junction or Corinth . . . Separated we can do but little; joined we may do much."[17]

General Price was just as headstrong as Van Dorn. Besides, he was following his commander's orders. He replied on September 5:

"I feel that General Bragg's instructions and the situation of affairs within my district alike compel me to keep near the line of this road. If I move toward Holly Springs, as you suggest, I not only endanger the safety of the road, which is essential to the supply of my army, but I expose my supplies of every kind and the valuable workshops and public property at Columbus and Gainesville to destruction by the enemy. I learn that a cavalry force of theirs, 1,700 strong, is even now within forty-eight hours' march of Columbus. General Bragg's orders also compel me to keep a close watch upon Rosecrans, and I hear that he is now at Iuka and crossing his army at Eastport. I am therefore pushing my army slowly forward, and shall remove my own headquarters to Guntown on Sunday. I shall then determine by what route to advance. I shall keep you fully advised of my movements, so that we may co-operate or unite our forces, as may be most advisable."[18]

On September 7 Price wrote: "Inform General Bragg that my army is marching. My advance guard is at Booneville, and I move my headquarters to Guntown tomorrow. Will push forward."[19] On the morning of September 8, General Price left his Tupelo headquarters going toward Iuka, hoping to spend the night in Guntown. His cavalry advance was at Booneville; Little's division at and near Baldwyn; Maury's division at Saltillo. Price hoped to move with his entire army in the direction of Iuka within 48 hours. The lack of sufficient transportation was causing him the most delay.[20]

In an effort to supersede General Bragg, General Van Dorn communicated with Secretary of War Randolph requesting that he be given command of General Price's Army. He also asked for Price's 5,000 returned prisoners which, he said, were necessary for his proposed campaign in west Tennessee. He continued: "I ought to have command of the movements of Price, that there may be concert of action . . . Bragg is out of reach; I refer to you." Randolph endorsed the letter to President Davis: "I suppose the matters would be regulated by General Bragg, and feel some hesitation in giving directions which might conflict with his plans. Something, however, should be done." President Jefferson Davis replied that the exchanged prisoners should join the headquarters of their regiments but that Van Dorn, being of higher rank, would be the commander whenever he and Price acted in concert. (Van Dorn was the senior major general by seven months.)[21] President Davis did not place Price under Van Dorn, however, when they were acting independently, which they would continue to do until after the Battle of Iuka. This correspondence from Van Dorn alerted the War Department that things were not going well in Mississippi and that General Bragg's departure had given rise to lack of co-ordination and confusion.[22]

General Price, on September 9, felt that he had been delayed long enough. He notified Van Dorn that General Bragg's repeated instructions compelled him to move immediately. "General Bragg has . . just ordered me to 'move rapidly' for Nashville," General Price related, "and I must obey his orders. I shall therefore move hence for Iuka Thursday morning, the 11th."[23] With his decision made,"Old Pap" and his army moved out.

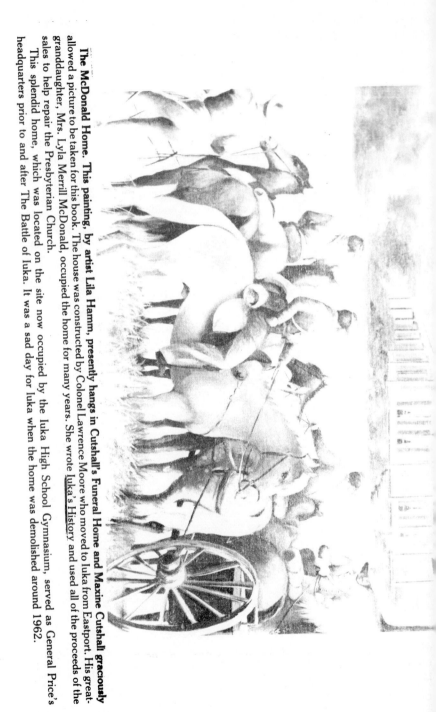

The McDonald Home. This painting, by artist Lila Hamm, presently hangs in Cutshall's Funeral Home and Maxine Cutshall graciously allowed a picture to be taken for this book. The house was constructed by Colonel Lawrence Moore who moved to Iuka from Eastport. His great-granddaughter, Mrs. Lyla Merrill McDonald, occupied the home for many years. She wrote Iuka's History and used all of the proceeds of the sales to help repair the Presbyterian Church.

This splendid home, which was located on the site now occupied by the Iuka High School Gymnasium, served as General Price's headquarters prior to and after The Battle of Iuka. It was a sad day for Iuka when the home was demolished around 1962.

24

THE MARCH BEGINS
CHAPTER THREE

Confederate General Little, one of General Price's division commanders, weak from several days of diarrhea, was against the move to Iuka. He had been taking quinine and was very nauseated but improved enough by the evening of the 10th to write General Price a letter trying to dissuade him from the northward march. Little felt that it was a mistake to abandon the rich country around Tupelo and leave it unprotected.[1]

A soldier who served under General Little described General Price's trustworthy right-hand man:

"of ordinary hight (sic) and slighty built, quick and active in his speech and movements, with a look and manner somewhat French; his forehead was rather broad, eyes black and piercing, nose small and Grecian, and lips thin; when speaking, under his black mustache, a very white and regular set of teeth was displayed; the chin was rather massive; his hair black and straight, worn long, and surmounted by a small military cap."[2]

General Price, however, was impatient to carry out Bragg's wishes and did not heed Little's advice. Very early on the morning of September 11, reveille was sounded and General Price's great army was placed in motion toward Iuka. At the light of day, the troops began moving out of camp. Some of his cavalrymen had been dehorsed and were not accustomed to rigorous marching. The troops were furnished transportation only for their cooking utensils and had to carry almost everything else in their knapsnack or on their person. The pack contained all clothing, combs, brushes, writing material and all else the soldier wished to carry in addition to his canteen, haversack, cap box, and gun. Some of the men were weak from the pervasive diarrheal diseases which had affected the camp while they were in Tupelo. There was also much worry and annoyance in regard to the beef and other stores and the men had a lot of trouble getting the wagons loaded. General Little summed it up in his diary when he wrote that there was "Great inefficiency somewheres."[3]

The marching conditions were very difficult. Hot weather and dry and dusty roads impeded the advance. Each regiment was followed by sluggish supply wagons, ordnance vehicles, and an ambulance. The commissary wagons, slow even when empty, were heavily loaded with at least seven days rations. Before the troops had proceeded very far, some of the roads on which they were marching converged, causing some units to have to wait until others had passed.[4]

Lieutenant Colonel Hubbell of the 3rd Missouri Regiment recorded in his diary:

"At twelve o'clock, we moved out in rear of the train; had a very tiresome and tedious march-wagon masters, teams, and teamsters all raw."[5]

Another soldier wrote:

"The country through which we passed was the poorest I ever saw - nothing but hills overgrown with sturdy oaks and tall pines."[6]

One of the men in the Third Texas Cavalry (which had recently been dismounted), describes the march toward Iuka:

"While I had been on full duty for some time I was very lean, physically weak, and far from being well, and starting out to make a march of several days, loaded down as I was, I had some misgivings as to my ability to make it; but I did not hesitate to try. As the object of the expedition was to move on Iuka and capture the force before General Grant could reinforce them from Corinth, a few miles west of that place, the troops were moved rapidly as practicable, the trains being left behind to follow on at their leisure."[7]

After a hot and dusty march of about fifteen miles, General Price's First Division (Little's Division) camped the night of the 11th in a bottom near Browns Creek, two miles east of Marietta. The campsite was in a valley watered by a babbling stream of clear, cool water. General Little wrote in his diary that there had not been as much straggling as he had expected.[8] After a good supper at a farm house about a mile beyond Marietta, General Little indulged in the amenities of his rank and found rest in a feather bed.[9]

While General Price was busily pushing his giant army toward the fashionable watering center of Iuka, Union General W. S. Rosecrans was hastily evacuating. With a loss of two divisions of his soldiers to General Buell, it was impossible for "Old Rosey" to hold the Memphis and Charleston Railroad and, on September 2, General Halleck ordered it relinquished east of Corinth.₁

"Railroad east of Corinth may be abandoned and Granger's Division sent to Louisville, Ky., with all possible dispatch," Halleck wired Grant on the 2nd. At this time General Stanley's division guarded the Memphis and Charleston Railroad from Iuka to Decatur, Alabama. Grant had proposed sending Stanley's division but General Halleck preferred Granger's to be forwarded.₂

Rosecrans wanted Iuka held because of the large military hospital that had been converted from the Iuka Springs Hotel. Also there was a huge stockpile of commissary supplies that Rosecrans certainly did not want Price to seize. He asked Grant to not let General Granger move until the hospitalized soldiers were transferred and the commissary supplies removed. Rosecrans also wanted Tuscumbia protected for several more days to allow the troops to remove the supply of tents and other public property there. Buell needed Granger's troops so urgently, however, that an immediate evacuation was ordered.

On September 2 Rosecrans telegraphed Grant from Tuscumbia saying that his dispatches had been received and orders had been issued accordingly. "One brigade will cover Iuka and points east," Rosecrans said. "Tuscumbia must be held till the tents of two divisions and other public property is taken away. Iuka covers Eastport and is the surest way of getting provisions. It must be well held. Have ordered troops to get ready to move. Will move them as soon as they can be replaced."₃

Union scouts began reporting increased Confederate activity and rumors of Price's Army moving northward. General Rosecrans, initially not expecting an attack from Price, now realized that one was almost certain. He forwarded instructions to General Stanley at Bear Creek to prepare to move west. He ordered General Stanley to have all of his units in Alabama across Bear Creek before stopping for the night on the 11th. The troops stationed at Iuka were to move to Burnsville. In order to travel with more haste, Rosecrans ordered the wagons loaded with tents to be dumped. Instead, ammunition and rations were to be carried.₄

Colonel Sprague of the 63rd Ohio, who in the absence of General

Stanley had charge of the division, rode up on September 3rd and informed the Iuka troops that he had just received orders for them to pack immediately and be ready to march with two days cooked rations. The men of the 39th Ohio hurriedly loaded their wagons and soon had everything packed except the tents, which they left standing until further orders were received. No more orders arrived, however, and the men camped again that night in Iuka. The following morning, as no orders had arrived, the men began taking their articles back out of the wagons. Two companies of the 39th that had been stationed at Cherokee arrived back in Iuka, having been relieved by the companies that they had relieved earlier.5

With no more orders to evacuate forthcoming, the men of the 39th Ohio began unpacking all of wagons to make themselves more comfortable. Several railcar loads of Negroes arrived from Tuscumbia, adding to the large number of contrabands that were already in Iuka. The black men were put to work and the women and children were kept together near the guard house. The following day more Negroes of both sexes were brought in and General Stanley came back from Tuscumbia.6

On Sunday, September 7, the Union soldiers had a religious service in the grove near the Iuka Springs. Father Tracy, a Catholic Priest, officiated. Generals Ord, Rosecrans, and Stanley attended the services as well as several lesser officers and a fair number of privates.7

On Monday, September 8, another train with slave women and their children arrived from Tuscumbia. The officers of the 39th Ohio invited General Stanley to dinner and formally presented to him a handsome sword which they had ordered from New York. The weapon cost $225.00 and was presented by Lieutenant Colonel Noyes.8

Contrabands continued to flood into Iuka. In addition to the large number which arrived in railcars, they came by foot in squads and delivered themselves to the Union pickets around Iuka. On September 9 another group arrived by train cars. "What are we to do with these poor creatures?" one of the Union officers asked.9 By this time the Union forces had all evacuated Tuscumbia and were concentrating in Iuka. The sick, some 800 or 900 in the hospital in Iuka, were being removed.10

During this time, Cincinnati, Ohio had become panic-stricken, its ctizens expecting a Rebel attack on the city. Colonel Gilbert, commanding the 39th Ohio, wrote his wife from Iuka on September 9, trying to assure her that there was no danger of surprise attack with such a river as the Ohio between Cincinnati and Kentucky. "If you could only believe this," he wrote, " . . . you would feel much more composed while listening to the thrilling accounts of the worst of the Rebels in Ky -- gotten

28

up many of them by secessionists & others by frightened cowardly soldiers running away from what they call danger. There is in fact not one tenth part danger from the hazards of battle that is generally felt and supposed. The real danger in the service arises from diseases."[11]

On September 9 a man by the name of Strode of Company H of the 39th Ohio came into Iuka, having been absent for some time. He said that he had been taken prisoner about two miles from camp on the Fulton Road while searching for melons and peaches. He said that he was unarmed and that four Rebels suddenly appeared and demanded his surrender. He related being carried to Guntown and Tupelo where he saw the Confederate forces. General Price, he said, was at Tupelo with "45,000 men." Strode reported seeing a lot of men, mostly cavalrymen, but that he was paroled and came back to Iuka in hopes of a discharge or to be sent home to await an exchange. Many of the men of his company, however, doubted his story and thought he might have let himself become captured in hopes of getting home.[12]

On September 10 another train load of sick men was sent to Corinth from Iuka. That left about one train load still in the hospital. Colonel Gilbert was appointed to take charge of the effects of the deceased soldiers at the hospital. Upon examination of their purses, he discovered many interesting mementoes and quite an amount of money. The 20 purses contained $481.78 in cash as well as various other articles such as promises to pay bills, bills due, charms, letters from children, and one contained an 1809 ½ cent piece. Colonel Gilbert gave a receipt for the funds to Dr. Crane, the hospital surgeon, and handed the purses containing the money to General Stanley. Plans were to offer the other personal effects, such as blankets, for sale the following day.[13]

The next day, while Colonel Gilbert was reading in his tent, an order arrived to strike tents and pack wagons and be ready to march at 4:00 a.m. on the 12th. The Iuka troops carried out their orders and were on the march toward Corinth by daylight. To speed General Hamilton's march from Jacinto to Corinth, Rosecrans ordered the troops to use three roads. The bridge over Hurricane Creek was to be destroyed after all of the men and wagons had crossed. General Rosecrans transferred his headquarters from Iuka back to Clear Creek, five miles southeast of Corinth, and there was joined by Hamilton's and Stanley's retreating divisions. Colonel Robert C. Murphy was left in Iuka, with about 1500 troops, to hold the garrison a few days longer in order to remove the remainder of the stores stockpiled there.[14]

Dave McKinney, a private in the 47th Illinois Infantry Regiment, briefly described his movement west pursuant to General Rosecrans' and

General Stanley's orders. In his diary he wrote:

"September 8

This Day has Beene Pleasant we Left our Camp at 7 & started west 9 miles & Campped for the night the Rods is verry Dusty & the heate oppressive

September 9

This Day we was in Line of march at 7 for iuca we had A Good Rane Last night & it is more Plasant travling we hav a trane of nigroess Allmoste as Longe as thare is of troops

September 10

This Day has Beene Plesant we marched 23 miles yesterday & Got to iuca At 10 P.M. & thare we Lay All Day to Day But to night we hav orders to march in the morning at 5

September 11

This Day has Beene Pleasant we Left our incampmen this morning at 5 & started for Burnsvill About 9 miles Distant At which Plase we Arrived About 12 N All is quiet"15

THE MULTICOLORED HORDE
CHAPTER FIVE

On September 12 General Little, feeling better from his illness, resumed his march from Marietta toward Iuka. A soldier in Green's Brigade recalled the slow progress that the army made that day: " . . . our Regt. was the guard for the wagon train, that day we made only two miles owing to the bad condition of the roads, - every wagon stalled ascending one big hill - that night I walked until daybreak."[1]

The division had to pass over an unstable bridge and it took a long time get all of the men and wagons over. Rain began to fall and the men camped one mile east of Bay Springs. Bay Springs was a small town on Mackey's Creek that had a fine grist mill. General Price, with Armstrong's dashing brigade of cavalry, pushed on ahead toward Iuka. General Price's other division (Maury's) had left Saltillo two days previously and, moving along the Saltillo-Bay Springs Road, rendezvoused with Little's Division near Bay Springs on the 12th.[2] General Price, unaware of Rosecrans' plans for evacuating Iuka, ordered the march to continue the next day. General Little wrote in his pocket-sized, leather-bound diary, " . . . nothing certain known of enemy at Iuka. Think we will have a battle at that place."[3]

General Little did not sleep very well in his ambulance the night of the 12th and the march came early the next morning. By 3:00 A.M. the men were in line and ready to continue the trek toward Iuka. They pushed forward but progress was slow. Dense clouds hung overhead. At one point the march was delayed in order to repair a troublesome bridge. The men marched steadily, however, and arrived tired and hungry at 5:00 P.M. at Peyton's Mills.[4]

General Little was quite impressed as he observed the men of his command cooking their food and preparing for the expected fight the next morning. "God give us victory." he wrote in his diary. Surely, he thought, the expected battle must come tomorrow![5]

Price's soldiers had barely finished their meals and their preparations for battle and had just begun to indulge in their much needed rest when orders were issued for resumption of the movement toward Iuka. Word was received of General Armstrong's attack and repulse at Iuka and the Confederate leaders deemed it necessary to push the men ahead, to try to surprise the Federals there. A Louisianan described his feelings:

"The tired and hungry soldiers had awaited their coming (to Peyton's Mills) ere thinking of sleep. Having partaken of their meal of beef and corn-bread, they thought to rest. Vain delusion! Scarcely had they thrown themselves upon the ground, when, at 10½ o'clock at night, the drum beat the call to 'fall in.' Knap sacks were left behind, and another night-march commenced, with the expectation of soon meeting the foe. The men were in good spirits, notwithstanding tired limbs and hunger."[6]

General Frank Armstrong's Cavalry Brigade was utilized by General Price to advance ahead of the slower moving infantry divisions and to screen them from attack and from Union scouts. These seasoned cavalrymen had recently returned from a sucessful raid up the Mississippi Central Railroad into West Tennessee and General Price was happy to have these brave horsemen under his command. The cavalry had to be on constant alert to prevent a Union raiding column from slipping through and attacking Price's men and supply trains.

General Price's men were generally optimistic and glad to be actively campaigning. A Missourian recalled:

"The men were in high spirits, and anticipated, with a feeling rather of pleasure, more exciting scenes than our long and protracted encampment during the summer offered. General Price was in command, and all were hopeful and confident while we saw him occupying this position."[7]

Price's "multicolored horde" was a strange sight indeed as the giant mass of Confederates pushed northward over the narrow roads toward Iuka. All along the march, women, old men, and boys too young to join the march, gathered along the route to view this remarkable amalgamation, joined together in defense of their homeland. William Lamers, in Rosecrans' biography, describes how every segment of Western and Southern life marched or rode with Price:

"old men and young boys, rich planters on blooded horses and Negro laborers on foot; farmers and clerks; grizzled hunters and tough keelboat men; prosperous merchants and plain backwoodsmen. Some had never been out of Mississippi; some had been bronzed in every latitude. Some wore black, full citizen's clothes, with beaver hats and frock coats; some in drab; some in gray, blue and streaked; some in red shirts, pants and high top boots; some in the old-fashioned militia uniform of their forefathers. On they came, glutting narrow roads, overflowing into the forest; undulating, talking in smooth drawls or emitting shrill, terrifying cries— as strangely assorted and colorful an army as ever human eye rested upon."[8]

The scenery along the route was described by a soldier from Missouri:
"a wild and uncultivated country, covered with a growth chiefly of pine .... Though the lands generally looked thin, in some localities fine fields

of corn were standing upon them."[9]

One of the most unusual sights in General Price's Army was a camel which belonged to a lieutenant in Company B of the 43rd Mississippi Infantry Regiment. The animal was used to carry the baggage of the officers' mess. The horses of the command were afraid of the camel and the driver was ordered to halt just outside the camp when the army stopped for the night. In the march toward Iuka, during one of the stops just after dark, the camel driver got in the line of march before they knew it. The result was that a frightened horse that had been tied to a fence rail bolted and ran through the camp, dragging the rail that was still attached to its halter. As it galloped through the campsite, men and animals stampeded in all directions. Although many of the men climbed trees or sought other protection, a lot of them and their animals were injured and the panic spread through much of the brigade. The camel was later in the Siege of Vicksburg and was killed there by a Yankee minie ball.[10]

John Young of Iuka, Mississippi, standing in the old Goyer Cemetery around which the Battle of Iuka raged. (Note the rough stone tombstones.)

"OLD ABE" COMES TO IUKA
CHAPTER SIX

When General Rosecrans and his staff vacated Iuka, the garrison there was placed under the control of Colonel Robert C. Murphy of the Eighth Wisconsin Infantry Regiment and Commander of the Second Brigade, Stanley's divison. Colonel Murphy had orders to hold Iuka until the huge stockpile of commissary goods and other government property was removed. Under Murphy's command were the 8th Wisconsin Regiment, seven companies of the 5th Minnesota Infantry Regiment, one section of Dee's Battery (consisting of two guns), and three companies of cavalry. Five companies of cavalry which had been left behind by mistake did not join Murphy's command until the day after his arrival.

The 8th Wisconsin Regiment was unique because of its unusual mascot, a pet bald eagle named "Old Abe". "Old Abe" was about one and a half years old at the time the 8th Wisconsin was garrisoned in Iuka and almost certainly was with the regiment in their camp south of Iuka in the area now known as Battleground Heights. The story of "Old Abe" is included in this history because of its interest and because of the 8th Wisconsin's involvement in the struggle for Iuka, both in defense against Armstrong's attack and later, in a supportive role in the Battle of Iuka. The story of this fascinating mascot begins in the words of Henry McCann, the son of Dan and Margaret McCann, who were the original purchasers of the eaglet from the Chippewa tribe of Indians:

"In the spring of '61 a band of Flambeau Indians (Chippewa Tribe), under the leadership of Chief Sky, were making their annual spring trip down the river in birch bark canoes with a quantity of maple sugar to trade supplies. One night while camped at the mouth of Jump River, which was known as Surveryor's Point, they saw an old Eagle hovering around a tall tree. One of the young bucks climbed the tree to the nest and while up there the old eagle charged on him and had to be shot. The young lad found two young eagles in the nest and brought them down.

On their way down the river they stopped at the Brunets to try to sell the little eagles, but they didn't want them. Then they came on down to old Dan McCanns whose home was on the flat about 12 rods above the west end of the present dam. The home sight is now under water.

The Indians wanted something to eat (an Indian is always hungry); Mother gave them some food which she had on hand. We had just finished planting corn and had about half a bushel left in a sack and the Indians wanted to trade maple sugar for the corn, but as we made our own maple sugar we had no use for theirs. Still persisting, the Indians wanted to trade one of the young eagles for the corn, but Mother when seeing them said they were crows, but to convince her they went to the canoe and brought up the old eagle. She finally traded for one of the young eagles. We never heard what became of the other

35

young bird.

The eagle became quite a pet during the time we had it which was a little more than a year. Father was a cripple. He used to play the fiddle for our amusement and the eagle seemed to like it. I recall one time that he played Bonapartes March, and the eagle would walk around when he played the slow part, but when he played the fast part he would flutter his wings and hop and dance as if he knew what it was all about.

In order to keep the eagle home, we clipped his wings while young and tied him with a fish line. As time went on we neglected to clip the wings again. One day he broke the line and flew to the river, where he managed to escape. He again flew north as far as Bruney Falls and was gone four days before his return home. Old Abe was recognized by some people who knew him by the blue ribbon we kept tied around his neck. After this escapade we kept him securely tied. It became quite a task to feed him; my brother and sister would go hunting every day for rabbits and partridge of which he would get his share. He could eat a rabbit or partridge in a day, and a mouse was like a pill; he would swallow it whole.

Sam and Porter Poppel were at our home talking about the regiment of soldiers that was about to leave Eau Claire, and suggested to "Dad" that he take the eagle to Eau Claire and present it to the soldiers for a mascot. He took the eagle, but Captain Perkins turned down his offer. In talking to the soldiers, "Dad" said that the bird was gentle and easy to train and knew many tricks, and if they would get him a fiddle he would show them what he could do. This they did and "Dad" played Bonapartes March and the bird performed and then they decided to take the bird as a mascot. Thus the Company was changed from the Badger Company to the Eagle Company. "Dad" was pleased to think they were going to take the bird in his place because he was crippled and unable to serve."[1]

The eagle soon became a great pet for the entire 8th Wisconsin Regiment and a center of attraction for thousands of visitors. Captain Perkins, of Company C gave him the name of "Abe" in honor of the President, Abraham Lincoln. He was consecrated by Company C to the country's service and no sum of money could purchase him. The men of the Company declared that "Old Abe" would never be captured by the Confederates.[2] Once when the regiment was in St. Louis, Missouri, the eagle was the center of attraction. One man offered $500 for the eagle, which Captain Perkins refused saying, "I would just as soon sell one of my men."[3]

Abe weighed over ten pounds, his breast was full, his head large and well developed, and his beak was nearly three inches in length. His legs were bright yellow, the feet were plump and on each foot were four talons with sharp ends which looked like steel. His wings measured from tip to tip six and a half feet. The color of his plumage was brown with a golden tinge and his head, the greater part of his neck, and his tail were white.[4]

The men of the Eighth Regiment took exemplary care of "Old Abe". They built a perch on top of a wooden pole on which they carried him into battle. To prevent "Old Abe" from flying away, he had to have his wings clipped frequently and was secured with a strong rope. As the Wisconsin soldiers participated in more and more campaigns, "Old Abe" became better known and recognized. He became a symbol of bravery and determination. He remained with Company C but the regiment (and the entire brigade) claimed him as their mascot. Whenever the regiment marched, citizens would line the streets to get a glimpse of the famous eagle.

"Old Abe's" first engagement was the Battle of Farmington, Mississippi. David McLain, a member of Company C, later wrote:

"The first fight the eagle was in was the battle of Farmington, Miss., where he showed a great deal of sagicity. When we were ordered to lie down on the ground, under a dreadful artillery fire from the enemy's batteries, he flew off his perch, getting as low as he could, and lay there until he saw the regiment rise to advance, when he flew upon his perch again, and remained there through the engagement."[5]

Several members of Company C served as Old Abe's bearer during the Civil War and none were ever injured while holding him. The first carrier was James McGinnis, a nineteen year old farmer who carried the mascot until May, 1862. David McLain was Abe's most famous carrier. He was officially given the duty on August 18, 1862, about a month before he carried "Old Abe" into Iuka.[6]

When Colonel Robert C. Murphy entered Iuka in the early afternoon of September 12th from the east with his command, Colonel Mizner still was there, as well as the large hoard of government property, but all of the troops had pulled out. Colonel Murphy inspected the stores, many of them located near the Iuka Depot, and estimated that about two trainloads or thirty carloads of property were still there.[7] (The depot at that time lay to the west of the later, brick depot. It was adjacent to the railroad, midway between Pearl and Main Streets.)

Shortly after his arrival in Iuka, Colonel T. K. Mizner delivered a communication to Murphy from Colonel H. G. Kennett, General Rosecrans' Chief of Staff. This notice instructed him to bivouac his troops at the most suitable places. The 5th Minnesota Regiment was to be placed adjacent to the Railroad Depot in Iuka to guard the stores which had been stockpiled there. They were also to place pickets around the town in the same positions formerly occupied by the 27th Illinois, to preserve order, and to give such assistance as might be required in loading the trains. Murphy was ordered to hold himself in readiness to march by "foot or rail". Colonel Murphy, however, felt very ill after the long march. He dispatched a message to General Rosecrans acknowledging receipt of his order and promising to act accordingly. "I am too sick to do more just now," the Colonel replied. "I must go to bed."[8]

Colonel Murphy spent most of the afternoon lying on the bed and complaining that he was sick. His staff engaged themselves in examining roads and stationing the command in the appropriate places. Murphy directed the Eagle Regiment and Dee's section of battery to be placed on a hill inside of the fortifications a short distance south of town. The 5th Minnesota was stationed in town as a provost guard. Rifle pits fifty yards long had been dug on the crest of the hill in the southeastern part of Iuka. The logs had rolled into the pits and had been raised more than 18 inches from the surface. According to Captain A. W. Dees, commanding the battery, there was no protection for the artillery. He said that, "It is one of the worst places to use artillery that I ever saw. The enemy can cover themselves in front of us within rifle shot."9

1st Lieutenant E. Y. Sprague of the 8th Wisconsin, who was acting assistant adjutant general of the 2nd Brigade, 2nd Division, spoke with Colonel Mizner that afternoon about the pickets and the approaches to Iuka. He also asked the same questions to General Nelson who was in command of the cavalry attached to Murphy's command. Sprague learned that there was no cavalry available in Iuka for picket duty. Infantry forces, therefore, were posted as pickets on the inside picket line. That evening the companies of cavalry at Buzzards Roost and Bear Creek Bridge were sent for. Also, Major Nelson summoned the cavalry troops commanded by Captain Webster. They arrived in Iuka on the night of the 12th or the morning of the 13th from the direction of Bay Springs.10

Captain Webster, who had camped at Barnetts' Crossroads eight miles south of Iuka, found no other cavalry in Iuka when he arrived. A total of eight companies of cavalry were subsequently posted in the vicinity of Iuka, including four companies of the 7th Illinois Cavalry, which were placed at the junction of the Tuscumbia and Jacinto and the Iuka road (Barnetts') and along the line of that road toward town. Major Nelson of the 7th Illinois Cavalry was in Iuka when Colonel Mizner left and received his instructions from him.11

Just after dark that evening (the 12th), Colonel Murphy went to the Telegraph office, accompanied by his aid-de-camp, 2nd Lieutenant John Woodworth of Company C, 8th Wisconsin Regiment. The Colonel still did not feel well and after sending a dispatch by telegraph, lay upon a cot and fell into a light sleep. Between the hours of 5 and 6 o'clock Colonel Murphy received orders to send his freshest infantry regiment and a battery to Burnsville that night and to let the other regiment follow the next morning. Murphy replied that neither of his regiments were fresh and that Dee's section of battery was poorly horsed. He informed General Rosecrans that the day's march had been severe but that he could move all of his command towards Burnsville before daylight of the 13th. "I am quite done myself," Colonel Murphy dispatched General Rosecrans.[12]

Lieutenant Woodworth and Colonel Murphy remained at the telegraph office until a little after 11 o'clock. During that period of time several telegrams were sent and received. After examining each dispatch, the aid-de-camp awoke the sick colonel and read the telegram to him. Woodworth read all of the telegrams that were sent and the ones that were received. Colonel Murphy received instructions from General Rosecrans by these telegrams to carefully guard all of the public property. All of the tents were to be packed and placed together where they could be easily loaded. The provost guard was to be strong and in attendence when the trains arrived and departed. All of the cots located in Iuka were to be gathered and sent to the hospitals in Corinth. Colonel Murphy was cautioned to keep everything in order, look for spies, reassure the fearful citizens of Iuka, and to be ready either to march or come by cars, sending the trains, with guard, by Burnsville towards the old camp at Clear Creek.[13]

General Rosecrans mistakenly thought that Colonel Murphy had the 43rd Ohio under his command at Iuka. As soon as the general learned from Colonel Mizner that Colonel Murphy had only two regiments, he directed that both remain at Iuka until further orders were given. He further directed Colonel Murphy to "have everything in readiness to move by railroad at short notice."[14]

The telegrams that Colonel Murphy received at the Iuka office on the evening of the 12th of September were quite disconcerting as they led him to believe two things: First, that an attack was expected at or near Corinth at any moment, and secondly, that he was left at Iuka weaker than in the judgement of the commanding general he should be or that he intended.[15]

UNKNOWN SOLDIERS
C.S.A.

Here lie 263 of Sterling Price's command who fell in Battle of Iuka, 1862. These unknown dead were once marked by a U.D.C. monument & an enclosing wall.

Monument in Shady Grove Cemetery in Iuka where the Confederate dead are buried in a trench.

ARMSTRONG'S ATTACK
CHAPTER SEVEN

Around September 10, acting General Frank Armstrong's brigade of Confederate cavalry returned to Baldwyn following a successful raid into West Tennessee and General Price immediately employed the brave horsemen as advance skirmishers for his march to Iuka. He wished to utilize patrols of the hard-riding troopers to sweep the countryside in front of his army's column. In addition to keeping a lookout for Union scouts, the cavalrymen could watch for Federal raiding parties which might try to slip through and attack the vulnerable supply trains. Several days previously, General Little had preferred charges against General Armstrong but General Price had prevailed upon him to drop the accusations.₁

General Frank Crawford Armstrong was a capable, rough, and ready cavalryman who had been born in the Indian Territory where his father, an army officer, was stationed. He had received an early taste of military life by accompanying his stepfather on a military expedition into New Mexico in 1854. After graduation from Holy Cross Academy in Massachusetts, he was commissioned directly into the regular U.S. Army the following year. He first fought for the Yankees during the Battle of First Manassas but later resigned and joined the Confederates. He was subsequently elected colonel of the 3rd Louisiana Infantry and thereafter was placed in command of a Confederate cavalry brigade.2

At about 2:00 a.m. on the morning of September 13, Colonel Murphy's command in Iuka was joined by seven additional companies of cavalry. Meanwhile, near Bay Springs, a day's march to the south, General Price's Army was about to begin an early morning march. General Armstrong's Cavalry Brigade was about a day's march in front of the footsoldiers and, by about 8:00 a.m. on the 13th, were already on the outskirts of Iuka. The swift horsemen quickly captured or drove in all of Colonel Murphy's pickets on the roads south and southeast of Iuka.

Just as Union 1st Lieutenant E. Y. Sprague of the 8th Wisconsin Regiment was suggesting to Major Nelson the possibility of sending out some Union cavalry pickets, some shots sounded near one of the Union picket stations. Suddenly a cloud of dust appeared in the same direction. Excitedly, Major Nelson rushed to form his cavalry for battle. About this time a large number of Armstrong's Confederate horsemen galloped up near the Union earthworks in the southeast portion of Iuka where the 8th Wisconsin and the section of Dee's Battery were placed. Major Jefferson of the 8th Wisconsin was in his tent when the firing commenced. He hurried to some earthworks that were about twenty feet from his tent. There he saw about fifty of Armstrong's cavalrymen riding in a direction opposite to his position. He quickly ordered his men to fall in. Some of Armstrong's men were wearing captured Union (blue) coats and Jefferson's first thought was that they were Union cavalry. Some of Jefferson's men that were near him wanted to shoot but the Major ordered them to hold their fire as he misjudged Armstrong's men for Yankees.[3]

About that time, near Colonel Murphy's headquarters one of the cannons of the 3rd Michigan light artillery opened fire. Shortly thereafter, Colonel Murphy went up to Major Jefferson's position and ordered one of Dee's guns sent two hundred yards from its previous emplacement. At the new position, the artillerymen opened fire on the Rebel cavalrymen. Several sallies between Murphy's men and Armstrong's occured within 100 yards of the Union breastworks.[4]

Finally, Captain Webster received orders from Major Nelson to charge the Rebels. The cavalrymen of the 4th Illinois moved through Iuka and met Armstrong's mounted horsemen. Within an hour, the infantry and cavalrymen, with the assistance of Dee's section of artillery, had forced the Rebel attackers back. As the Union cavalrymen pursued the retreating Confederate horsemen, they were soon met with a superior force of Armstrong's men, supposed by the Yankees to be not less than eight hundred strong. They encountered this large body of men about a mile from town.[5]

The large contingent of Confederate cavalry, moving in close column, charged Captain Webster's center and left and flanked the men of the 4th Illinois when they fell back. In that action, Captain Webster lost both of his lieutenants and three men were taken prisoners by Armstrong. The Confederates also placed flanking parties on the Federal's right and left. The rough terrain and hills prevented the Yankees from detecting the flanking movements early.[6]

Three companies of the 8th Wisconsin were sent out as skirmishers. The company that was sent to the front returned and brought in some captured horses and other trophies. Some of Armstrong's cavalrymen that attacked the Federals on their left and front and attempted to penetrate their lines were repulsed by F Company of the 8th Wisconsin and some of the Rebel cavalrymen were unhorsed. Shortly after this skirmish, Armstrong's men again appeared harassingly on the left and the rear. The guns were opened on them and Union skirmishers were forwarded in their direction and the Rebel attackers were again repulsed.[7]

On the afternoon of the 13th, Armstrong's men moved across the railroad to the north of Iuka and another party of 200 horsemen crossed the old Eastport road between Burnsville and Iuka. In the skirmishes, Armstrong's cavalrymen captured 23 men (pickets) from Colonel Murphy's regiment. Only two Confederate prisoners were taken by the Yankees, an officer and a private.

The two Confederate prisoners were brought in by Major Nelson's command. The private was turned over to Lieutenant Sprague of the 8th Wisconsin and taken to Colonel Murphy. On the way to see the Colonel, Lieutenant Sprague inquired as to what unit the prisoner belonged. His reply was "Armstrong's Brigade of cavalry." Next Sprague inquired about the infantry and the Rebel prisoner replied that they were one or two days march behind. The prisoners subsequently stated their force to be General Armstrong's Brigade of cavalry, 2,000 strong, the advance guard of General Price's Army. They told their captors that General Price and his staff were at Bay Springs the night before and that the Confederate infantry and artillery were one day behind. The two prisoners were examined separately. The private's story was thought to be clear and, from fear, apparently honest. The captain was more guarded and less communicative.[8]

One of the men taken prisoner on September 13th by General Armstrong's Cavalrymen was a servant of Captain Dees, a man of part Indian blood named James Platt. He, along with a sergeant and three other men, were out from Iuka getting forage for the horses when General Armstrong attacked. The men were out as far as the first picket which was manned by infantrymen. The men were halted and advised that no one could pass the picket line except the Union cavalry. The picket men advised them, however, of an area about eighty yards to the left where they could obtain some forage. The men went over to the designated area and were in the process of loading the forage when they heard the sounds of Armstrong's Cavalry. At first they thought it was Union cavalry but changed their minds when the horsemen began firing at the men on the picket line. When the gunfire began, the men left the fodder pen and began running from the Confederates. When the other men began running away, James Platt's mule followed them and before James could catch and mount it, he was captured by the Rebels. James was taken back and placed with the picket men that had been captured and some of Armstrong's horsemen continued after the Union artillerymen. They captured at least one, a private, who was in Captain Dee's Battery. The prisoners were taken to the Colonel who ordered the men to the Confederate rear. The men marched back past one cavalry regiment where they were turned off of the road. As far as James could see, Confederate horsemen were drawn up in line of battle. He estimated that there were three or four regiments of cavalry there. Then the prisoners were marched through the woods about two miles until they came to the road again and halted. There the Confederate cavalry was drawn up in line of battle on both sides of the road. The horsemen were positioned where they exited the woods and also off to the left in three or four ranks. The prisoners were kept at that point for fifteen or twenty minutes, then they were marched back to meet the Confederate baggage train. They walked for another seven miles and then were halted for two or three hours. Three or four regiments of Armstrong's cavalry passed them marching towards Iuka. When the prisoners met the baggage train they saw two captured lieutenants of the 7th Illinois Cavalry. The lieutenants asked some of the Rebels how many men they had. At first the greyclads would not tell and, instead, asked the lieutenant's opinion of the Confederate numbers. One of the lieutenants said he had seen a good many cavalry and could judge as well as anyone he saw and he should say there were between eight and ten thousand cavalry. The Rebel soldier said the lieutenant was "about right". The Rebel soldier was a private, one of the guards. The prisoners later were returned to Iuka on Sunday, September 15, the day after General Price entered Iuka with his infantry force.9

General Armstrong reported the skirmish to General Price who was at Peyton's Mill. General Price was giving his infantry soldiers a short rest, before beginning a night march. At moonrise, Price's infantry would begin their trek toward Iuka again.

COLONEL MURPHY EVACUATES
CHAPTER EIGHT

Following General Armstrong's cavalry attack on the garrison at Iuka, Union Lieutenant Sprague wrote a telegraphic dispatch stating briefly what had occured and sent it to the telegraph office to be forwarded to General Rosecrans. Soon thereafter, Sprague received word that the wires between Iuka and Corinth had been cut. He assumed that the wires had been cut by some of Armstrong's Cavalrymen early that morning. 1st Lieutenant F. L. Billings of the 8th Wisconsin had been at the telegraphic office since 9:00 that morning, trying to get some information relative to the arrival of the trains. He remained in the office until Doctor Murta arrived with a dispatch from Colonel Murphy. After repeated attempts to forward the message, the operator told Billings that the wires must have been transected. Billings had been at the office from the time it had opened that morning and there had been no message received or sent except a conversation with a Mr. Coolbough concerning the train. Previous to the arrival of Colonel Murphy's dispatch, the operator had expressed fears to Lieutenant Billings that the wires were cut or down.[1]

Being almost certain that Armstrong's men had transected the telegraphic lines and obstructed the railroad, Colonel Murphy sent the dispatch by a courier, escorted by three men. The courier was instructed to have the message telegraphed from the Burnsville headquarters to Rosecrans at Corinth. If he could not send it by wire from that point, the dispatch was to be forwarded by fresh couriers to Corinth. The courier was never heard from! In exasperation, Colonel Murphy then sent a repairman toward Burnsville to find the break in the line and repair it. Like the courier, the repairman was never heard from and was presumed to have been killed or captured by Armstrong's men.[2]

Feeling endangered, Colonel Murphy became more anxious with each passing hour. At 4:00 p.m. he ordered a single courier on a fast horse to hurry a dispatch to Burnsville and to either hand it over to the commanding officer there or to send it forward by telegraph or courier. About an hour later, at 5 o'clock in the afternoon, Colonel Murphy gave orders to the brigade quartermaster, 1st Lieutenant F. L. Billings, to get all of the transportation of the forces together and pack them near the spring in such a manner that they could be readily moved in case of a withdrawal.[3]

Lieutenant Billings did as he was directed. He gathered about seventy-five six-mule wagons and about two hundred horses belonging to the cavalry and artillery. He loaded the wagons with the camp and garrison equipage and supplies usual to an army of that size. Its value was between seventy-five and one hundred twenty-five thousand dollars. His task completed, Billings reported back to Colonel Murphy and was with him during the evening of the 13th.4

At 8:00 p.m., the courier on the fast horse that Colonel Murphy had sent to Burnsville at 4:00 p.m. returned to Iuka with the astounding news that there was not a Union soldier in Burnsville! He had been informed that the last men had left by railcars for Corinth that day.

The following is a copy of the dispatch brought back by the courier.5

Iuka, Miss. Sept. 13th 1862
3:45 p.m.

Genl Rosecrans
  Comg. Army Miss.

Have tried to communicate with you by telegraph, have sent courier By indications, I fear he will not get through. I now send another.

My force on the hill 8th Wis. and two guns Dees Battery were attacked from the south by Armstrong's brigade of cavalry said to be 2000 strong at 8 a.m. today. Our cavalry were sometime getting ready and on the ground, the officers behaved very well the men very poorly. I cannot rely on them must have more cavalry. The 8th Wis. and the rifled guns of Dee's repulsed their various attacks for an hour and a half. The enemy now made a detour to our left- their right and made their appearance on the Buzzard Roost and R Roads. Our pickets being very strong opened on them and some well directed shells from Dees battery drove them off. They have not annoyed me since but from indications and information acquired from prisoners now in my hands, this force is but the advance of Price's army, he (Price) and staff having been seen by the prisoners last night at Bay Springs (as they say). They allege the infantry is one or two day's march behind them.

I only regret that I have not my entire Brigade and a regiment of cavalry as the fate of my small but brave command would not then be so uncertain.

I send this to Burnsville to be telegraphed or expressed to you at Corinth.

Reinforcements can be of no service unless they reach me before daylight tomorrow morning.

Very Respectfully
Your Obb. Servt.

R. C. Murphy
Col Comg at Iuka

Following the return of the messenger from Burnsville, Colonel Murphy became more insecure and apprehensive about his troops welfare. Burnsville was his nearest support and it was vacated! The absence of any support troops at Burnsville, the cautionary message by General Rosecrans to be ready to move by "rail or foot", the severance of the telegraph lines and blockage of the railroad, and the fact that he was beseiged by a superior force which was only the advance guard of a large army, caused Colonel Murphy to make further preparations for an evacuation from Iuka.[6]

About 9:00 p.m., Captain Simmons and Captain Mott visited Colonel Murphy at his camp on the hill at Iuka. Captain Simmons informed the Colonel that General Rosecrans had given orders that all of the stores should be removed and, in case this became impossible, they should be destroyed. They then discussed the destruction of the stores, in the eventuality they could not be moved. Captain Simmons told Colonel Murphy that the stores were in such a condition that they could not be destroyed effectively without placing them in a building and setting it on fire. Colonel Murphy told Captain Simmons that he should put the stores in a building and that if a withdrawal from Iuka became expedient, he would notify him in plenty of time to have the stores burned. At that time, Colonel Murphy still held hopes that a courier would arrive announcing reinforcements or that possibly an order would reach him directing him to hold the Iuka garrison. Captain Simmons informed the Colonel that there were plenty of contrabands around to help put the stores into some buildings. Captain Mott and Captain Simmons, however, did not understand that Colonel Murphy had any immediate plans for evacuation or that they should make the precautionary preparations of moving the stores into buildings that night. The two captains departed Colonel Murphy's camp on the hill south of Iuka and went into town and retired to bed in the quartermaster's building, leaving the large cache of commissary stores in the open by the depot.[7]

Feeling that his troops were in jeopardy and still having received no word from his superiors at Clear Creek, at 10:00 p.m. Colonel Murphy ordered Lieutenant Billings to set the entire quartermaster's train in motion towards Farmington. Billings had already gone to bed and was asleep but quickly arose and carried out the Colonel's orders. He procured invalid soldiers and Negroes to ride and lead the seventy-five wagons and two hundred horses and as quickly and as quietly as possible, set out on the Farmington Road. Billings told Colonel Murphy that he should have at least half a company of cavalry as an advance guard. Colonel Murphy declined the request saying, "You don't want them. If you meet anything you will meet a whole army and they will do you no good. And I have no men to spare." Colonel Murphy ordered Lieutenant Billings to move as quietly and secretly as possible. He was not to let a single person know what he was doing! In case of an inquiry by a regimental quartermaster or someone else, he was to say that he was moving out a few miles to get out of the range of shot and shells in case of an engagement. Billings was ordered to keep the train as tightly together as possible and to move steadily to Farmington unless he met reinforcements coming to Iuka or a courier with dispatches. In case he met a courier, he was to stop him and learn what instructions he conveyed. If the dispatch carried by the messenger ordered Murphy to stay in Iuka or if reinforcements were met, Billings was to stop the train at the first watering hole. Lieutenant Billings executed Colonel Murphy's orders in a most creditable manner and took the train safely by a line of Confederate cavalry strung out along the railroad without being discovered.[8]

Colonel Murphy remained extremely apprehensive. He still had not received a courier or any orders from General Rosecrans and felt that he was isolated and very vulnerable to capture by the large Confederate army moving from the South. The following telegraphic message was sent by General Rosecrans but was never received by Murphy because of the transected lines:[9]

Headquarters, Army of the Mississippi
Corinth September 12, 1862

Col. Murphy.

Happy to get word from you. The cavalry has been ordered to cover your front. The stores must be sent to Corinth. You may move when that is done. An office will be opened at Burnsville. Give me particulars where the troops appeared. The exact position and what they did. I hope in future you will lay ambushes for Cavalry. order your men to hold their fire and hold the fellows until you can spring a trap on them.

Signed   W. S. Rosecrans
                Brig. General U.S.A.

During the night, signal rockets fired by General Armstrong's men were continually observed by the queasy Yankees in the Iuka garrison in their front, their left, and rear.

At 2:00 a.m. on the 14th, Colonel Murphy sent Lieutenant Woodworth down to the town to notify Captain Simmons and Mott that he would destroy all of the government property and evacuate with his whole command at daylight. The lieutenant and aid-de-camp did as directed. He went to Captain Simmons' quarters and awoke him and delivered the order. The captain was very anxious to find out what news had been received during the night. Woodworth informed Simmons to make the necessary preparations or get his matters there in readiness. He also told Captain Simmons that the infantry would move out in advance and for him to be ready to "apply the torch" to the government stores when he saw the Union cavalrymen riding over the hill. Captain Mott was sleeping in a nearby bed and overheard Lieutenant Woodworth give the orders to destroy the stores, which were still out in the open and had not been placed into houses as had been discussed several hours earlier.[10]

At about the same time, Captain Webster (who was in command of the cavalry force-Major Nelson had hurt his ankle in a fall from his horse the day before) was notified to not withdraw his pickets until some time after the infantry had been withdrawn and not to march until at least one hour after the infantry had departed Iuka. He was to be responsible for protecting Captain Simmons while he was destroying the government stores and to assist in their destruction.[11]

After giving Captain Simmons the order to prepare the stores for destruction, Woodworth went to the hospital and half an hour afterwards returned. He came upon Captain Simmons and a sutler named Cones. He asked Captain Simmons what progress he was making in getting ready to destroy the stores. Simmons replied that he was getting along "as well as he could". The town had the appearance of being abandoned by the stragglers who usually laid about on the sidewalks at night. About this time, Colonel Murphy rode up to the railroad track on his horse and gave an order regarding destruction of the stores. This was about daylight. Then he went into the Iuka House for a few minutes and had a cup of tea. After about ten or fifteen minutes, he came out of the Iuka House and some of the soldiers began chopping the hoops from the salt barrels. Captain Simmons and Captain Carpenter each took an axe and began bursting the barrels and scattering the salt. Several of the wooden barrels were broken and the salt scattered on the ground. A large number of flour barrels, which had been rolled out of the building, sat along the railroad track where they would be convenient for loading onto the cars. The hard bread was also along the track and sand had been thrown over it to make it easier to ignite.[12]

About daybreak, Colonel Murphy ordered the infantry troops to move toward Burnsville and in a short time the Iuka Square was almost deserted. Lieutenant Woodworth observed Captain Simmons knocking open the barrels and then rode forward and overtook Colonel Murphy.

Immediately after Colonel Murphy marched, Captain Webster reported to Captain Simmons in accordance with Colonel Murphy's orders and said that he was ordered to march in one hour. Captain Simmons said that he would prepare the property to be immediately destroyed by pouring lard or tar over the flour. Captain Webster then left and began getting his men in line. Several minutes later, Captain Webster sent a messenger to Captain Simmons saying that he should march in fifteen minutes, that this outposts were being driven in and that Simmons must be prompt! Captain Webster left one company on the other side of Iuka as a vanguard and formed a second line on the west side about three hundred yards from where the commissary stores were located. He then called in his pickets and waited about twenty-five minutes for Captain Simmons to destroy the property. Getting no report from Simmons, Webster forwarded his troops through Iuka towards Burnsville.13

Captain Simmons and Carpenter had done very little toward destruction of the Federal stores when the cavalry galloped through town. Perhaps twenty-five or thirty barrels of salt had been destroyed by knocking in the heads of the barrels and spilling the salt on the ground. The value of the stores was thirteen thousand dollars, a considerable sum in 1862, and there was also a large pile of corn and oats left behind. A small amount of additional stores, consisting of desks, scales, etc., was destroyed by order of Captain Simmons.

About an hour after daylight, Captain Simmons and Carpenter heard several shots fired from the south, about one half to three fourths mile away. Immediately thereafter, the 7th Illinois Cavalry appeared in a cloud of dust and galloped through town. They rode north up the road past the hospital, onto the railroad track and through the square. One of the officers rode back about half way and beckoned for the captains to follow, saying that the Confederates were upon them in full force. Simmons and Carpenter quickly mounted their horses and followed the cavalry. The southwest corner of the square in Iuka was quite elevated and Captain Simmons looked for the enemy as he crossed that point but did not see any of them. After passing two or three hundred yards through the square, the cavalry came to a halt and formed into regular order for the purpose of marching on toward Corinth, leaving the huge accumulation of stores in Iuka unguarded and undestroyed.14

RETREAT TO FARMINGTON
CHAPTER NINE

When Colonel Murphy moved his troops out onto the Burnsville Road at daybreak on September 14, the 8th Wisconsin was in the advance. Next was the section of artillery. The 5th Minnesota brought up the rear. The cavalry, whose withdrawal had been delayed to assist in the unsuccessful destruction of the stores, left about an hour after daylight.[1]

Colonel Murphy told Captain Webster (in command of the cavalry) that he was fearful of an attack during the march to Farmington and that it would probably occur at Burnsville. He delegated to Captain Webster the responsibility of covering the rear during the march and offered to give him a 12 lb. gun and any other assistance that he might require. Murphy feared the unknown Confederate force between him and Burnsville more than the Iuka attackers. After marching four miles, Colonel Murphy learned that the rear of the 5th Minnesota, Colonel L. T. Hubbard commanding, had been fired upon. Murphy immediately halted and placed one gun of Dee's Battery in the rear of Hubbard's regiment.[2]

Captain A. W. Dees, however, did not get a chance to fire any of his cannons during the march. In fact, he later said that he did not see a Rebel during the entire trek to Farmington. His battery had a strength of 52 men and he had two guns - a Parrot and one howitzer. He lost one man during the march. Joseph Robe was taken prisoner by the Southerners.[3]

Captain Simmons, traveling with the cavalry, after passing about two and a half miles from Iuka, did not observe anything particularly except a few Negroes and a few citizens' wagons. They soon came to a swamp about three fourths of a mile wide. There he saw bundles of clothing and a few knapsnacks and one family of white people with a wagon and one dead man. The deceased was lying on his face and someone remarked that he had "died in a fit." All of the people he saw seemed to be panic stricken and some said that the rear of their column had been fired into, although Simmons did not hear any firing at that point.[4]

The cavalry received fire from the Rebels at about two miles and again about five miles from Iuka. Captain Webster forwarded word to Colonel Murphy that his 250 man detachment was being pressed from the rear. Agreeable to orders from Colonel Murphy, Captain Webster destroyed a bridge near Burnsville, supervising the wrecking of it himself. While doing so, Captain Webster discovered a force of about 200 of

Armstrong's Cavalry to the rear on the eastern side of the bridge.[5]

Captain Carpenter traveled in the rear of the cavalry until they reached a point about 2 miles from Burnsville. Earlier in the morning, he had attempted to save his books, papers, and desks and had told his clerk to prepare a team to haul them to Corinth to prevent them from falling into the Confederates' hands. The wagon team had been late in leaving and did not reach the bridge until it had already been demolished by Captain Webster's men. Carpenter went up on the hill where his command had halted and discovered that the team that was transporting his official book and papers was not there! He then returned to the bridge and found that it had been stranded on the other side. He tried to make arrangements to get it over, but was unsuccessful. There were also some trains belonging to citizens which did not get over.[6]

As Colonel Murphy approached Burnsville with his column, he expected to meet a large Confederate force. He sent Major Jefferson of the 8th Wisconsin Regiment with four companies, at double-quick time, to cross a bottom and deploy on the right and the left side of the road at the base of a hill. Meanwhile, Colonel Murphy planned to follow with six companies of the 8th Wisconsin and one gun of Dee's Battery. He planned to leave the 5th Minnesota Regiment and one gun of the battery as a reserve in the bottom under the hill. The cavalry was to cover the rear. These dispositions were carried out but no Confederates were seen.[7]

As the bridge was being destroyed by Captain Webster's men, Colonel Murphy formed a line of battle and placed the guns in battery. The 5th Minnesota was on the left and rear of the battery and the 8th Wisconsin on the right. The cavalry was in the rear of the 8th Wisconsin. Three companies of the 8th Wisconsin were sent by Major Jefferson, upon order of Colonel Murphy, to scout the village of Burnsville. They returned with the information that there were only two or three companies of Rebel sharpshooters there.[8]

Colonel Murphy kept his men in line of battle for about an hour. They had no forage and only one day's rations. The wagons had already passed on to Farmington. No Rebels appeared, much to Colonel Murphy's relief, and he ordered the movement to continue. Some of the men had already finished cooking when the march was resumed toward Farmington, in the same order as before.

As soon as Colonel Murphy got his column stretched out toward Farmington and no troops remained in Burnsville but the cavalry, a few shots were fired from the swamp by some Rebels. Captain Webster met Colonel Murphy at about the middle of the column as Murphy was going to the rear and said that he wished for him to get his column out of his way and move on so that he could manage his men. Captain Webster said that he could deal with them successfully if Murphy would only get the infantry troops out of the way. Accordingly, Colonel Murphy moved on with his men and did not hear anything else from the rear except that "everything was getting along alright". The march to Farmington was "tolerably quick" but in no great haste. The men moved in good order and marched well. They arrived in Farmington about three or four o'clock in the afternoon of the 14th.[9]

Old Abe, the Yankee war eagle. This is the way Old Abe appeared in 1865 when he was photographed for a soldier's aid fair.

General Price's march from Peyton's Mill toward Iuka during the night of September 13 and early morning hours of the 14th was agonizingly slow, as the Confederates were unaware that Colonel Murphy was pulling his troops from Iuka and were wary of an ambush. The march began at 11:00 P.M. and at daylight on September 14 General Little's soldiers were disgusted that they had covered only eight miles and were still five miles from Iuka.[1] The movement was especially hard on disabled General Little, as he was hardly able to ride horseback. He was still weak from his febrile illness and the boil in his rectal area that had given him so much pain several weeks before was probably still bothering him. He did manage to sleep some in the saddle, however, which was usual for him during night marches.[2]

Just before daylight, Price's fatigued troops halted for a rest and ate roasted field peas and beef for breakfast. They also had some hard corn, but no bread or salt. This was the first meal that some of the men had received since the previous day at about the same time.[3] General Price was unaware that Colonel Murphy was at that time evacuating Iuka and he had hopes of capturing his unit there. He therefore allowed the men only an hour's rest before ordering them, at 5:00 a.m., to move as rapidly as possible toward Iuka. The troops were directed, about an hour after daylight to "quick time" it to Iuka. The men could move faster since it was daylight and because Armstrong's Cavalry was available to screen their advance. To a trooper in He'bert's Brigade "quick time" meant:

". . . for us to get over that piece of road as rapidly as our tired legs could carry us. To keep up with this march was the supreme effort of the expedition on my part. I do not think I could have kept up if Lieutenant Germany had not relieved me of my gun for three or four miles of the distance."[4]

Several miles south of Iuka, General Armstrong's Cavalry was fired upon by some Union cavalrymen. Armstrong's men pursued them as far as Burnsville and reported that they killed and wounded a number of the retreating Union horsemen. This report may have been in error as Colonel Murphy said in his official report that he "did not lose a man" in the retreat. When Armstrong's Rebels approached, two companies of Union troops hurriedly evacuated Burnsville. (These were the two companies of sharpshooters that Colonel Murphy had left in Burnsville when he retreated to Farmington.) Union General Rosecrans later reported to his superior, General Grant, "sharpshooters scared out of Burnsville by a few rebel pickets, stray scalawags from the Armstrong command."5

When Price's advance entered Iuka, mounted patrols of Armstrong's Cavalry were sent eastward to try to establish contact with Confederate Colonel Philip D. Roddey. Other men were posted on the west side of town to watch for Union movement from the direction of Corinth, toward which Murphy's men were retreating.6

At about sunrise on Sunday, September 14, as General Price's hungry, footsore, and ill clad infantrymen approached the town of Iuka, they received news that the Yanks had evacuated without a struggle and that General Armstrong's Confederate Cavalry was in possession. This gave the men added vigor and they marched eagerly and rapidly toward the village. As the vicinity of Iuka was approached, the Confederates observed that many of the farmhouses, including all improvements, had been burned by the Yankees, albeit a few had been left unscathed. The men were given the explanation that the burned houses had been the homes of the Southern sympathizers and those untouched by the torch were the homes of Unionists. Groups of women and children, thinly clad and barefooted, were seen gathered around the ashes of their beloved homes. These pitiful sights were obviously sufficient to arouse strong feelings of retaliation among the Southern troops.7 When the Confederates were about one and a half miles from Iuka, the men loaded their guns8 and the army was formed in column of brigades. General Little said in his diary that he entered the town at about 8 o'clock a.m.9 and Maury's Division tramped in several hours later. The men had covered ground rapidly by the forced marching; the last forty-five miles in thirty hours and the last five miles at the "double quick".10

A surgeon of the Fifth Minnesota Volunteers who was in Iuka when General Price's Army arrived on the morning of the 14th of September had this to say:

"I was in Iuka on the 14th of September. I got up about six o'clock and went to the hospital. I was told that our people had left. I found the hospital empty and our own people gone but two or three. I found one soldier of the Eighth Wisconsin in charge of things. He said he had been left by Doctor _____ . I then returned to my boarding house and remained there until 7 o'clock by half past six. I saw people coming in to the stretch shaking hands with the citizens. The people where I was boarding said it was the cavalry coming in. By 7 o'clock, they began to come in more freely and call at the houses. An officer came to the house where I was and asked me to go and report to General Armstrong. I was

56

taken prisoner. They came in in constantly increasing numbers for about three hours. About 9:00 quite a body of infantry came into town. The infantry came from the direction of the northwest, at least they passed the town in that direction. They came upon a road that led to Burnsville, running nearly parallel with the railroad and north of it. It was styled the Army of the West commanded by General Price and their numbers were stated by young officers to be from 30 to 40 thousand. I should say perhaps 15 or 20 thousand. At half past nine I was taken to General Price and saw him."[11]

A private citizen named William Johnson who was present when General Price arrived in Iuka gave this report:

" . . . . I then went over to town in three fourths of an hour (after sun up) and then saw three men whom I recognized as enemies armed. Those two men were about the only ones I saw. I went immediately home. Was there perhaps half an hour when I was arrested and brought back to town by another party. The enemy (Confederates) did appear in force on the 14th. The advance entered town about 7 or 8 o'clock. Price's whole army was in there by 9 or 10 o'clock. I should judge his army to be from 15 to 18,000. Price's army came in on one road. They marched in columns of twos. The column of Price's Cavalry was one half or three fourths of an hour passing the point where I was. At a walk. It was still passing when I left."[12]

A soldier in the Third Texas Cavalry Regiment, a regiment in He'bert's Brigade, who had to "quick-time" it into Iuka that morning, had this to say:

"Unfortunately for me, I was on guard duty the last night before reaching our destination, and as we moved on soon after midnight I got no sleep.

Next morning after daylight, being within six or seven miles of Iuka, the Third Texas and Third Louisiana were placed in front, with orders to march at quick time into Iuka. Now, literally, this means thirty inches at a step and 116 steps per minute . . . At the end of the march my strength was exhausted, and my vitality nearly so. The excitement being at an end, I collapsed, as it were, and as soon as we went into camp I fell down on the ground in the shade of a tree where I slept in a kind of stupor until nearly midnight."[13]

When the Confederates entered Iuka, they discovered that the Union retreat had been so hurried that large amounts of commissary and quartermaster's stores had been left behind. The commissary stores were valued at approximately $14,000.[14] Even their tents had been left standing. In many instances, nothing had been removed, although

57

several of the salt barrels had been broken and the salt scattered on the ground. Several of the very large tents were filled with sutlers' stores of all kinds which the eager and hungry Rebels readily appropriated. Corn, salt, cheese, crackers, bacon, and a "little of most everything"[15] was left behind in their rapid retreat. One report said that six hundred and eighty barrels of flour were confiscated.[16] The large Iuka Springs Hotel, utilized as a Federal hospital,. also contained large amounts of commissary and quartermasters' stores. A long train of cars was left on the tracks by the depot, loaded with every variety of articles for army use, which the soldiers eagerly confiscated.[17] Several wagons and about one hundred bales of cotton had been abandoned.

John W. Gillespie, the ordnance officer of General Maury's Division, reported the capture of the following ordnance stores at Iuka:

> Stands of small-arms . . . 295
> Rounds of small-arm ammunition . . . 18,500
> Rounds of artillery ammunition . . . 10
> Pairs privates' epaulettes . . . 600
> Tarpaulins for ordance wagons . . . 19
> Knapsacks . . . 100

He said that the guns that were captured were in good condition and ready for service.[18]

Lt. A. W. Simpson of Missouri entered Iuka with General Price's main army on September 14. He wrote in his diary:

"the Yankees got up and dusted — got all their commissary stores and many other things."[19]

One of the troops of the 3rd Louisiana Infantry Regiment, who had been marching since around 10:30 p.m. the night before, gave this exaggerated report:

"The army captured about $200,000 worth of stores, consisting of arms, ammunition, and commissary supplies of every description, including such luxuries as coffee, tea, sugar, condensed milk, cheese, mackerel, canned fruit and preserves, brandy, lager beer, whiskey, Claret and Catawba wines, etc. The ragged and half-starved soldiers feasted on 'good things' for once, and had more than a 'square meal'. Among other things, the regiment found some hand-cars, which the men would push up the road, an up-hill grade, and, getting on them, come down at break-neck speed. Iuka is situated in a valley, on the Memphis and Charleston Railroad, and is quite a pretty place. It is noted for its fine mineral springs, and was a fashionable resort previous to the war. The people received the Southern troops with every demonstration of joy; the ladies especially, of which there were large numbers residing here, and handsome ones at that."[20]

About one hundred or one hundred fifty prisoners were taken by the Confederates, several of them Negroes which had been armed by the Federals. After a short time, guards were stationed to protect the stores and the soldiers had to leave them alone, but not until they had taken a large amount. That night the men had a rare treat - good coffee, biscuits and ham. They had not enjoyed such rations for a long time (General Price estimated the Federal stores to be worth "several hundred thousand dollars)."[21]

The men discovered that the Union Army had constructed breastworks all around and in town but the only formidable fortification had been constructed upon a hill south of the town. A Union cemetery contained about two hundred graves, in all conditions, some not nearly filled. Several fresh graves were found. The army camped in and around Iuka that night. Gates' Brigade marched out and camped in a pasture half a mile from town.[22] The soldiers were much fatigued and in want of sleep, having marched all night. One soldier wrote in his diary that "we got so sleepy we almost fell asleep in marching. I would march a mile sometimes and not be wide awake."[23]

After a rest of only two or three hours, the Second Texas was ordered out on the skirmish line west of town, just south of the Memphis and Charleston Railroad, to feel the strength of the Unionists. The other regiments of Moore's Brigade and Bledsoe's Battery were held in reserve. Their haversacks were well filled with bread, crackers, cheese, and canned goods removed from the confiscated stores in Iuka.[24] A soldier of Ross' Texas Cavalry Brigade reported that they received "full rations of bacon and crackers."[25]

Upon arrival in Iuka, some of the soldiers discovered a lot of Northern newspapers of recent date and letters written to the Union soldiers. These they enjoyed reading. One soldier wrote, " . . it appears the people (Yankees) are as deluded as ever."[26]

General Little, upon reading one of the captured Union papers, had his fears confirmed. In it was an account of the capture of Absalom Grimes, a secret courier used by the Missouri Confederates to communicate with their friends and families in St. Louis, where General Little's wife and four year old daughter had gone to live. "Good bye to hearing from my darling wife & child," a sorrowful General Little wrote in his September 14th diary entry.[27]

General Price selected as his headquarters one of the largest and most handsome homes in town, the Moore House. It had been constructed by Colonel Lawrence Moore who had relocated to Iuka from Eastport when

General Sterling Price

the railroad bypassed the old river port. It had a high porch with square columns all around the house. The wide hall running the length of the house had attractive hand-painted walls. It was strategically located on the south side of town on the street leading west into the Jacinto road (the present site of the Iuka High School Gymnasium). Lamers described the residence:

"An encircling veranda, shaded its wide, floor-length windows, and the glazed doors in the long central hallway overlooked miles of rolling wooded country to the south. The bedroom, with its fifteen-foot-high ceilings, was simply furnished, but the front parlor was as lavish as any "secesh Palace" in town. Elaborately patterned silk draperies with brass clasps and heavy, tasseled silk cords hung at the windows. The unobtrusive fireplace was faced with slate, and a coal-oil lamp, shaded with amethyst glass, spread a dim, violet glow on fragile sofas and on the lush tulips and roses of the velvet carpeting."[28]

General Little went into the house of a Mr. Pride, where he received pampering from Pride's wife and daughter.[29]

"Old Pap" remained unsure of the correct course to follow; whether to move toward Nashville to reinforce General Bragg or to join with Van Dorn in an attack on Rosecrans and Corinth. On September 14 Price received a telegram from General Bragg, dated September 6, instructing him to "march rapidly for Nashville", as Buell was falling back and "Rosecrans must follow." In the meantime, General Van Dorn was doing some political manuvering, trying to become General Price's commander. He had wired Secretary of War George Randolph on September 9: "I ought to have command of the movements of Price, that there may be concert of action."[30] General Price reasoned that since Rosecrans had retreated westward, there was no pressing need for him to cross the Tennessee and move upon Nashville, as had been ordered by General Bragg. Instead, he would try to continue to hold Rosecrans in check and prevent his possible junction with Buell. Accordingly, General Price dispatched couriers (on the 14th) to General Van Dorn, announcing his occupation of Iuka and Rosecran's retreat westward and proposing again to unite the two armies and move against Corinth. He also sent Brigadier-General Moore to Tupelo to try to hasten forward the exchanged prisoners that General Bragg had ordered to be sent there for Price's Army.[31]

Still exhausted by their rapid march to Iuka and lack of adequate rest, the men of the 2nd Texas spent the night of the 14th on the skirmish line west of Iuka. General Price expected Grant to attack from that direction and the men had been thrown out in lines of skirmishers to meet them when they approached. It was about dark when the men of the 2nd Texas were deployed at double distance; that is, with eight paces between each two men. The soldiers were permitted to assemble by fours at night, so that three could sleep while the others remained on duty.[32]

The next day some of the inquisitive Confederate soldiers explored their newly captured town and found it to be an attractive village of about three hundred inhabitants. The men examined the beautiful pavilions that shaded the several fine springs of different mineral content that had made Iuka a tourist center during the watering season each year. Beautiful grounds had been arranged, ornamented by trees and shrubbery with graveled walks winding among them. They discovered the large and elegant buildings that had been used as hotels for the accommodation of guests seeking to drink and to bathe in the health-giving waters. One of the hotels was found to have been occupied by Negroes, many of whom were left lying dead and unburied in the building. The Confederates could not ascertain why they had died or why they had been left unburied.[33] Some of the troops spent a part of their free time reading the Northern papers and letters they found on their arrival in the town. One of the Confederates wrote in his diary:

"Think this would be a nice town in time of peace but everything is ruined by the enemy now. The best houses have been used for negro barracks."[34]

One of the Confederate regiments went to Eastport, Mississippi, eight miles to the northeast, where the Union Army had stockpiled large quantities of stores. The port was at the head of all year navigation on the Tennessee River and was used by the Federals as a shipping terminal for river transports. Rosecrans had made an effort to remove the stores at Eastport but in the haste of the withdrawal, the depot there was prematurely abandoned. The Confederates were surprised to find so many goods stockpiled at Eastport. One soldier wrote in his diary that Price's men captured about three times as many provisions and commissaries as they had taken in Iuka. It was reported to him that "1 million of dollars worth" was confiscated.[35] This is, most surely, a gross exaggeration although there probably were a lot of stores captured at that port.

The Confederate cavalry, on September 15, brought in about fifty more prisoners. Also a number of Negro children were found that had been abandoned in the woods on the side of a road by, according to one observer, "these inhuman, Yankee, pretended, philanthropists."[36] Lieutenant Colonel Hubbell of the 3rd Regiment Missouri Infantry also stated in his diary:

"Their (Yankee) atrocities are disgraceful to civilization. In one neighborhood we passed through, they had burned every house, and in one instance the occupants in it."[37]

SKIRMISHING ON THE BURNSVILLE ROAD
CHAPTER ELEVEN

Following the occupation of Iuka by General Price, the Confederate forces remained tense and unsettled as they expected an attack from General Rosecrans at any instant. The men slept on the battlelines, within reach of their rifles and were ordered to be prepared for any Union offensive. Many false rumors circulated through the Confederate camps and along the battleline as the leaders tried to maintain readiness for the impending assault. On several occasions Yankee troops were reported to be advancing in force from the direction of Burnsville and Price's soldiers were ordered out from their camps to meet the foe, only to discover that the "force" was a small band of marauding cavalrymen or outposts of the enemy picketlines. Once during this period of time some of the soldiers remained in line of battle for two days and a night, during which they endured heavy and drenching rains.

Samuel Barron of the Third Texas Cavalry wrote:

"We remained about a week in and around Iuka, in line of battle nearly all the time, expecting an attack by forces from Corinth; and as it was uncertain by which one of three roads they would come, we were hurried out on first one road and then another. One afternoon we were hurriedly moved out a mile or two on what proved to be a false alarm, and were allowed to return to camps. On returning we found a poor soldier lying in our company camp with a fearful hole in his head, where a buck and ball cartridge had gone through it. A musket was lying near him, and we could only suppose he was behind in starting on the march, and had killed himself accidentally."[1]

On the afternoon of September 15, just before sundown, the alarm was sounded that the Federals were moving toward Iuka. The Confederates grabbed their arms and marched out to meet the foe. One of the men later said, "It seems like they was all as keen to fight as if they was going to eat breakfast."[2]

The men of Ross' Texas Cavalry Brigade were cooking two days rations when they received the warning that the Yankees were approaching from two directions. The excited men were ordered "into line on quick" and spent the night in line of battle. They were forbidden to light any fires so that the Federals could not determine their position. When no attack materialized, the following morning the men were directed back to their camp and ordered to resume the preparation of rations.[3]

Some of the Missourians bivouacked in the woods about a mile from

Iuka.[4] Other men sent their cooks back to camp to cook rations as they were expecting a movement the next morning. General Little, having taken his quarters at Mr. Prides, was elated about the news of General Lee's northern advance from Maryland and optimistic about the prospect of battle the next day.[5]

Meanwhile on the Union side, General Rosecrans was still attempting to ascertain the whereabouts of General Price's infantry troops. His intelligence was scanty. All that he had were the stories told by the two Confederate cavalrymen captured by Colonel Murphy's command during the skirmish on the 13th. They had told that Price's infantry troops were two days behind Armstrong's Brigade. Rosecrans' Federals had tried vigorously to penetrate the screen of outposts that Armstrong had established to shield Price's movements but they had been unsuccessful. With each attempt, the Yankee cavalrymen were met by Armstrong's omnipresent horsemen and repulsed without gaining any significant information.[6]

The unsubstantiated stories presented by the Union scouts only served to confuse Rosecrans and the other Yankee Generals. One tale alleged that General Price intended to invade Middle Tennessee, and if Grant sought to pursue him, Van Dorn would attack Corinth. Another rumor that was circulating had it that General Van Dorn would attack via Ripley, while Price moved against Corinth from the east or northeast. A third report indicated that General Price planned to cross Bear Creek and the Tennessee River and join forces with General Bragg in Kentucky.[7]

As late as September 15, General Rosecrans still did not know the location of the Confederate infantry. General Grant was disgusted with the lack of reliable intelligence and issued orders for Colonel Marcellus M. Crocker to lead a three-regiment combat team on a forced reconnaissance from Glendale to Iuka. When Colonel Crocker failed to reach Rosecran's Clear Creek headquarters by nightfall, Colonel Joseph A. Mower was placed in charge of the expedition.[8]

The morning of September 16 arrived and General Grant was still puzzled as to the whereabouts of the Confederate infantry. He wrote to General Halleck at 8:00 A.M. from his headquarters near Corinth reporting:

"For ten (10) days or more the enemy have been hovering on our front in reported large force -- I have watched their moves closely until I could concentrate my forces -- All are now in good shape . . . Gen. Price is south east from us near Bay Springs moving north east. It is reported that Van Dorn & Breckinridge are to join and attack. From the best information they cannot reach here under four (4) days. My view is they are covering

Confederate General P. G. T. Beauregard

66

a move to get Gen. Price into East Tennessee. If I can I will attack Price before he crosses Bear Creek. If he can be beaten there it will prevent either the design to go north or to unite forces and an attack here".9

General Little's troops, which had slept on their arms during the night, returned to their camps soon after sunup. General Little, who had been nearly "devoured" by fleas during the night, had breakfast at Mr. Pride's and slept most of the morning.10

Colonel Mower, meanwhile, with his three regiments of infantry, two companies of sharpshooters, several companies of cavalry and battery of four guns, was on his way, by rail, to Burnsville from Clear Creek. When the train reached Burnsville, Colonel Mower was informed that General Price was at Iuka with a large force. Mower decided to push ahead to verify the information. It was windy and dusty. The force departed Burnsville early in the forenoon. They penetrated to within six miles of Iuka before they encountered Armstrong's pickets. After a few shots had been exchanged, Armstrong's men retreated toward Iuka. Colonel Mower's force continued their advance, although at a more cautious pace.11

When the excited Confederate horsemen reached the Iuka camps and sounded the alarm, the infantry troops rallied and marched toward the invaders. General Maury positioned his division a half mile west of Iuka, across the Burnsville Road. The 2nd Texas and Ripley's Arkansas Sharpshooter Battalion were deployed and advanced toward the Unionists. A squadron from Colonel W. Wirt Adams' Mississippi Cavalry Regiment covered the flanks of General Maury's skirmish line.12 One of the Missourians later wrote:

"Once their cavalry approached and came in contact with ours three miles from the place . . . The boys buckled on their cartridge-boxes without waiting orders, which were soon received, and the command double-quicked out in that direction."13

As soon as his scouts reported that they had sighted the Confederate footsoldiers, Colonel Mower ordered his column to halt. The Federals were formed in line of battle on a ridge, which commanded the countryside for about a mile. As Mower's men double-timed into position, the roar of musketry was audible in their front, indicating that the Union advance was in contact with the Confederates.14 Captain Alexander W. Dees, commanding the Third Battery of Michigan light Artillery, placed two of his guns (one 10-pounder Parrot and one 12-pounder howitzer) on the brow of the hill and threw shells to the right, left, and front into the heavy clouds of dust that were moving from Iuka. The other two guns of his battery were soon thereafter placed into position and the firing continued for about fifteen minutes.[15]

Under the cover of cannon fire, Colonel Mower ordered his team forward. After crossing the field at the foot of the hill where they had formed, the advancing Federals entered the woods beyond. They did not advance very far into the woods before they met the hardy Arkansasans and Texans. A brisk skirmish developed and Colonel Mower soon decided that his men were getting the worst of it. The Rebels began to feel for Mower's right flank and the Union colonel ordered his men to fall back to the protective ridge.[16]

The Union retreat was in good order. Captain Dees covered the withdrawal with a howitzer and cannister. The narrow road did not allow him to deploy more than one gun. After reaching the protective ridge again, the Federals halted and Colonel Mower ordered Dees to replace the howitzer and one Parrott gun in position and to resume firing. Captain Dees again shelled in several directions for a short time and, when everything seemed quiet, he ordered the battery to cease firing.[17]

A Confederate soldier of Ross' Cavalry Brigade entered into his diary that the Federals' "rifled shells cut the trees very close to our position but (did) us no harm". The men of the 6th Texas were having problems of their own. General William C. Cabell apparently became confused and ordered sharpshooters of the 2nd Brigade to fire into their own men. A man of the 6th Texas was severely wounded.[18]

When everything remained quiet, Colonel Mower again advanced the sharpshooters and skirmishers in the field below the hill. The field was about a mile wide toward the east. As the Union skirmishers advanced across the flat and approached the forest beyond, they were greeted by a brisk volley from the Rebels. Captain Dees then reopened fire from his 10-pounder Parrott gun and the Confederate firing ceased. Mower then advanced his entire force in line of battle. Skirmishing between the bluecoats and greyclads continued until nightfall put an end to the fighting.[19] General Maury reported that the Confederate loss was only five slightly wounded.[20]

Colonel Rogers, commanding the 2nd Texas Regiment, gave this eyewitness account of the skirmish in his September 24th letter to his wife:

". . . on Tuesday evening at 2 P.M. the booming of cannon announced the enemy was returning. I formed the old Reg. and advanced it deployed as skirmishers in front of the 1st Brig. -- The enemy soon greeted us with minnie balls -- we returned their fire for two hours drove them before us, until night put a stop to our work. Second Texas was the only Reg. in the fight and during 2½ or 3 hours was exposed to the fire of the enemies' sharpshooters and artillery. About sundown their cavalry made a dash at the Reg. which we repulsed in fine style -- our loss was only 2 killed and 3 wounded. We were from a half to ¾ of a mile ahead of the Brigade all the time . . ."[21]

Colonel Mower decided that his combat team should spend the night on the field and issued orders for the soldiers to sleep on their arms. The Confederates also slept in line of battle. A deserter from the 2nd Texas was discovered and taken to Mower's command post. He informed the Federals that General Price was in Iuka with "at least 12,000 men" and five four-gun batteries. He also told that the Rebels planned a night attack. This revelation caused the Colonel to revoke his orders. The Federals were quietly withdrawn and advanced westward under cover of darkness. By 11:00 P.M. Mower's men were in camp at Burnsville.

General Little made his headquarters at an old delapidated house which he wrote in his diary "looks like ruin." He doubted if the big confrontation with the Federals would come the following day but knew that there was the possibility and the men were instructed to sleep on their arms again all night. Little slept in the "delapidated house" without receiving any alarm during the hours of rest.[22]

At dawn on Wednesday, September 17 Colonel Rogers sounded the advance to pursue Colonel Mower's Yankees. The Confederates went forward for a mile or more through forest, fields, and brush looking for the enemy but they were far in their front. That day Mower's team fell back to Glendale from Burnsville, leaving the train that had carried them to Burnsville about one mile east of the village.[23]

It rained all morning and most of the day of the 17th, stopping about two hours before sunset. The rainwater caused spoilage of some of the Confederate rations and details had to be sent to camp to cook more.[24] At one point an alarm was sounded among the Confederates when some of their own men shot their guns.[25] General Little was given another Union "Dragoons coat". He took his breakfast and dinner at Mr. Pride's. Various rumors circulated in the Confederate camps of Yankees in the vicinity and some cannonading was heard in the direction of Corinth.[26]

During the day, Colonel Wirt Adams, accompanied by two cavalry regiments (his own and the 2nd Arkansas), made a forced reconnaissance toward Burnsville. As they neared the village they sighted the train that for some unknown reason, had been foolishly left on the tracks east of Burnsville by the conductor. The Confederates struck swiftly and ran off the small detachment of Federal cavalry which sought to protect the train. The train of cars and crew were captured. After burning the cars and exploding the locomotive, Colonel Adams and his cavalrymen returned to Iuka.[27]

Meanwhile General Little, feeling "bad and weak"[28] from his illness, was also very worried about his dear wife and child because of the Grimes' arrest with the letters. He was afraid that she would be banished from St. Louis. The Rebels endured rain again that night (the 17th) in line of battle.[29] One of the soldiers wrote in his diary:

"I hear musketry now though it rains so hard can't tell whether or not the engagement is general."[30]

Iuka, facing northeast. This photograph was taken near the site where the 11th Ohio Battery stood.

AWAITING ATTACK
CHAPTER TWELVE

General Grant, having satisfied himself that Confederate General Van Dorn could not reach Corinth in less than four days with his large army, decided to leave Corinth with a force sufficient to resist a cavalry attack and to engage General Price at Iuka.[1]

On the morning of September 18, by General Grant's orders, General Ord advanced his column eastward from Glendale toward Iuka. It rained some that morning but the weather cleared by noon. By that time Ord had reached Burnsville, where he was joined by General Grant. That afternoon, the Union column was placed forward on a fairly wide front. Ross' Division was posted at Burnsville; Davies was on the right; McArthur's was massed north of the railroad.[2]

A detail consisting of the 7th Illinois Cavalry and two infantry regiments was ordered to make a reconnaissance toward Iuka. The patrol advanced along the road south of the railroad and soon met Armstrong's pickets. A few shots were fired and the Rebel pickets were driven in. When General Grant learned that the combat patrol had met the greyclads, he issued orders for the Federals to secure a defensible position and hold their ground. The patrol found such a position within six miles of Iuka.[3]

Meanwhile, life went on in the Confederate camps. General Little returned to his quarters, took a bath, and put on some clean clothes. He had received several gifts; pickles, preserves, marmalade, etc., of which he was quite proud. His division was ordered in from the front and he rode up to visit with General Price.[4]

A lot of excitement was produced in the Rebel camps when pickets reported that Grant's men were in force three miles away, that they had "heard the drums and seen the smoke."[5] To add to the frenzy, General Green's son (General Green was the commanding officer of one of the brigades of Little's Division) was playing with an artillery shell that the Federals had fired at them a day or two previously. The foolish soldier got the shell too close to a fire and the powder exploded! There were several men near the explosion but apparently only one man and a horse were wounded.[6]

At about 8:00 P.M. when General Price received the alarm raised by Armstrong's pickets about the movement of the Federal force from Burnsville, he believed that it was the major advance that he had been expecting, and ordered out his army to meet them. About nine o'clock on the night of the eighteenth Generals Little and Maury turned out their divisions upon the road running between Iuka and Burnsville and camped about four miles from Iuka. Little's men were placed more than a mile in advance of their older position, with an open field to their front and the men protected by a rise of ground. General Little wrote in his diary: ". . . feel very hopeful and think if they attack us we will not only repulse them but gain a victory! 'God grant it.'"7 The soldiers remained in that position until daylight, when they formed into lines of battle. The center lines of the defense were placed a short distance in a field, upon some very advantageous ground, near the suspected approach route from Corinth. From their position the road sloped gently in an undulating manner toward a small creek, about half a mile to the west. The artillery was placed so as to command and sweep the ground in front of the Confederate line and the wings of the defense were concealed in the woods on the right and left flank. Green's, Martin's, and Gates' Brigades were positioned to counter the oncoming Federals. General Maury's Division was held in reserve and posted in the woods to the rear.8 General He'bert's Brigade was posted closer to Iuka, about two miles north of town.

On the morning of the 19th, some skirmishing took place between the Rebel and Yankee outposts west of the creek, but no marked or decided attack was made by either side. By afternoon, everything had become quiet in the Confederate camps.9

While General Price was preparing for the imminent Federal attack, he was also having to make some important decisions. The night before (the night of the 18th) after he had received the information from Armstrong that the Federals were moving on the Burnsville road, two couriers from Van Dorn arrived with dispatches requesting Price to fall back towards Rienzi in order to form a junction of the two armies for a campaign into West Tennessee. One of the couriers also informed Price that Van Dorn was now his commanding officer; that President Davis had given Van Dorn command of the Army of the West! On the morning of the 19th, while many of the men were expecting an attack, General Price wrote that he would move to Rienzi at once. He would order his troops to prepare to leave Iuka. His and Van Dorn's armies would join and attack Corinth!10

In part, General Price wrote General Van Dorn:

"I will move my army as quickly as I can in the direction proposed by you. I am, however, expecting an attack to-day, as it seems, from the most reliable information which I can procure, that they are concentrating their forces against me. Ross' division is said to have gotten here yesterday from Bolivar. General Ord, commanding the left wing of Grant's army, is in front of me. A demonstration by you upon Rienzi would greatly facilitate the execution of the movement . ."[11]

President Jefferson Davis had become very concerned about the lack of cooperation between Van Dorn and Price. In a message to General Bragg on September 19, he wrote:

"Telegrams from Tennessee and Mississippi indicate a want of co-intelligence and co-operation among the generals of the several columns. No copy of your instructions in regard to operations in Tennessee has been received, and I am at a loss to know how to remedy evils without damaging your plans. If Van Dorn, Price, and Breckinridge each act for himself disaster to all must be the possible result . . . Van Dorn, with three divisions, might perform valuable service. If to act alone, he had better have remained in Jackson."[12]

On the same day, the Confederate Secretary of War, G. W. Randolph, expressed the same fears to Van Dorn:

"We fear that a serious misunderstanding exists with reference to the movements of Price, Breckinridge, and yourself. General Bragg, we are informed, expected Breckinridge to follow Kirby Smith with 7,000 men, and that Price and yourself should act in concert. This co-operation seems to us essential to success, and nothing should be allowed to obstruct it . . . When in company with Price you will, by virtue of seniority, direct the movements of the embodied forces."[13]

On the 19th a telegram from Cairo reached General Grant's headquarters giving a greatly distorted account of the battle of Antietam, which had been fought two days previously. In part, the telegraph read:

"Longstreet and his entire division prisoners. General Hill killed. Entire rebel army of Virginia destroyed, Burnside having reoccupied Harper's Ferry and cut off retreat."[14]

Reading these words, Grant reasoned that the war could be in its final days. He asked General Ord to send General Price the news of the battle. Possibly, Grant thought, General Price might realize that further conflict was unnecessary and lay down his arms and avoid further bloodshed.

Within a short time the truce party reached the Confederate lines and the telegram was in General Price's hands. He read Ord's dispatch asking him to lay down his arms because Lee's Army had been routed in Maryland and that the war would soon be over. "Old Pap" answered that he did not credit the telegram, but that even "if the facts were as described . . . they would only move him and his soldiers to greater exertions in behalf of their country, and that neither he nor they will ever lay down their arms . . . until the independence of the Confederate States shall have been acknowledged by the United States."[15]

At about 10:00 a.m. on the morning of the 19th, General Price called a council of war. At the time Generals Maury and Little were occupying with both of their divisions a line of battle about two miles west of Iuka on the Burnsville Road. The battleline faced Burnsville with the left resting on the Memphis and Charleston Railroad. At the council General Price disclosed to Maury and Little the information in Ord's and Van Dorn's letters as well as other pertinent facts. It was evident to all in attendence that the Federals were not attempting to move into Tennessee at all, but lay in heavy force on their immediate left and in a position to possibly cut them off from their lines of supplies on the Mobile and Ohio railroad. Both generals apparently agreed with General Price's decision to march back the next morning toward Baldwin and thence unite with Van Dorn in a combined attack on Corinth. Orders were at once issued for the trains to be packed and the whole army to move at dawn.[16]

General Little wrote in his diary: "Think we will return to Baldwin or Jacinto - dread another night march."[17] This was General Little's final entry in his diary. In a few hours he would become a casualty in the great battle.

The Brinkley Home served as General Grant's and General Rosecrans' headquarters during the War Between the States. It is Iuka's grandest antebellum home and has been kept in excellent condition by the Brinkley family since the war. Current residents (pictured) are Mrs. Bill Brinkley and her daughter-in-law, Mrs. Frank Brinkley. Frank Jr. (center) now resides in Ripley, Mississippi where he works for the FHA. The original structure was begun in 1837 by David Hubbard. He sold the unfinished house to Robert C. Brinkley who completed it in the early 1840s.

GRANT'S TRAP
CHAPTER THIRTEEN

Unbeknown to General Price, Grant and his subordinate commanders had agreed on a plan to annihilate his army before he left Iuka. It was to be a classic pincers attack with Rosecrans attacking from the south and Ord from northwest. Price had about 15,000 men. Rosecrans' two divisions that had been left at Corinth contained 9,000 effectives. General Ord was to advance from Corinth with another two divisions, giving the Federals a total attacking force of 17,000 men. This was not a great preponderance of men but Grant thought that by use of the pincers convergence, Price's Army could be either captured or destroyed. General Grant said later, "It looked to me that, if Price would remain in Iuka until we could get there, his annihilation was inevitable."[1] Grant's goal was to destroy Price before he and Van Dorn could concentrate and then get back to Corinth and protect it against Van Dorn.

The tactics were to be as follows: General Ord would swing north and descend toward Iuka with 8,000 men. Rosecrans would attack from the south on the Jacinto and Fulton Roads with 9,000 men. When Price's Army was concentrating on and fighting Ord, Rosecrans would fall on his rear. It was expected that Price's Army, demoralized and cut off from their route of escape, would have to choose between death and surrender. General Grant advised both of his subordinate commanders of the plan and they were was optimistic as he was. General Rosecrans warned, however, that "Price is an old woodpecker," meaning that he was clever and difficult to trick.[2]

While General Rosecrans had his headquarters in Iuka, he had an excellent map prepared, showing all of the roads and streams in the country surrounding Iuka. He was also very familiar with the ground and aided General Grant greatly in the plans to ensnarl General Price. A few miles east of the Fulton Road lay Bear Creek, a formidable obstacle to the movement of large numbers of troops and wagons. All bridges across the creek had been destroyed at that time. Also, not many miles away to the northeast lay the Tennessee River, an even more formidable obstacle for an army pursued by another force.

According to the master plan, Generals Ord and Rosecrans were to attack simultaneously at daylight on September 19. Rosecrans planned for all of his units that were to join in the attack to be at Jacinto by 2 p.m. on September 18. He wished for his force to move at that time and camp for the night near the Bay Springs' road. Since all his troops, except

Stanley's division, were already at Jacinto, Rosecrans did not anticipate any difficulty in meeting this schedule.₃ It was to be a very difficult maneuver, however, as the terrain was rough and unfavorable and communciations between Rosecrans and Grant would have to be by courier over a long and circuitous route.

General Grant expected from the following dispatch that General Rosecrans would be near enough by the night of the 18th to make it safe for Ord to press forward on the morning of the 19th and bring on an engagement:

September 18, 1862

General GRANT:

One of my spies, in from Reardon's, on the Bay Springs road, tells of a continuous movement since last Friday of forces eastward. They say Van Dorn is to defend Vicksburg, Breckinridge to make his way to Kentucky, and Price to attack Iuka or to go to Tennessee. If Price's forces are at Iuka the plan I propose is to move up as close as we can to-night and conceal our movements; Ord to advance from Burnsville, commence the attack, and draw their attention that way, while I move in on the Jacinto and Fulton roads, massing heavily on the Fulton road, and crushing in their left and cutting off their retreat eastward. I propose to leave in ten minutes for Jacinto, from whence I will dispatch you, by line of vedettes, to Burnsville. Will await a few minutes to hear from you before I start. What news from Burnsville?₄

W. S. ROSECRANS,
Brigadier-General

To which was sent the following in reply:

Headquarters District of West Tennessee,
Burnsville, Miss., September 18, 1862—6:45 p.m.

General ROSECRANS:

General Ross' command is at this place. McArthur's division is north of the road, 2 miles to the rear, and Davies' division south of the road near by. I sent forward two regiments of infantry, with cavalry, by the road north of the railroad, toward Iuka, with instructions for them to bivouac for the night at a point which was designated about 4 miles from here if not interrupted, and have the cavalry feel where the enemy are. Before they reached the point of the road (you will see it on the map, the road north of the railroad) they met what is supposed to be Armstrong's cavalry. The rebel cavalry was forced back, and I sent

78

instructions then to have them stop for the night where they thought they could safely hold. In the morning troops will advance from here at 4:30 a.m. An anonymous dispatch, just received, states that Price, Magruder, and Breckinridge have a force of 60,000 between Iuka and Tupelo. This I have no doubt is the understanding of citizens, but I very much doubt their information being correct. Your reconnaissances prove that there is but little force south of Corinth for a long distance and no great force between Bay Springs and the railroad. Make as rapid an advance as you can and let us do to-morrow all we can. It may be necessary to fall back the day following. I look upon the showing of a cavalry force so near us as an indication of a retreat and they a force to cover it.5

U. S. GRANT,
Major-General

General Ord prepared all of his forces in the Jackson-Bolivar, Tennessee Command - the divisions of Generals McArthur, Ross, and Davies - to form the northwestern wing of the pincer. With adequate rail transportation, he had his troops in Corinth on September 17 within 24 hours after receiving his orders.

On the morning of the 18th of September, General Ord moved by rail to Burnsville where the troops exited the cars and moved out to perform their part of the attack. His plan was to get as near the Confederate line as possible during the day and intrench and hold the position until the following morning. Grant left some troops at Jacinto and Rienzi to counter any cavalry that Van Dorn might send out against Corinth. Grant remained at Burnsville with a detachment of about 900 men from Ord's command and communicated with the two advancing armies by courier. Ord met the Confederate advance of Armstrong's pickets and an engagement ensued. The Federals intrenched about six miles from Iuka opposing the Confederate line about four miles out. Ord maintained his position and was ready to attack at daylight the morning of the 19th, as planned.6

General Stanley, however, ran into a lot of difficulties on his march from Clear Creek. His guide turned him onto the wrong road and they followed Ross' troops toward Burnsville, losing a lot of valuable time. General Stanley had to backtrack and take another road. It was 9:00 p.m. before the wary marchers reached the Jacinto area, seven hours late. General Rosecrans wrote General Grant, explaining the difficulties and informing him that he could begin the march toward Iuka by 4:30 a.m. on the 19th. General Grant did not receive the dispatch until after

midnight:

"Headquarters Encampment.
Sept. 18th 1862.

GENERAL:

Your dispatch received: General Stanley's Division arrived after dark having been detained by falling in the rear of Ross through fault of guide. Our Cavalry six miles this side of Barnetts, Hamiltons 1st Brigade, nine miles this side, Stanleys near Davenports Mills. We shall move as early as practicable, say 4½ A.M. This will give 20 miles march for Stanley to Iuka. Shall not therefore be in before one or two O'Clock. But when we come in will endeavor to do it strongly.

(Signed)   W. S. ROSECRANS,
Brig. General. U. S. A."

When General Rosecrans' letter was handed to him, General Grant was quite disturbed to discover that Rosecrans' troops had not left the vicinity of Jacinto. Due to the distance and the bad condition of the roads, Grant doubted that Rosecrans could reach Iuka by 2:00 p.m. the next day as he had indicated. Grant later wrote in his memoirs:

"I did not believe this possible because of the distance and the condition of the roads, which was bad; besides, troops after a forced march of twenty miles are not in a good condition for fighting the moment they get through. It might do in marching to relieve a beleaguered garrison, but not to make an assault."[7]

This news of the delay in movement of Rosecrans' troops caused Grant to have to issue new orders to General Ord. Instead of attacking at daybreak, Grant instructed Ord not to attack "until Rosecrans arrived or he should hear firing to the south of Iuka."[8] He also informed Rosecrans of the change by a dispatch sent with his return messenger.[9]

General Grant later wrote:

"Receiving this dispatch as I did at night and when I expected these troops were far on their way towards Iuka, and had made plans accordingly, caused some disappointment, and made change of plan necessary. I immediately dispatched to General Ord giving him the substance of the above, and directions not to move on the enemy until Rosecrans arrived, or he should hear firing to the South of Iuka. Of this change General Rosecrans was promptly informed by dispatch sent with his return Messenger. During the day General Ord returned to my Headquarters, and in consultation we both agreed that it would be impossible for General Rosecrans to get his troops up in time to make an attack that day. The General was instructed, however, to move forward driving in the enemy's advanced guards, but not to bring on an engagement unless he should hear firing."[10]

The two roads running south of Iuka were approximately two miles apart. The most eastern road known as the Fulton Road entered Iuka at the site of the famous springs, part of the route being near the present Airport Road. The more western approach was known as the Jacinto or Bay Springs Road and generally followed old Highway 25 south of Iuka. Grant's plan called for an invasion on both roads to prevent Price's escape.[11]

General Rosecrans' entire column, consisting of Stanley's and Hamilton's Divisions, with five batteries, moved by daybreak on the 19th on the Tuscumbia Road toward Barnett's. At 7:00 a.m. on September 19 Rosecrans sent Grant a telegram and at that time planned to send divisions up both roads:[12]

"Troops are all on the way, in fine spirits by reason of news—Eighteen miles to Iuka — but think I shall make it by time mentioned 2 o'clock P.M. If Price is there he will have become well engaged by time we come up & if so twenty Regiments, and thirty pcs. cannon will finish him. Hamilton will go up Fulton & Iuka road, Stanley up Jacinto road from Barnetts & when we get near will be governed by circumstances. Cav. will press in on the right to cut off their retreat, if you can spare any of the 7th Ill. Cav. send them up to report on front as soon as possible— Country on our side is open: closed on yours."[13]

On the march to Iuka, two of Colonel Mizner's cavalry regiments screened the advance and Colonel Edward Hatch's 2d Iowans shielded the right flank of the column. Carrying out his mission, Hatch proceeded toward Peyton's Mill. As they drew near the mill, his men were fired on by Rebel pickets belonging to Colonel William C. Falkner's 1st Mississippi Partisan Rangers. Falkner's men were unable to check the Iowans' advance and fell back to the mill where their regiment was camped. The Federals pressed hard on the Rebels as they retreated toward the camp. The bluecoats quickly opened fire on Falkner's troops but Falkner succeeded in forming a part of his regiment and skirmished with the Iowans for the better part of the next half-hour. Finally, Colonel Falkner discontinued the engagement and retreated to Bay Springs.[14]

Hatch's Iowans were soon reinforced by two companies of the 7th Kansas Cavalry. From Peyton's Mill, Hatch's enlarged command advanced up the Fulton Road. They burned a small Southern commissary depot near Thompson's Corners. The march was then continued and they camped for the night at Barnett's.[15]

Meanwhile General Ord, by General Grant's orders, was readying his three divisions for the impending attack. This force numbered about 8,000 and consisted of Davies', Ross', and MacArthur's Divisions. The troops had moved to Glendale on the 17th of September and to Burnsville on the morning of the 18th.16

Approximately two miles from Burnsville, the road leading east forked with the upper road leading to Eastport and the lower road to Iuka, lying north of the Memphis and Charleston Railroad. Early on the morning of the 19th, Ord advanced Ross' Division to within 6 miles of Iuka, to hold the Confederates' advance guard and skirmishers in check. This was on the direct or lower road between Burnsville and Iuka. McArthur's division was ordered to move a like distance from Iuka on the Eastport Road. General Grant, having received intelligence that the Confederates were making demonstrations upon Corinth from the south and west, directed General Ord to leave Davies' Division at Burnsville, to be ready to return to Corinth by rail at a moment's notice.17

During the 19th of September, from 9 o'clock in the morning until 3 in the afternoon, General Ord made a careful reconnaissance of the Confederates' western front, in preparation of the anticipated offensive. Confederate General Dabney H. Maury marched his First Division toward Burnsville, where he knew the Federals were located. About 3:00 p.m., General Ord's reconnaissance force met Maury's Confederates. The reconnaissance was so "handsomely conducted" that General Maury was somewhat deceived, thinking that Grant's entire army was about to attack.18

U. S. Brig.-General Jeremiah C. Sullivan, Commander of the 2nd
Brigade of Hamilton's Division. Courtesy of Massachusetts
Commandery Military Order of the Loyal Legion and the U. S. Army
Military History Institute.

SKIRMISH AT BARNETT'S
CHAPTER FOURTEEN

One-half mile west of Barnett's Corner, the Union movement first encountered the advance Rebel pickets. General Price's cavalrymen were hidden in a deep ravine. When the head of the Federal column arrived at the brow of a hill, they were warmly greeted by a Confederate volley. The Rebel force was well supported and Captain Willcox, commanding the Third Michigan Cavalry that was leading the column, immediately dismounted twenty of his cavalrymen. He then ordered the men into the woods to the right of the road. Twenty other dismounted horsemen were sent into a cornfield to the left under command of Lieutenant Mix. Two other companies, under Captain Dyckman, were sent forward on the Tuscumbia Road. After a sharp skirmish of about fifteen minutes, the Confederates were driven from their stand in the woods, leaving one man and one horse killed. Also, one man and a horse were captured by Captain Latimer. [1]

Following the brief skirmish, with the Third Michigan Cavalry in the advance, Rosecrans continued his march toward Barnett's in the following order:

"First Brigade: (Buford's, commanded by Col. John B. Sanborn), Fifth Iowa, Eleventh Ohio Battery, Twenty-Sixth Missouri, Forty-Eighth Indiana, Fourth Minnesota, Sixteenth Iowa; Second Brigade: (commanded by Brig. Gen. Jerry C. Sullivan), Tenth Iowa, Seventeenth Iowa, Eightieth Ohio, two sections (four guns) Twelfth Wisconsin Battery, Tenth Missouri. These troops comprised the Third Division commanded by Brig. Gen. Charles S. Hamilton. Next came the Second Division, commanded by Brig. Gen. David S. Stanley—Second Brigade: (commanded by Col. Joseph A. Mower of Eleventh Missouri), Forty-seven Illinois, Twenty-sixth Illinois, Eleventh Missouri, Eighth Wisconsin, Spoor's Second Iowa Light Artillery, Third Michigan Light Artillery, Fifth Minnesota (the Fifth guarded the train on the march and during the battle). First Brigade: (commanded by Col. John W. Fuller of Twenty-seventh Ohio), Thirty-ninth Ohio, Company F (Second United States Light Artillery), Twenty-seventh Ohio, Sixty-third Ohio, Capt. Albert M. Powell's battery (M First Missouri Light Artillery), section of battery Eighth Wisconsin Light Artillery, Forty-third Ohio. This force, with a small amount of cavalry, numbered about nine thousand men." [2]

Rosecrans' column of men arrived at Barnett's at noon after a rapid, 12 mile march. Barnett's was 8 miles from Iuka, where the Tuscumbia

Road crossed the Jacinto or Bay Springs Road. Until then, the plans had called for one of the Union divisions (Hamilton's) to march up the Fulton Road and the other Union division (Stanley's) to take the Jacinto approach. At Barnett's, Sanborn's Brigade, which was in the advance of Hamilton's Division, halted as they thought they were to turn to the east on the Tuscumbia Road to get to the Fulton Road. The troops rested at Barnett's about an hour. Rosecrans soon arrived and he and his brother (a priest who accompanied him) and staff examined a map of the country which showed them the distance over to the Fulton road. This being found to be about five miles, and too far away to leave the two columns in supporting distance of each other in case of a battle, he ordered the entire army to proceed up the Bay Springs (or Jacinto) Road. He, no doubt, expected that he would be able to cross over to the Fulton Road on a crossroad about one mile south of the garrisoned town. Eight companies of the Third Michigan Cavalry, under command of Captain Willcox, formed the advance.₃ Sanborn's Brigade of Hamilton's Division continued the lead of the infantry troops; the rest of Hamilton's Division came next, and Stanley's Division followed. Rosecrans still hoped to attack the Rebels at 2:00 p.m.₄

From Barnett's, General Rosecrans sent another dispatch to General Grant. He informed him that Hamilton's Division was already a mile past Barnett's and that the second division (Stanley's) was just passing. In a round about way, Rosecrans told Grant of his change in the plans. Although he did not tell his superior that the second division would not go up the Fulton Road, he hinted the same by saying that Hatch's Cavalry would cover the Fulton Road. He sent the dispatch at 12:40 p.m. but due to the rugged landscape between Barnett's and Burnsville, the courier had to **backtrack** to Jacinto so that it was after dark before General Grant heard about Rosecrans' change in plans.₅ The battle was over before Grant received the following telegraph:

"Reached here at 12—Cavalry advance drove pickets from near here. Met another stand at about one mile from here—Hamilton's Division is advancing—Head of column a mile to the front now—Head of Stanley's column is here—Hatch at Peyton's Mills—Was skirmishing with cavalry. Killed orderly sgt. & brought up his book — belongs to Faulkner—numbered 45 men for duty—Cavalry gone east towards Fulton road—one hour—one of Hamilton's brigades went over to Cartersville. it will turn up into Jacinto & Iuka road above widow Moore's—Cols. Dickey & Lagow arrived here half an hour ago—says you have had no skirmishing since three o'clock—"₆

A strong wind was blowing from the north as General Rosecrans moved closer to Iuka with his two divisions and General Ord's skirmishers met those of the Rebels within 4 miles of Burnsville. Meanwhile, General Grant, at Burnsville, was waiting for the noises of the muskets and cannons.[7]

Major General Joseph A. Mower. In the Battle of Iuka he was a colonel and commanded the 2nd Brigade of Stanley's Division. Courtesy of Massachusetts Commandery Military Order of the Loyal Legion and the U. S. Army Military History Institute.

THE BURNING OF WIDOW MOORE'S
CHAPTER FIFTEEN

After departing Barnett's, Captain Willcox's Third Michigan Cavalry was constantly harassed by Lieutenant E. B. Trezevant's Confederate horsemen. According to Captain Willcox,[1] a running fight was kept up until the Rebels fell back to a branch of Cripple Deer Creek, a distance of about four miles. Trezevant's men had taken a stand at the home of Widow Moore, a lovely house which had been constructed on an elevation four hundred yards from the branch and overlooking the road. The house was on the east side of Jacinto Road and just north of the point where the road from the west entered. In addition to what one of the Yankees described as "the finest residence I had ever seen in this state,"[2] Mrs. Moore had large barns, cotton houses, a cotton gin and presses, Negro quarters, and a carriage house with a fine carriage in it. It was situated about 4 miles from Iuka on the Jacinto Road.

Colonel Oscar Jackson, in his diary, stated that a few days previously, three or four Union scouts had passed Widow Moore's residence and were fired upon from the house. One man was killed and one wounded. The other two were apparently able to assist their wounded comrade and escaped.[3]

Willcox's advance, under Sergeant H. D. Cutting, Company K, charged up the road at full gallop and drove the Confederates from their position at the house into the woods. Two squadrons of Trezevant's men rallied, however, and forced the Union cavalry advance to retire. Sergeant Cutting's horse was shot but he was unhurt. The Rebels fired a number of shots into the head of the Union column, killing one of General Hamilton's bodyguards, Lieutenant Schraum of the Benton Hussars. Willcox, at once, wheeled his cavalry into line on the road-side.[4] About this time, General Hamilton, commanding the Third Division, rode up angry about Lieutenant Schraum's death.

Little did General Hamilton know that he would be confirmed as major general as of that date, September 19, 1862. General Hamilton, originally from New York, had graduated from the United States Military Academy in 1843 but had resigned from the U. S. Army in 1853. He had settled in Fond du Lac, Wisconsin and worked as a farmer and flour manufacturer. After the outbreak of hostilities, he was appointed colonel, 3rd Wisconsin, on May 11, 1861 and confirmed as brigadier general to rank from May 17, 1861. Hamilton served in the Army of the Potomac until removed by Major General George B. McClellan, who called him "not fit to command a Division." He was subsequently dispatched to the western theater where he was given command of a division under General Rosecrans. On March 19, 1863, Hamilton was confirmed as major general to rank from September 19, 1862, the date of the Battle of Iuka.[5] (This last promotion was supposedly upon the interposition of General Grant. At the same time that Hamilton was assuring Grant of his esteem and devotion, he was privately assuring Senator James R. Doolittle of Wisconsin that "Grant is a drunkard." After other criticisms of superiors as well as trying to get command of James B. McPherson's XVII Corps, General Grant protested strongly to Washington and Hamilton's resignation was accepted on April 13, 1863.)[6]

General Hamilton ordered Sanborn to relieve Willcox's cavalry with infantry troops. Colonel Matthies then threw forward three or four companies of the 5th Iowa Regiment as skirmishers. These crack troopers, under the command of Lieutenant Colonel Ezekiel S. Sampson, moved forward on the double and, crossing the branch of Crippled Deer, engaged the Confederates and forced them to give up their position at Mrs. Moore's residence. General Hamilton was so mad over the death of his staff officer, he had a patrol put fire to Mrs. Moore's beautiful home. He must have felt justified in taking this action because Trezevant's sharpshooters had taken their position there.[7]

Dudley says in his account:

"Here (at Mrs. Moore's) the Confederate cavalry had again taken a stand and as the Federal column came in sight fired a volley which killed Lieut. Schraum, a member of Gen. Hamilton's staff. This infuriated the Federal commander, who ordered the torch applied to the handsome residence of Mrs. Moore and it was in a few minutes reduced to ashes. This deed of vandalism was totally without excuse, as Mrs. Moore was not responsible for the fact that the commander of the Confederate force had chosen to make a stand in front of her home, and the burning of her dwelling was an unworthy and disgraceful act."[8]

The heat was uncomfortable for the troops as the long line marched past her burning home. The skirmishers of the 5th Iowa moved forward up the road and the balance of the 5th moved along in a flank movement close behind them.[9]

ROSECRAN'S ADVANCE
CHAPTER SIXTEEN

With the Confederate cavalry driven back, the Iowans marched on toward Iuka on the Jacinto Road. Trezevant's men remained in sight much of the time and several shots were exchanged. At one point the dismounted cavalry rallied in a house on the west side of the road in the center of an open field. The position completely commanded the field through which the Union skirmishers had to approach. A flank movement by the left of the Iowan skirmish line soon convinced the Rebels that to remain in their position meant death or capture, however, and the Confederates broke for the rear. One of the men fell dead in a peach orchard near the house and another was killed in the woods on the other side of the road. Apparently two others were killed and other Rebels wounded but only one of the Union men injured.[1]

At about four o'clock, and when the Union Army was about three miles from Iuka, the skirmish line of the Fifth Iowa was relieved by Companies A, B, G, and I of the Twenty-sixth Missouri Regiment, under Lieutenant Colonel Holman. Hamilton's Division of two brigades (Sanborns and Sullivan's) of five regiments and a battery each had marched all of the way from Jacinto and Stanley's Division, also of two brigades of five regiments each, was following on the same road. The bluecoat army of 9,000 men was within three miles of General Price's headquarters and no more than a couple of very limited and transient stands had been taken by the Confederates against them.

A correspondent of the <u>Mississippian</u> wrote in his paper:

"Don't see how, with woods full of cavalry, the Yankees could get so close to General Price's headquarters without his knowledge."[2]

In General Price's report he simply states that at 2:00 P.M. his pickets were driven in on the Iuka road and that they reported to him at 2:30 P.M. that the enemy were advancing in force on the Jacinto Road. Dudley, in his account, states his belief the messengers were infantrymen although they very well could have been some of the dismounted cavalry that had taken a stand at the house in the field.

"These pickets were undoubtedly infantry pickets from all the circumstances," Dudley said. "Their outpost was about a mile from Mrs. Moore's and about three miles from Iuka. Two men were on this picket post. One was slain and the other made his escape, covered with the blood of his slain comrade, and he it was probably who brought to Gen. Price the first information that convinced him that the movement on the

Jacinto road was a serious one."[3]

A short distance further along the Jacinto Road the Union column passed Dick Rick's log plantation house. It was on the west side of the road adjacent to a large, irregularly shaped field on the east side of the road. The surface of the field was quite level. Its width in front of the house was nearly a quarter of a mile and its entire length was nearly a half mile. Some of the thirsty bluecoats stopped for a drink from the well in the yard of the Rick House. Over the gate to the yard was a little circular board which read, "Iuka 2 miles".[4]

A quarter of a mile beyond the Dick Rick House, the Missourians came to a log church building on the west side of the road and at that point the roads forked. The right fork passed through timber and was quite narrow and followed a ridge. On the left just beyond the forks was a shallow ravine, the ground being low and covered with long grass and bushes at first, and young, straight timber further on.[5]

Across from the church and on the south side of the road, a few rods away, was a graveyard. The narrow road ran east-northeast for some two hundred yards at which point it turned again to the north. Where the road turned north again it descended from the ridge toward Iuka. This high ridge ran east and west with an inclination to northwest and southeast. The eastern edge of the ridge was divided into three spurs, one running nearly south, one running east-southeast, and the other intermediate. This ridge was about a quarter of a mile beyond the forks of the road and an old abandoned road passed along it.[6]

The Union scouts told Lieutenant Colonel Holman, who commanded the advance guard, that the road which branched to the right from the log meeting house gave access to the Fulton Road. The left branch ran out a ridge in a northward direction toward the Armstrong (or Yow) house. Going ahead along the narrow ridge road to the right, Holman's Missourians topped the high ridge beyond the log house. Here the advance was halted. Only a few hundred yards ahead the Confederates lay concealed in the woods. A great and furious battle was about to commence.[7]

U. S. General David S. Stanley, Commander of General Rosecrans' 2nd Division at the Battle of Iuka. Courtesy of Massachusetts Commandery Military Order of the Loyal Legion and the U. S. Army Military History Institute.

THE BATTLE BEGINS
CHAPTER SEVENTEEN

Around 2:30 p.m. on September 19, an excited Confederate rode up to General Price's command post on the Burnsville-Iuka Road. The scout informed the General that a large force of Federal troops was approaching Iuka on the Jacinto Road and that the cavalry patrols were unable to check their advance and were falling back toward Iuka. At the time, General Price was expecting the Federal attack to come from the west, from Burnsville, where General Grant had his headquarters, and from which direction all of the action and skirmishing had occurred. The southern approach had been left essentially unguarded and, except for some skirmishing from the Confederate horsemen under Lieutenant E. B. Trezevant, the two divisions of Union infantrymen had advanced to within a few miles of Iuka unnoticed and uncontested. Of General Price's two divisions, the First, Third, and Fourth Brigades of Little's Division were in line of battle on the Burnsville Road and General Maury's Division was posted in reserve in the woods a little distance to the rear.

Little's Second Brigade, He'bert's, was also posted to guard the Burnsville Road but was nearer to town, in a position to move to any threatened point. Apparently the brigade was about two miles or so north of Iuka when General Price received word that the Federal troops were approaching from the south. According to Dudley, [1] He'bert's Brigade's campground was near Oak Grove Cemetery and they were in this area when they were ordered forward by General Price. (Oak Grove Cemetery was deeded to the Town of Iuka in 1866 by Colonel Lawrence Moore, the same man that built the residence that General Price selected as his headquarters.)[2]

Ephraim McD. Anderson, a member of another brigade (the First), had this to say about the position of He'bert's Brigade:

"General He'bert's Brigade was posted on another road, the one on which we had advanced upon the place, and though it was improbable that anything more than a cavalry demonstration would be made here, and perhaps doubtful if even that were done, nevertheless it was deemed prudent to place a respectable force "en potence," to guard against attack from this quarter: the position it occupied was about a mile and a half from the town, in which our train was left."[3]

W. H. Tunnard of the 3rd Louisiana Infantry Regiment, a regiment in He'bert's Brigade, confirms that his regiment was posted almost two miles north of Iuka on the Burnsville Road. He says in his remembrances:

"The regiment continued in line of battle until the 19th, when they returned to camp, to remain only a short time, being ordered out on the Byrneville (sic) road once more. While on this road, Sept. 19th, news arrived that the enemy, under command of General Rosecrans, was advancing on the Baldwin (sic) road. General He'bert received orders to proceed with his brigade at a double-quick to meet them. The command, at almost a full run for nearly three miles, hastened forward. Over the railroad, through Iuka, and out on the Baldwin (sic) or Bay Springs road; when about a mile from Iuka, the brigade was formed into line of battle."4

A portion of He'bert's Brigade might have been posted further out the Burnsville Road as Samuel Barron, a member of the Third Texas Cavalry, suggests:

"On the night of September 18 we marched out about four miles on the Corinth road, leading west, and lay in line of battle until about 4 P.M. the next day, when a courier came in great haste, with the information that the enemy was advancing on the Bay Springs road from the south, with only a company of cavalry in front of them. We had then to double-quick back about three miles in order to get into the road they were on. We found them among the hills about one and a half miles from the town. . ."5

He'bert's Brigade was well disciplined and represented the best of General Price's troops. It was also called the Second Brigade (of General Little's Division) and consisted of the 3rd Texas (dismounted cavalry) Regiment, the 1st Texas (Whitfield's) Legion (dismounted cavalry), the 3rd Louisiana Regiment, the 40th Mississippi Regiment, and the 14th and 17th (consolidated) Arkansas Regiments.

The 40th Mississippi was the only one of He'bert's units that had never been in combat. It was a new regiment that had been added to General Price's command just before Little's Division had been ordered to the Guntown area. It was quite unusual and is remembered for some distinct peculiarities. The unit contained the tallest man and the largest boy in the Confederate Army. Also, the men carried an extraordinary amount of luggage. It seemed to some of the other soldiers in the other regiments that the Mississippi boys had brought all of their household goods along when they joined the Division. The tallest man was rather slender and appeared to be about seven feet high, which was very tall for that time. The largest boy was about seventeen years old and weighed more than three hundred pounds.6

Upon hearing of the Union advance south of Iuka, General Price immediately sent for his trusted division commander, General Lewis Henry Little. Price had overwhelming confidence in General Little and it was upon his and General Van Dorn's recommendations that Little had been promoted to brigadier general a few months earlier. Little had been assigned to the command of a division by General Bragg after the evacuation of Corinth and had performed his duties remarkably well. General Little was only forty-five years old and was Price's right hand man. General Price told General Little to send He'bert's Brigade immediately and swiftly to meet the advancing Unionists. As General He'bert formed his brigade, Little gave him his instructions. He was to proceed out the Bay Springs or Jacinto Road to check the heavy Union column which was advancing rapidly northward toward Iuka. Two batteries, the St. Louis Artillery and the Clark Missouri Battery were sent to accompany General He'bert's Brigade.7

It was fortunate that He'bert's Brigade was posted so near Iuka and within quick striking distance of Rosecrans' troops, which had only a few cavalrymen between them and the town. General He'bert ordered the men to double-quick in the direction of the advancing Union troops. In a very short period of time the brigade formed and started in a trot, passing west of the Iuka Depot and taking the Jacinto road (Old Highway 25 as it lies south of town, passing by Elm Shopping Center, The Church of Christ, The Tishomingo County Courthouse, and Walmart approximates the old Jacinto Road.) They crossed Hubbard Branch (or West Indian Creek) which now flows between Iuka Discount Drugstore and Elm Shopping Center. When they reached the top of the hill beyond Hubbard Branch (probably somewhere near the Tishomingo County Courthouse), the Confederates were deployed in line of the battle and moved steadily forward through the woods, on both sides of the Jacinto road.8

The excited soldiers of Whitfield's Texas Legion covered both sides of the Jacinto Road as they moved toward the Yankees in their front. About one mile southwest of town, He'bert's vanguard caught sight of the retreating Confederate cavalrymen who were falling back in the face of Rosecrans' powerful force. The horsemen cheered He'bert's infantrymen as they rushed to meet the oncoming Unionists. After moving forward only a few hundred more yards, the Confederates met the Federal skirmishers who they drove back rapidly upon the main body, which was approaching on the ridge just back of the forks of the road.7 At the summit of the second hill south of Iuka the Jacinto Road veered almost at right angles toward the east. It was here that the large forces of Unionists and Rebels met.10

Within a few minutes of General He'bert's departure from north of town to meet Rosecran's advancing force, General Price correctly deduced that more troops would soon be needed. He quickly ordered

General Little to take the Fourth Brigade (Martin's) to the front. This brigade was composed of three Mississippi regiments and one Alabama regiment. Some of the men in the 37th Alabama, thinking that they were being deployed by another false alarm, began to make jokes directed at General Price and the other officers who happened to be nearby. Their laughter soon turned to sobriety, however, as they double-timed it toward the battle which had begun to rage south of Iuka.11 General Maury was placed in charge of the troops massed against General Ord on the Burnsville Road.

After marching eighteen miles, Rosecran's tired but excited body of troops encountered the Confederates defense at about 4:30 p.m. with Hamilton's Division leading and Stanley's Division in the rear. Each division had two brigades of five regiments each. Of Hamilton's Division, Sanborn's Brigade was in front, followed by Sullivan's. Sanborn's and Sullivan's Brigades each had a battery as well as five regiments. They had traveled in light marching order and only wagons carrying forage, extra rations, ammunition, and hospital supplies had been allowed to accompany the columns. Each soldier was supplied with 100 rounds of ammunition, 40 of which was carried in the individual's cartridge-box. Rosecrans' total marching force was 9,000 men but Stanley's Division was some distance in the rear and only three of his regiments reached the field in time to take any part in the battle.

Major General C. S. Hamilton, commanding the leading Union division, had just halted his men in the order in which they had been marching. The head of the column (Sanborn's Brigade) had just finished ascending a long hill, from the top of which the ground sloped in undulations toward the front. General Hamilton was at the front of the main column and just to the rear of his skirmishers. When he saw the Union skirmishers giving way, he dashed back to the head of his column. He reasoned that if the column should become enveloped by the Confederates, a rout would be inevitable and the division would be doubled back on itself.12

As soon as General He'bert saw Holman's Missourians advancing, he yelled for Lieutenant James L. Faris of the Clark Battery to unlimber a section of his guns. He wanted the lieutenant to place the artillery on a knoll to be in range of the ridge held by Colonel Holman's Union skirmishers. Unhitching the cannons, the Confederate artillerists pushed the fieldpieces up the rise to the knoll. Bullets whizzed by from Holman's snipers, coming too close for comfort. As the artillerists were well in front of the infantrymen, Lieutenant Faris decided that it would be foolish to expose his men to possible capture by the Missourians and ordered the section to fall back. The Confederate artillerymen withdrew their cannons about one hundred fifty yards and waited for the infantry to advance and drive back the Union skirmishers. They placed the battery just below the brow of the hill (near the site occupied by Billy Gann's Construction Company), awaiting the development of the Confederate line. In the meantime, the second section of the Clark Battery (Lieutenant Henry S. Johnston, commanding) took position west of the Jacinto Road with its cannons aimed toward the open fields, in case the Union advance would come from that direction.[13]

By the time the Confederate artillerists had unlimbered their cannons, He'bert's lead regiment, the 3rd Texas Cavalry, had started to form. General He'bert ordered the regiment deployed as skirmishers to drive back the Federal sharpshooters.[14] The Third Texas was the first regiment to leave the State of Texas and was one of the best regiments ever in the Confederate service. Unfortunately, all of their men were not brave and trustworthy, for they had men that were too cowardly to fight and they had some men unprincipled enough to desert, but taken all in all, for gallantry and for fighting qualities under any and all circumstances, either in advance or retreat, the 3rd Texas deservedly stood in front rank and would soon prove themselves on the Iuka Battlefield.[15]

General He'bert formed his 2nd Brigade with the 3rd Louisiana on the left, the 3rd Texas (dismounted cavalry) in the center, and Whitfield's 1st Texas Legion (dismounted cavalry) on the right. The 40th Mississippi and battalions of the 14th and 17th Arkansas were formed in rear of the 3rd Texas and 3rd Louisiana.[16] A member of the 3rd Louisiana Infantry Regiment claimed that skirmishers from Company F of that regiment fired the "first gun" that was shot during the Battle of Iuka.[17] The following account was given by a soldier in the 3rd Louisiana:

"After General Herbert (sic) made disposition of his brigade for battle, the Third Louisiana being on the extreme of the line, Colonel Gilmore ordered forward as skirmishers the left wing of his regiment. Company F, being on the right, came in contact with the enemy . . . . This little skirmish lasted about fifteen minutes, the enemy losing four or five men killed. I must state a circumstance that occurred during the affair. Two of the enemy took shelter behind a large tree directly in front of Company F. The tree, however, was not large enough to protect the two, one of whom was instantly killed by private Hudson; the other begged for his life most piteously, which would undoubtedly have been granted him had he relied on the word of a rebel. He was ordered several times to come to the company and his life should be spared, but he was afraid to expose his person. During the conversation between him and the captain, private J. Jus, it seems, became rather restless, left his position in the line, and slipped around until he came in view of the Yankee, then raised his gun and shot him through the head, at the same time remarking, 'Damned if I don't fetch him'. The Federal proved to be a lieutenant.[18]

The brave men of the 3rd Texas were also utilized as skirmishers. Colonel Hinchie P. Mabry led them forward. As the dismounted Rebel cavalrymen moved ahead, one of the officers asked General He'bert, who was supervising the advance, "General, must we fix bayonets?"

"Yes sir! the native of Iberville Parish, Louisiana shouted. "What for you have ze bayonet if you no fix him? Yes, by gar; fix him!" He'bert's men charged and Holman's Missourian skirmishers gave way, falling back on the Union main line of resistance about four hundred yards to the rear.[19] Holmon's Company A then rallied on the right and Captain Rice brought up his reserve. The three Union companies fired a round into the Rebels and almost instantly drew the fire of the Confederates' artillery and two regiments of infantry. The Union skirmishers held their ground until their front line was formed, then fell back and formed with their regiment.[20]

The ground occupied by the head of the Union column was on the brow of a densely wooded hill which fell off abruptly to the right and left. The timber and underbrush were too thick to easily deploy troops or cannonry. The most that General Hamilton thought could be done was to take a position across the road, by marching the leading regiments into position by flank movements. This he attempted to do, under the blazing Confederate firing of musketry and grape, canister, and shell.[21]

General Hamilton quickly ordered his leading regiment, the 5th Iowa, across the road and moved it a short distance to the right. He formed it along the top of the ridge in line of battle with the right wing slightly behind, to prevent, as far as was possible, it being flanked on that side by Price's troops before the other Union regiments were deployed.[22] The right wing extended down the slope of the ridge.

General Little arrived from the north with Martin's Brigade just as General He'bert had deployed his brigade, unlimbered his artillery, and advanced his skirmishers. As the Mississippians and Alabamans of Martin's Brigade reached the site of the action, some of the men made remarks about "buzzards passing", this being their first experience with enemy shells.[23] In accordance with General Little's orders, General Martin immediately formed his brigade in the rear of General He'bert's battle line.

To counter the rapidly developing Confederate fire and manpower,

Colonel Wirt Adams, Commander of the Mississippi Regiment of Armstrong's Cavalry. Courtesy of Massachusetts Commandery Military Order of the Loyal Legion and the U. S. Army Military History Institute.

Union General John Sanborn ordered up his battery, the 11th Ohio, to take position immediately to the left of 5th Iowa. The Eleventh Ohio Battery, commanded by Lieutenant Sears, was situated near the front of the column behind the 5th Iowa. They marched through a defile at the crest of a thickly wooded hill and heard heavy gunfire in their immediate front. As the battery exited this defile they found themselves within range of the Confederates, who instantly opened fire on them.[24]

As soon as the Texans drove in the Union sharpshooters, Faris' Confederate gunners replaced their guns on the commanding knoll. Charging their two guns with case shot and canister, the Missourians poured deadly fire into the developing Union battle line.[25]

One of the junior first lieutenants of the 11th Ohio said that it gave him the impression of being in a violent hail storm. He was riding at the head of the column and turned his head to look for his men, expecting to see half of them and the horses on the ground. To his great joy, none had been injured by the rain of Rebel bullets; all had apparently passed just over their heads. The cannoners of the 11th Ohio scrambled to get into position and unlimber their guns before the Confederates could get their range. Just in front of the artillerymen, the road turned to the right. The men turned to the right into the brush and took position facing this road on the only available suitable ground. A small log house, surrounded by a clearing, was just in front of the site selected by the cannoneers.

Taking careful aim, Faris' Confederate gunners working "coolly and calmly" made almost every round count. Within a few minutes, the Union troops had taken cover, either in the woods or on the ground. Lieutenant Faris, not wanting to waste any ammunition, shouted for his gun captains to hold their fire. Lieutenant Johnston's section had also gone into action. The rounds of canister caused the skirmishers from the 48th Indiana to scamper back into the woods for cover.[26]

Under Lieutenant Sears' command, the 11th Ohio was now into position to return the deadly cannon fire. Junior First Lieutenant Henry M. Neil was in charge of the right section, Second Lieutenant Alger the center, acting Second Lieutenant Perrine the left section, and acting Second Lieutenant Bauer the line of caissons. The six guns consisted of the following:

(2) 4.62 caliber twelve pounder Howitzers; (2) 3.67 caliber smooth-bore 6 pounders with a 14 lb. ball; and (2) 3.67 caliber rifled, bronze 6 pounders (James pattern) with a 14 lb. ball.[27]

Colonel Sanborn formed his line of battle on the crest of the ridge. The 48th Indiana Infantry (434 men) was brought into position to the left of the battery with the left wing slightly held back. The line was prolonged on the left by the placement of the 4th Minnesota (408 men). These regiments were ordered to hold their position at all hazards until further orders. The 26th Missouri Infantry was formed in order of battle below the crest of the ridge, with its left nearly in rear of the center of the 5th Iowa and its right down a steep side of the hill to a ravine. Colonel Boomer, commanding the 26th Missouri, was ordered by Colonel Sanborn to move immediately to the right of the 5th Iowa if the Rebels should move in that direction. Colonel Boomer was given discretionary authority, however, to move to the relief of any point in the Federal line that was strongly assailed.[28]

The 16th Iowa (350 men) was formed behind the battery for support. It was placed below the crest of the hill with its right behind the battery and the left flank of the 5th Iowa. The left of the 16th Iowa was about 20 yards behind the three right companies of the 48th Indiana. All of these formations and movement's were made under a steady fire of canister from the Rebel batteries.[29]

Although the adrenalin-charged Confederates had advanced to within 200 yards of the Federal battleline, the 11th Ohio Battery still had not received orders to commence firing. Becoming extremely anxious, a sergeant screamed: "By God, I guess we're going to let them gobble the whole damned shooting match before we strike a lick." A corporal replied: "I guess we are obeying orders." "Damn the orders," the sergeant yelled back. "It was the last straw," the battery commander later said. "Give them hell as fast as you can! . . . The guns of this battery became the bone of contention"; Sears remembered, "everything else, both flags, Union and Confederacy . . . were forgotten in that all-absorbing handspike-and-ramrod, rough-and-tumble, devil-take-the hindmost fight for those six guns."[30]

Sears' artillerymen opened first with shell directed at the Confederates 200-400 yards across the deep ravine, in areas now occupied by Iuka Monument Company, McNatt's Ford Company, and Billy Gann's Construction. (Highway 25 Bypass now traverses what was then the deep ravine.) Shells from the Confederate batteries continued to crash through the Union battle line.[31] Mrs. Woodley, who lived close by, said "they shot so fast it sounded like corn a 'poppin'."[32]

W. P. Helm, a member of Company I, 3rd Texas Cavalry and acting commissary of the regiment, said that he could never forget the moment his unit was fired upon by the 11th Ohio Battery. His regiment was down in the valley between the hills when they received enormous and sudden fire from the enemy. "It came like lightning from a clear sky," he later wrote. "The roaring of artillery, the rattle of musketry, the hailstorm of grape and ball were mowing us down like grain before we could locate from whence it came. We were trapped; there could be no retreat, and certain death was in our advance. We fell prostrate on the ground."[33]

One of the men in his unit, Captain Green of Company I, arose on his knees to give the troops an order. Just as he said, "Steady, boys, steady," he was decapitated by a cannon ball. Another officer, Lieutenant Ingram, arose to stop one of the men from retreating and he and the private were both cut in two with grape shot. "Our ranks were shattered in the twinkling of an eye," Helms said. The men dared not retreat because the hill in their back was steep and would certainly expose them to heavier and more accurate fire from the battery. They had to advance up the hill, which they did, attempting to protect themselves from positions behind trees and logs. Helms got behind a log and Lieutenant Alf Hunt was next to him. From these tenuous positions the men shot at the Federal gunners on the hill.[34]

General Price planned to strike Hamilton's troops in the center and to flank them on the right and the left. When the fight commenced, General Rosecrans was riding with General Stanley about a mile to the rear of the head of General Hamilton's column. He quickly galloped forward along the clogged wagon road to the front.[35] "Old Rosy" inspected General Hamilton's and Colonel Sanborn's placement of troops on the front line and, finding them to his satisfaction considering the disadvantages of the terrain, ordered Colonel Mizner to send a battalion of the Third Michigan Cavalry to reconnoiter the Union right. He also ordered Colonel Perezel, with the Tenth Iowa Infantry and a section of artillery to take position on the Union left, on the road leading north toward the Yow house.[36] These two guns belonged to the Twelfth Wisconsin Battery under command of Lieutenant L. D. Immell and Sergeant Jones.

Due to the nature of the Union Army's position on the brow of the hill, General Rosecrans and Hamilton were unable to rapidly commit their troops. This was of considerable advantage to the Confederates. As the battle commenced, General He'bert's Brigade was opposed only by Colonel John Sanborn's Brigade of Brigadier General Charles S. Hamilton's Division. Before Rosecrans was able to send up any additional units, Colonel John D. Martin's Brigade had arrived and was massed in support of General He'bert's battle line.[37] The remainder of Hamilton's Division formed in rear of the first line and the head of Stanley's Division stood in column below the Federal hospital (Rick's House) awaiting the developments on the front before being moved into line.[38]

On the morning of the battle, Lieutenant T. B. Hunt, the 4th

Minnesota regimental quartermaster, and Commissary Sergeant T. P. Wilson were in Corinth, where they had gone for supplies for the regiment. About noon, hearing that a battle was about to occur, they left for Iuka. After riding about 40 miles, they arrived in Iuka while the battle was still raging.[39]

During the progress of the battle, a great many of the officers' colored servants "fell back on the base" as it was called. In other words, they ran for the rear as fast as they could. Humorous scenes were created as the scared servants sheltered themselves behind trees and logs. Some of the best runners seemed to act as if they had urgent business in Corinth. Before Hunt and Wilson reached the Union lines they met one of the colored servants running as fast as his legs could carry him. They stopped him and inquired as to how the battle was progressing. He replied:

"Oh, Lord, Massa! Big fight up dah; an I'se gitten to de r'ar. I'se dest trowed way a big key, and a knife dat I paid five cents fur, ter lighten me up, so I kin go faster. Yer bettah look out up dar!"[40]

Sergeant Wilson rode on to the front and suddenly found himself in the presence of a line of Confederate soldiers, who were lying on the ground behind a fence with their arms all ready to fire. "Where are you going?" one of the Rebels asked. "Oh, I am just looking around a little," Wilson replied as he wheeled his horse partly around and looked back up the road from which he had come. "You had better not go very far in that direction," the Rebel advised. He had not observed Wilson's blue uniform. "I'll be careful," Wilson answered as he turned his horse to the left and rode away to make his escape.[41]

Iuka, Mississippi in 1862. From Harper's Weekly, September 13, 1862.

IUKA, MISSISSIPPI.

GENERAL HE'BERT'S CHARGE
CHAPTER EIGHTEEN

With the battlelines of the opposing armies formed on opposite ridges, the men of the 3rd Louisiana Infantry Regiment heard the Union order to advance, "Forward--guide centre, march!" yelled loudly. Hardly had the words died away, when the same command, loud and clear, rang in their ears from their commanding officer. Colonel Gilmore immediately ordered forward Company K of the regiment as skirmishers. This company rapidly threw themselves in front of the rest of 3rd Louisiana Regiment, and advanced double-quick up the hill, followed closely by the regiment. Directly in their front was a long sloping hill, covered with large trees with very little underbrush. Rosecrans' line soon appeared, and was immediately warmly received by the skirmishers, who held their ground until the rest of the regiments came to their assistance. The firing immediately opened from both lines like a "sudden clap of thunder" and continued without abatement. At the commencement of the firing the Louisiana boys dropped down on their knees and the greatest portion of the Union firepower flew harmlessly over their heads, while their shooting had a telling effect on the Federals. The firing was fearful -- the smoke enveloped both lines, so that the Rebels could not see the Yankees and vice versa. The enemy's lines could only be distinguised by the flash of the guns. The evening was damp, dull, and cloudy and the black powder smoke settled and hung at about head level.[1]

The Federal's 11th Ohio Battery, under the command of Lieutenant Sears, was sandwiched between the Fifth Iowa on the right and the Forty-eighth Indiana on the left. The battery had opened with shell, which were hollow projectiles used against animate objects in distinction from solid shot which were intended to batter down walls or heavy obstructions. The shell fire proved so effective against the Confederates that General He'bert ordered a massive assault on the battery.[2]

With Martin's troops massed in the rear of He'bert's, General Little gave the order to attack. The Confederates, with the terror-striking Rebel yell, moved off the ridge to the south of the Yankees and then advanced in double line of battle, slowly at first, down the hill on which they had formed, across the little valley, to begin the ascent of the hill on which the 5th Iowa Regiment and the 11th Ohio Battery were posted. As soon as the battle line started forward, Colonel Mabry called back the men of the 3rd Texas that had been sent out as skirmishers. Assembling, Colonel Mabry's men fell in to the left of the 1st Texas Legion. As they moved across the ravine, one of the Texans recalled, "a little dog was observed trotting along in advance of the line, apparently oblivious to the thunders of artillery, the rattle of rifles, and the whizzing of missiles that literally filled the air. The fate of the brave little rebel dog was never known."[3] As soon as He'bert's men reached the bottom of the valley, the command "double-quick" was given. Soon the greyclads were across the valley and had begun driving up the ridge where Hamilton had formed his battle line.

When He'bert's men ascended the hill, they came in range of the artillerists of the Clark Battery and to prevent killing their own men, the Confederate cannoners had to stop firing. As He'bert's Brigade charged up the hill, the 11th Ohio changed from shell to double charges of canister. Canister was simply a sheet iron case filled with bullets and was very effective against men and animals at very short ranges. The Rebel method of charging in masses made the effects of the canister much more devastating. One of the Texans describes what it was like:

"As we ascended the hill we came in range of our own artillery, and the guns had to be silenced. The entire Federal artillery fire was soon turned on us, using grape and canister shot, and as their battery was directly in front of the Third Texas, their grape shot and musketry fire soon began to play havoc with our people, four of our men, the two files just to my right, being killed."[4]

While Lieutenant Feris' gunners were waiting to begin firing again, their positions were raked with the deadly canister from the 11th Ohio Battery. They could not defend themselves without firing into the backs of He'bert's charging troops. In addition, they were within range of the Yankee's small arm fire. The deadly minies swept through both Johnston's and Faris' Batteries. Finally, General Hebert gave word for the artillerists to withdraw their guns to a less exposed position. The men withdrew their pieces from the knoll and placed them on the right of the road.[5]

"Charge!" the brave Louisianan from Iberville Parish yelled, and Colonel Whitfield echoed his command. By this time, Whitfield's regiment and the 3rd Texas had pushed to within 150 yards of the Union battery. The Texans shouted loudly and fought toward the canister-blasting cannons. "On, men, on!" General He'bert shouted and the Confederate battle-line surged forward, men falling at every step. The men that were left standing struggled ahead, leaving their fallen comrades behind, firing volleys into General Hamilton's ranks. Louder and louder sounded the roar of the cannons and musketry. "Double charges of grape and canister," screamed someone from the Union line.

106

It was a scene never to be forgotten by both Yankee and Rebel participants. The ground trembled as Lieutenant Sears' cannoneers of the 11th Ohio sent round after round crashing into General He'bert's advancing Confederates. Many of the Third Texas dismounted cavalry were armed with double-barreled shotguns and fired the deadly buckshot at close range into the embattered Unionists. Brave young Lieutenant Dan Alley of Company G, Third Texas, during the hottest time of the clash, yelled "Come on boys!" and charged the unyielding Federals.6

About this time, with the battle raging and the rugged hillside becoming more and more littered with the lifeless and struggling blue and greyclad bodies, General Little ordered Colonel Martin to split his brigade and reinforce the right and left flanks. General Little said that he would take command of the 37th and 38th Mississippi Regiments and use them to support He'bert's Brigade on the right. Martin was to take the two regiments on the left, the 36th Mississippi and the 37th Alabama, and support He'bert on that side. This would form a long Confederate battleline, commanded (from left to right) by Colonel Martin, General He'bert, and General Little.

Meanwhile, the 3rd Louisiana Infantry Regiment, also having received the order to charge, rushed up the hillside into the Union Line and drove them from the rise. On the hill, however, the regiment suffered. A new line of the enemy opened fire on them and one of the other Confederate groups in their rear also mistakenly shot into their line. It was a terrible moment for the brave men of this regiment.7

Major Russell rode up to the Confederate line and told them that they were firing on their friends. About this time, the Colonel's horse was shot from under him and he was wounded in the shoulder. Not to be outdone, the Colonel, now on foot, ordered a charge down the hill and led it in person. Here the fighting was desperate; a number of the men in the 3rd Louisiana were wounded and a large number killed.8

Some of the troops of the 3rd Texas Regiment also received rounds from their friends. General Whitfield's troops, mistaking the 3rd Texas for the enemy, fired into them. Lieutenant Hunt was among those wounded in the charge. The men of the 3rd Texas, seeing only certain death between friend and foe, heard the order: "Boys, if we are to die, let it be by Yankee bullets, not by our friends. So let us charge the cannon!" The men of the 3rd gave a shout and leaped forward. One of the men described the fierce hand to hand combat that ensued:

"Sword and bayonet were crossed. Muskets, revolvers, knives, ramrods, gun swabs--all mingled in the death-dealing fray. All the furies of torment seemed turned loose in that smoke-blinding boom of cannon and rattle of musketry".9

Union General Hamilton gave the following perspective from his side of the battle:

"The Confederate line had moved forward, concentrating their fire on our little front, and stretching out their wings to the right and left, as though we were to be taken in at once. Our men stood their ground bravely, yielding nothing for a long time, but the pressure began to grow severe and I feared we might be driven from our ground . . . All the while the battle waxed hotter and more furious. The dead lay in lines along the regiments, while some of our troops gave signs of yielding . . . Our troops, as yet, had not given way. The battery under Sears was doing noble service, but had lost nearly half its men. Sanborn's brigade was held by him to their work like Roman veterans, but without help we could not much longer hold out."10

Captain Henry Little. This photograph was taken 16 years before the Battle of Iuka when Little served with the 7th U. S. Infantry. Courtesy of Massachusetts Commandery Military Order of the Loyal Legion and the U. S. Army Military History Institute.

THE DEATH OF GENERAL LITTLE
CHAPTER NINETEEN

As the terrible battle on the hills south of Iuka waxed hot and furious and General He'bert's troops met unyielding resistence from the determined Yankees, General Price realized that the Union force he had encountered was stronger than what he had originally thought. Reinforcements were needed immediately and he sought his trusted division commander, General Henry Little, for consultation.

General Little was born Lewis Henry Little on March 19, 1817. He was a native of Baltimore, Maryland and the son of a long-time Maryland Congressman and War of 1812 veteran, Peter Little. In 1839, after attending St. Mary's College in Baltimore, he was commissioned directly into the U. S. Army and was awarded for meritorious and gallant conduct at the Battle of Monterey in the Mexican War. In 1858 he participated in Colonel Albert Sidney Johnston's expedition to Utah.[1] His marriage in 1855 produced two daughters, Kate and Irene. Kate died at the age of 4 in 1860. In 1861 he resigned his U. S. commission and cast his lot with the Confederacy. Initially, he was commissioned as a major of artillery in the regular service. He soon, however, became attached to the staff of General Price as a colonel and assistant adjutant general and became one of General Price's favorite officers. Little distinguished himself while commanding a brigade at the Battle of Elkhorn. Upon recommendations of General Price and General Van Dorn, Little was promoted to brigadier general on April 16, 1862. After the evacuation of Corinth, General Braxton Bragg assigned General Little the command of a division.[2] He grew to become General Price's "most trusted lieutenant", the best division commander he ever knew.[3]

In August, 1862, General Price highly recommended Little's appointment to Major General. In part, he said:

"General Little commanded this (First) brigade during my retreat from Springfield and at the battle of Elkhorn, and on both occasions displayed distinguished coolness, and skill, and the military ability of a very high character, thus demonstrating his ability not only as an organizer and disciplinarian but as a commander upon the field. His officers and men place the greatest confidence in him, and every one from Missouri has appeared willing to yield precedence to him, though he is not and has never been a resident of that State. I cannot commend him too highly . ."[4]

General Price and General Little met at the base of a hill about 100 yards east of the Jacinto Road near the battleline, close to the sector held by the 3rd Texas.[5] Price ordered Little to immediately bring forward the other two brigades of his division, Gates' and Greens' which were about two miles distant. This meeting occurred around 5:45 p.m. The whole party was close together at that moment, General Price and General Little were both mounted. The two generals were only a few feet apart. General Price had his back toward the Yankees' line and General Little was facing Price. Before General Price had finished speaking and just as General Little was preparing to go after the two brigades, a minie ball passed under General Price's arm and stuck General Little "square in the forehead."[6] This occured approximately three-fourths of an hour after the fight commenced. The projectile entered on the line of the scalp over the left eye, passed through his skull, and stopped under the skin on the posterior portion of his head. His death was without pain and his passage was instantaneous. He did not speak nor move after he was shot.[9] When he was hit, General Little threw up his arms, the reins dropping to the horse's neck, and he fell limp and lifeless into the arms of a comrade.[9] Victor Rose says that Little's body was caught by Sergeant T. J. Cellum of Company A, 3rd Texas[9] while Dudley, in his account, says that Colonel Celsus Price, the son of General Price who was a member of General Price's staff, caught the dead general.[10] The accident occured just as General Little's aide-de-camp, Frank Von Phul, reached the scene.

Horrified over the loss of his dear friend and faithful subordinate, General Price jumped from his saddle and knelt over the lifeless body of General Little, weeping "as he would for a son."[11] With teary eyes and a husky voice, the General ordered Sergeant Cellum: "Bear his body from the field, my son; and remain with it, yourself, until I can join you."[12] Then, pulling himself together, "Old Pap" remounted and took personal charge of the battle, at the same time sending word to Brigadier General He'bert that he now commanded Little's division.[13]

Reverend Johnathan Bannon of St. Louis took charge of General Little's body and conveyed it to Little's headquarters, a small cottage in the center of Iuka. There the body was laid out and afterwards decently buried.[14]

The fall of General Little was immediately known throughout the Confederate lines, but, far from creating consternation, panic, or confusion, most of the officers and soldiers seemed to become filled with new determination to win. The leader whom they had learned to love and esteem and in whom they had full confidence had fallen. The Yankees had deprived them of him and revenge was within their grasp![15] The men of He'bert's Division pushed steadily ahead up the hill, selling their lives dearly for each yard of the hillside that was gained.

General Price later said in his official report:

"It will thus be seen that our success was obtained at the sacrifice of many a brave officer and patriot soldier. Chief among them was Brig. Gen. Henry Little, commanding the First Division of this army. Than this brave Marylander, no one could have fallen more dear to me or whose memory should be more fondly cherished by his countrymen. Than him, no more skilled officer or more devoted patriot has drawn his sword in this war of independence. He died in the day of his greatest usefulness, lamented by his friends, by the brigade of his love, by the division which he so ably commanded, and by the Army of the West, of which he had from the beginning been one of the chief ornaments."[16]

One of the Missourians later wrote:

"In Henry Little our brigade lost its main stay and support, and the army its best subordinate general. He did more, both while belonging to the Missouri State Guard and in the Confederate service, towards organizing and disciplining the Missouri troops than any man connected with them. To him it owed its proficiency, steadiness in danger and excellency of drill, and to his labors it was greatly indebted for the high rank it achieved among the armies of the South. His death was an irreparable loss to the army, to his State, and to the Confederacy.[17]

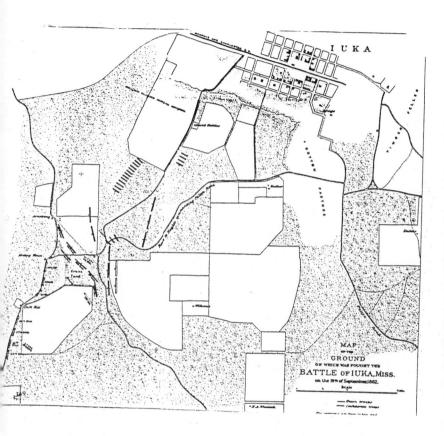

From: The Atlas to Accompany the Official Records of the Union and Confederate Armies, plate XXV.

HAMILTON'S TROOPS RESIST
CHAPTER TWENTY

The battleground on the Union side was an old abandoned field, which was about fifty yards square. The line of battle, from the Ohio battery west, ran across its southeast corner. The 48th Indiana was about 60 feet in front of the woods, which extended along the rear of the Union line. The 4th Minnesota was about 160 to 170 feet in front of the woods. There was a ravine in front of the 5th Iowa, with a small fill for the public road which ran across it. On the opposite side of the ravine was a heavy stand of timber which covered the long hillside. This cover effectually hid the Rebel movements until they were within 50 feet or so of the Union line at that point. The ravine ran out into the old field, the surface of which was uneven and rolling.[1]

COLLAPSE OF THE 48TH INDIANA

The 48th Indiana Regiment was formed on a line nearly with and to the left of the 11th Ohio Battery, on the crest of a hill receding to the left and semicircular in form. The sixteenth Iowa was in the rear for their support and not more than 20 yards to their left was the 4th Minnesota. The men had been ordered to lie down and hold their fire until they could make it effective. There was a deep ravine between the regiment line and the Rebels on the opposite hill. In front of the right wing of the regiment the slope of the hill was very abrupt; on the left it was more rolling and at many points offered a cover to the Confederates' attack. When Clark's Battery had commenced firing, the first and second companies of the regiment who were on the right wing suffered a lot of casualities. The fire from the Confederate batteries was from converging points and the troops that were to the right and left of the 11th Ohio Battery suffered the most. After the Rebel cannoning had lasted about half an hour, He'bert's men had begun their advance toward the section of the Union line that was held by the 48th Indiana and the 5th Iowa Regiments. He'bert's greyclads advanced in three lines, two men deep each.[2] As soon as the Confederates appeared on the opposite ridge, Colonel Eddy's men began firing and continued it until the Rebels disappeared into the hollow separating the armies. For several minutes the Confederates were out of sight but then they reappeared, screaming and storming from the valley below. Hamilton's bluecoats opened fire from the ridge above. He'bert's men halted and returned the volley. Then, with another Rebel yell, the men from the South charged and the line of the 48th Indiana gave away against the powerful surge of Whitfield's Texans. The Federals fell back nearly 100 yards before they were rallied.

Alonzo L. Brown of the 4th Minnesota observed the disorganization in the 48th Indiana. He later wrote:

"We (saw) a part of its rear rank go back to the edge of the woods and return a couple of times, and then the whole regiment broke and fled into the woods in its rear. They had discovered the enemy advancing on them three lines deep, and instead of stopping on our line to fight, left it.

When the 48th ran into the woods the enemy was advancing on them . . . . and followed them into the woods and got on the left flank of the battery. While the 48th was in the woods, in front of the 16th Iowa, and their officers were endeavoring to rally and form them into line, the 16th Iowa fired a volley into the disorganized mass, which killed and wounded nearly one hundred of them."[3]

At the time the line of the 48th Indiana broke, Colonel Eddy was wounded and compelled to retire to the rear. Lieutenant William W. Townsend of the 27th Texas was given credit for shooting Colonel Eddy with a dragoon pistol.[4] The Colonel was badly injured and had to be helped to the rear of the line by several of his men.

Lieutenant - Colonel De Witt C. Rugg then took command of the regiment and restored order. The regiment was reformed on the right of the road on which the battery was placed but the damage had already been done and the 11th Ohio Battery was now exposed and vulnerable to the Confederate's blazing attack. The 48th Indiana Regiment went into battle 434 strong and sustained 37 deaths, 56 wounded, and 8 missing.[5]

Many years following the battle, after the Official Records had been published, General Sanborn was questioned as to the losses of the 48th Indiana. He gave the following astonishing reply:

"The great lost made by the Forty-eighth Indiana was the result of a full volley fired by the Sixteenth Iowa, which was in reserve and immediately in their rear when the rebels broke the right of their line. The rebels and the Forty-eighth men came back absolutely intermingled, with the troops of the Forty-eighth but a few paces in advance in any place. I was near Colonel Eddy between the lines and near the right of both regiments, which was about on the same line. The colonel and his horse fell at the same time that the line broke, shot with from three to five balls each. The Sixteenth Iowa rose up and both ranks brought their guns down to the shoulder, took aim and made ready to fire, and I shouted over and over again at the top of my voice for the men to hold their fire until the Forty-eighth had passed. The troops of the Sixteenth Iowa were cool and looked up intelligently as if they understood the command. I rode to the right of their line, which was but a few paces, and when about half of the Forty-eighth Indiana men that had broken from their own line had got through or over the line in some way, and a few butternuts were getting very close, the Sixteenth Iowa delivered its volley and everything was swept down in its front to the crest of the ridge where the Forty-eighth was first formed, and the Sixteenth Iowa immediately rushed forward and took that position; the rebels were still the other side of the crest and Colonel Chambers was soon shot and fell into their hands; but this accounts for the great loss in that regiment. You may want to know, and the world may want to know, why these facts were not embodied in my official report of the battle. I did embody them in my first report, and both Generals Hamilton and Rosecrans recommended that they be omitted and I redrafted the report and omitted them. They thought that these facts might tend to humiliate some of the officers and men when there was no ground for such humiliation, and both stated that veteran troops could not have been expected to hold the position or to have done better, and that although the fire of the Sixteenth Iowa seemed cruel, that regiment could no longer have been expected to withhold its fire, as rebel troops were within a few rods or a few feet of them. The discharge of that volley by the Sixteenth Iowa was the most cruel and destructive sight that I witnessed in the war, and is as vivid now as when the men brought their guns down to the shoulder, took aim and made ready to fire."[6]

After Colonel Eddy was shot and his Indiana Regiment swept back, the left flank of the 11th Ohio Battery was bare and vulnerable. General He'bert turned his right flank regiments to the left, toward Lieutenant Sears' unprotected cannoneers. As the Confederates drew closer, the artillerists of the 11th Ohio blasted the Southerners with double charges of canister, tearing gaps in the Confederate lines. Enduring the carnage, Whitfield's and Mabry's brave Texans pressed steadily toward the endangered battery. Ensign Ivey Cook, who was carrying the colors of the 27th Texas, was severely wounded in this charge. His brother, Samuel, snatched up and held the treasured Texas banner. Before he could advance more than a few steps, he also was shot down. The third brother, Andrew, then grabbed the staff of the banner shouting, "The flag shall wave, though the entire Cook family is exterminated in the attempt."[7]

As Lieutenant Sears' cannoneers continued to pump cannister into the Confederates at close range, they saw the regiment to their right, the 5th Iowa, being cut to pieces by He'bert's men. Colonel Matthies realized that his left flank companies were being hard-pressed and shouted for the Iowans to charge. "Cheering lustily" the men of the 5th Iowa Regiment pressed forward toward the Confederates. He'bert's men quickly learned that the Iowans would not be driven back as easily as the Indianans. Several deadly volleys from the rugged Iowans drove the men of the 14th and 17th Arkansas Regiments back down into the valley between the hills. Supported by the Texans on their right and the Louisianians on their left, the men from Arkansas charged up the hill toward the Yankees a second time, cheering as they came. Again Colonel Matthies yelled "Forward" and the Arkansans were forced to retreat down the hill. In this attempt, several of the Confederates tired to seize the colors of the 5th Iowa from the standard bearer. Trying to deceive the Iowans, one of the Confederates displayed a United States flag and shouted, "Don't fire at us; we are your friends."[8]

General Rosecrans sent an order for Colonel Matthies to hold his position at all hazards. "That's what I calculate to do," "Old Dutchie" answered.[9] A loud cheer was heard as General He'bert ordered his long battleline forward again, attempting to capture the Unionists on their narrow front. Basically, the lengthy formation had placed the 3rd Louisiana in front of the 5th Iowa and the Third Texas and the Arkansas troops in proximity to the Ohio battery. Whitfield's Texas Legion had faced the 48th Indiana. When Martin's Brigade had been split, the 37th and 38th Mississippi Regiments had been thrown to the right of the Texans and the 36th Mississippi and 37th Alabama to the left. The battle, which had become a bloody infantry duel, continued with great intensity. General Price, in his official report, later said, "The fight began, and was waged with a severity I have never seen surpassed."[10] Many men, both blue and grey, were giving their lives in what would prove to be an indecisive struggle. General Hamilton's men had begun to fall back, but General Price's Confederates were paying dearly for every foot of battleground that had been gained. General Matthies of the 5th Iowa, realizing that his three left flank companies had been decimated, sent a runner to ask Colonel Boomer of the 26th Missouri for help. He could see that something had to be done at once or General He'bert's men would capture the six guns of the Ohio battery. Boomer ordered Major Ladislaus E. Koniuszeski to support the battery with the left wing of the regiment and sent word to Colonel Holman to hold the right battalion ready to counterattack. Watching Major Koniuszeski, Colonel Boomer was not satisfied with the way he was defending the left wing and hastened to the battlefront, taking charge himself.[11]

The left flank of the 11th Ohio Battery had been left bare and unsupported when the 48th Indiana collapsed. Now the right flank, the 5th Iowa, was being cut to pieces. Only about eleven officers and a handful of men remained to man the cannons. With the line melted away, the battery found itself facing in three directions and battling with masses on three fronts. It had a rear but no flanks. The guns were being worked with greater speed and smaller crews. Cannoneers were falling. Other cannoneers replaced them as they were killed or wounded and performed double duty. Drivers left their dead horses and took the places of injured comrades, only to be struck down in turn. Of eighty horses, only three remained standing and a withdrawal of the guns was impossible. The surviving men were too few to do more than work the guns. The few brave Ohio artillerists that were left standing continued to fight, however, blasting the advancing Confederates at short range.12

The four companies of the Twenty-sixth Missouri Infantry that came to support Colonel Matthies and his 5th Iowan Infantrymen, assisted them in holding the ground to the right of the Ohio battery for more than an hour until Colonel Matthies discovered that his ammunition was exhausted and ordered the 5th Iowa Regiment to retire to a field about 100 yards to the rear. This was done in good order. The regiment was then reformed under a "galling" fire. At this time the 11th Missouri advanced in order of battle and the 5th Iowa retired further to the rear. There, under the direction of an aide-de-camp, the regiment was reformed in line, ammunition distributed to the men, and then they were ordered to rest on their arms for the night.13

The 5th Iowa sustained high losses with 7 commissioned officers killed and 8 wounded and 33 enlisted men killed and 168 wounded.14

DISORDER IN THE 26th MISSOURI

The 26th Missouri Infantry had been formed in the rear of the Fifth Iowa, the right wing extending down into a steep ravine and the left resting near the 11th Ohio Battery. Colonel Boomer had orders that, in case the Rebels should attempt a flanking movement on the right, he should move the regiment in that direction into an open field. Colonel Boomer had reconnoitered the position on the right and had found no indication of a flank movement. He therefore had remained in position awaiting further orders. Colonel Matthies had called on him for assistance because the left wing of his regiment, next to the 11th Ohio Battery, was being decimated. Colonel Boomer responded by ordering Major Koniuszeski to reinforce him with the left wing, composed of four companies (162 men). At the same time he ordered the right wing to remain where it was and to await further orders. Seeing Koniuszeski dismount and give inadequate orders, Boomer took command himself. The companies soon came under heavy Rebel fire and Boomer went back to bring up the other wing but found that, under Lieutenant-Colonel Holman, it had retreated to the rear. Unable to find his other companies, Colonel Boomer immediately returned to the left wing where he remained, mixed up with the disabled battery, until he was severely wounded. After the injury, he ordered the men to retreat down the ravine and he was carried off the field. The left wing of the 26th Missouri had encountered the heat of the battle. The position, in the midst of tangled horses struggling to get away, was difficult both to take and to maintain in order.[15]

When the 26th Missouri fell back, the officers found it very difficult to maintain order. The wreckage of the 11th Ohio Battery was all around with abandoned guns and caissons and many dead horses. Also, the Texans poured fire into Boomer's left flank as they followed their leader's orders to retreat.[16]

The right flank of Holman's battalion was caught in a deadly crossfire when the 48th Indiana collapsed. Suddenly, a team hitched to one of the caissons began to run down the hill on Holman's left and threw that part of his line into confusion. The men broke and ran for the rear and he was unable to rally them. He saw that it would not be possible to reallign the left flank and ordered the men on the right to pull back. He later reformed his battalion and placed it to the right of the 10th Missouri but it was not engaged again during the battle.[17]

Possibly, an explanation by Captain Brown explains why Colonel Boomer could not find the right wing of his regiment. Captain Brown, a Union officer, commanded a company of the 26th Missouri and took part in the Battle of Iuka. In his official report he says:

"The 11th Ohio Battery was placed on right of road and near an unoccupied house. My command laid down for protection until a Confederate officer cried out with a loud voice, 'shoot low', which caused the right of the regiment to falter and start to run."[18]

For several days after the battle, Colonel Boomer's wounds were considered lethal. In thinking of death, he said that if it was God's will that he should end his earthly career at that time he was satisfied, and knew that he should not be left to tread "the dark valley" alone. One of his friends expressed her fear that he had sacrificed his life. He replied: "And you call this sacrifice, if I lose my life or become disabled? It is a price to be paid, but not too dear for the blessings of a good government. I would not have my country go through such a struggle without feeling the satisfaction that I had, in thought and in act, given my entire, my most hearty sympathy. Our nationality must be maintained."[19]

COLONEL PERCZEL DEFENDS THE LEFT RIDGE

At the same time that the attack was being made on the 5th Iowa and the 11th Ohio Battery, a brigade of Confederates on the Rebel's right consisting of the 37th and 38th Mississippi Regiments, attempted to cross the road toward Colonel Perczel. The Colonel had taken position with seven companies of the 10th Iowa Infantry and a section of the 12th Wisconsin Battery (under Lieutenant Immell, First Missouri Light Artillery), on the Iuka road about a quarter of a mile ahead of the Federal's left wing. His position was in an open field just to the east of the Yow or Armstrong House and west of the area where the old Woodley House now stands overlooking Hiway 25 South. He first had sent three of his companies to his right into a dense wooded area and then placed his two cannons into position and threw a few shells in an oblique direction toward the Confederate lines. His three companies in the woods reported a full brigade of Rebels advancing on the Union left wing. He promptly withdrew the soldiers, leaving only one company for observation of the Mississippians and changed his front perpendicular to the Union line of battle on the Iuka road. Colonel Perczel then repositioned his cannons and obtained a dominating flanking position. Being on the ridge, Colonel Perczel could observe the Confederate movements for they had to cross a broken open field in order to attack his forces.[20]

The 37th and 38th Mississippi Regiments had been ordered to move forward on the extreme of the Confederate line but not to fire, as He'bert's Brigade was between them and the Federals. After moving forward through a dense thicket about 250 yards in the direction of the Yankee's lines, the 37th Mississippi came to an opening, enclosed by a high fence, which they had to mount. Just as the Rebels were passing over the fence, Colonel Perczel's bluecoats responded with a heavy crossfire upon the Mississippian's right and front. Exposed to this sudden and unexpected heavy fire from an enemy in a superior position and without a positive command for action, Colonel McLain ordered his men to fall back in rear of the fence they had just crossed. The men fell back in some confusion, but were promptly rallied by Lieutenant-Colonel Holland and Colonel McLain and brought again into line of battle about 75 yards in the rear of the position they had previously occupied. They were now parallel to the steep ridge held by the 10th Iowa.[21]

Twice the Rebels attempted to advance but were driven back each time. Colonel Perczel had the great advantage of being on the high ridge and the firepower from the cannons and muskets tore heavily into the Confederate ranks while their firing did very little damage to Perczel's troops.[22]

The battle wavered to and fro and, at times, almost reached the Iuka Road which was Colonel Perczel's only road of retreat. He became concerned that his route of escape would be severed and he might lose his two cannons. About this time one of General Hamilton's aides-de-camp rode up and inquired how matters stood. He informed the Colonel that the Iuka Road, although raked by the Confederate's fire, was still in Federal possession. At this time Colonel Perczel ordered the cannons back and they were withdrawn safely.[23] The 37th Mississippi and the 10th Iowa fought with one another until it became too dark to see.

The 38th Mississippi Regiment advanced on the left of the 37th Mississippi. The command moved steadily forward until they reached the top of the hill, in full view of Immell's Battery. Someone gave the word to halt and the regiment stopped and lay down, where they remained under a heavy fire from Perczel's men. Then someone on the left of the regiment gave a command for the unit to fall back. The commander, Colonel F. W. Adams, was unable to ascertain who had given the order but the regiment fell back some 50 or 60 yards in confusion. Colonel Adams then reformed the regiment and ordered it forward to reinforce Whitfield's Texans. Colonel Adams said that the 38th never fired a shot, because he had been so ordered, but had received very heavy fire and his men, with few exceptions, had acted with coolness and courage.[24]

As night approached, Colonel Perczel moved his troops closer to the main body but left Company I to observe the Confederate movements. Soon thereafter, Company I reported that a new body of Rebels was advancing and Colonel Perczel again advanced with three companies. Hearing the noise of the Union advance, the Rebels fired several tremendous volleys. Owing to the darkness, however, and to their uphill firing, not a Yankee was hit. Colonel Perczel's men returned the fire. Darkness put an end to the fighting which had been much in the Federal's favor due to their advantageous position on the high ridge.[25] Colonel Perczel withdrew the 10th Iowa and moved it near the hospital building. Lieutenant Immell also withdrew his two guns and moved them near the log church building where he had at first left his other two guns, the teams to which during a stampede had run away and broken out the tongue.[26]

THE 16th IOWA FALTERS

This regiment, under the command of Colonel A. Chambers, was positioned in rear of the 11th Ohio Battery, the left of the regiment extending across the road leading to the battery's position. After the initial shelling by the Confederates had killed six or seven men, the soldiers were ordered to lie down and, in this position, few or none were injured by the repeated discharges of grape and shell. The men of the 16th Iowa held their fire for fear of injuring a man or horse in the battery. When the battery became greatly endangered, however, by He'bert's charging hordes and the Confederates became better targets, Colonel Chambers ordered his men to rise and fire. Due to the trees and thick underbrush, the greyclads were not visible until they were quite close. The volley from the 16th Iowa transiently stopped their charge, but killed many men of the 48th Indiana who were in their front. He'bert's men regrouped and reloaded and the battery was attacked again. After a tough battle, the center companies of the 16th Iowa (which were situated behind the left section of the battery) retreated. The left of the regiment was holding a comparatively safe position and did not retire until they were fired into by one of the other Union regiments in the rear. The entire right companies, although under a remarkably heavy fire, held their position longest and experienced the heaviest loss. For a time, the right regiments held their ground alone after the 5th Iowa and the 26th Missouri had retreated. Toward the close of the action, Colonel Chambers was shot in the neck and shoulder and was captured by the Confederates. Subsequently, Lieutenant Colonel Addison H. Sanders reassembled the disheartened men of the regiment and they took a position near the battlefield but it was starting to become dark and the regiment did not engage in any more fighting that night.27

THE 4th MINNESOTA

The 4th Minnesota Regiment was placed in position to the left of the 48th Indiana. Captain E. Le Gro was commanding and Captain Edson took charge of the left wing. Their line faced the dense body of timber on the hill to the front which essentially hid everything from their view.

Soon after the front line was formed, the regiment marched 100 feet or so to the front, where they fixed the sword bayonets to their Whitney rifles and remained a few minutes. While they were in that position, Colonel Perczel made the demonstration on their left to uncover the Rebels. When the brigade of Confederates advanced, the 4th returned to their former position on the left of the 48th Indiana. Soon thereafter, General Rosecrans walked in rear of their formation, from right to left. At that time the left of their line rested in front of a little log house (Yow House) on the Iuka Road. An old abandoned road in their front passed from this point across the old field and off to the southeast on the ridge by the 5th Iowa.[28]

When General He'bert's long line attacked, one of the Minnesotans said that "bullets flew in all directions like hailstones."[29] Fortunately for the Minnesotans, most were on low ground and the majority of the bullets flew over their heads. A constant shower of the bullets, many fired by other Federal troops, whizzed overhead through the air. At the beginning of the action, Lieutenant James A. Goodwin of Company E was shot through the hip and four men carried him off the field in an army blanket to the hospital at the Rick House. J. W. Dunn, the orderly sergeant of Company B, and several others were soon wounded. The ground in front of the 4th's position was higher than that on which they were standing and this helped to protect them, but the land gradually rose to where the 48th Indiana was stationed.[30]

Shortly after the 48th Indiana fell back in confusion, Captain Le Gro ordered the Minnesota right wing to move back to the woods. He did this because the regiment was exposed to an oblique fire from the rear and also because he did not want the Confederates to get around his right flank. This order was apparently a blunder because it better allowed He'bert's men to attack and conquer the beleaguered battery. Lieutenant Snyder, who commanded Company B on the right, yelled to the Minnesotans, "Men! the order is to fall back to the edge of the woods. Go back in good order now!" Before he had time to say anything more, the frightened Unionists "flew for that brush." One of the soldiers at first started to walk, feeling disgusted, then took three of four jumps as the bullets flew in swarms from all directions just over his head. His cap fell off and he returned and got it. The men of the right flank reached the edge of the timber safely but were terribly disorganized. While Lieutenant Snyder was attempting to preserve order and form his company, every other man in the company was trying to do the same thing with his neighbor. They seemed to have lost all reason as various orders were heard: "Form here, men! form here!" "Stand where you are!" "There now, form on this man!." Two of the men crouched behind the dirt-filled roots of a fallen tree and watched for the Confederates as, to that time, they had not seen one. In a few moments they saw He'bert's men entering the woods to their right. One of them fired at a tall man who wore a straw hat and he fell.[31]

The movement made by Le Gro's order virtually withdrew the 4th Minnesota Regiment from the battle scene. Snyder soon formed the company and they moved 50 or 75 feet further to the rear into the road running north from the log meeting house which was called the main Iuka road. The balance of the regiment soon joined them. Colonel Perczel and Immell's two guns also changed front with them. At this time, the fighting for the battery was raging furiously. Volleys could not be distinguished. One of the participants in the battle said that it sounded like "one continued roar or clap of thunder."[32]

While the men of the 4th Minnesota Regiment were standing in the main Iuka road, the cheers to their right informed them that He'bert's troopers had overwhelmed the battery. Not long afterward, the regiment began their movement to the right. Led by Company B, the regiment marched by the right flank south on the main Iuka road toward the log meeting house. They marched about forty rods or more toward the church and then moved in line of battle through the small timber in front of the road. By this time, the fighting had entirely ceased. On their way to the front, the men stepped over several wounded men of other regiments, some of whom begged to be shot to put them out of their suffering. The troops were halted before reaching their destination. It had already become very dark. A part of the left wing became detached from the regiment and got between the 80th Ohio and the Rebels. The right wing halted within 50 or 75 feet of the Confederate line, which was concealed in the woods. At this time the 4th Minnesota's right was in rear of the 80th Ohio, which had previous to this time moved some distance to the front. The Rebels fired into and over the left wing and into the 80th Ohio and the Ohioans -- not having been informed that the Minnesotans were in their rear -- returned the fire! The volleys from the Ohioans killed and wounded more of the men of the 4th Minnesota than the Confederates had done before![33]

On the right, the Minnesotans were on lower ground than either of the commands that did the firing, otherwise their loss would have been much greater than it was. When the shooting commenced, commands were at once given by several in a loud voice to "Lie down!" and most of the men were willing to obey. Captain Inman of Company D, in the right wing, demanded, "Who are you? What regiment is this that is shooting into us?" It was several minutes before the responsible regiment was identified. The extreme right of the 4th Minnesota Regiment had passed just beyond the right of the 80th. Soon after the firing occured, Captain Lueg of Company G, in the darkness, walked against a wounded horse which fell on him. Several of the men of the regiment ran over and released him from beneath the injured animal.[34]

When the shots were fired, the right flank of the 4th was halted and was not over 50 feet in the rear of the 80th. The blaze from their guns went into their faces and over their hands and they sighed, "Thank God! they are on higher ground than we are." One man was seen crouched behind a tree about three inches in diameter.[35]

Not long after they were fired into, Quartermaster Hunt arrived with orders and at 8:30 P.M. most of the regiment marched by the right flank to the rear and into the field across the road from and southeast of the hospital, where, with the right of the regiment resting against the rail fence on the east side of the field, they remained the night in line, facing the Confederates. The night was cold and the dew was heavy and some of the men became chilled, having left their coats in the wagon train.[36]

SULLIVAN COMMITS HIS RESERVES

Seeing that Sanborn's Brigade was collapsing under General He'berts's repeated thrusts, Union General Sullivan raced to the rear to throw forward his reserve troops. The 17th Iowa and the 80th Ohio had been posted near the log church west of the cemetery, the 80th Ohio on the left and the 17th Iowa on the right.[37]

The left of the Ohioans' position was near the old church and the right rested a few rods across the Iuka road, where it turned down the hill. In that position, they were exposed to a heavy fire of musketry and grape shot. Lieutenant Bartilson, commanding the regiment, received orders to advance down hill, eastward through the thick woods and brush. He executed the order by advancing his command down the ridge, across the ravine, and up the next rise. Bartilson had been informed by General Hamilton that he would find the Federal line at that point. Instead, when he was within 30 paces of the Rebels' line, they raised up from their concealed position in Bartilson's front and right and fired into them. Bartilson's Ohioans returned the fire and the battle lasted about 10 minutes, at which time the Confederates fell back to the edge of the field in Bartilson's front. During the firing, the Colonel's horse was killed under him and he received a severe wound through his right thigh by a buck-shot. In such condition, Bartilson felt that he was unable to command any longer and ordered the company commanders to hold their positions.[38]

Due to the thick brush, Companies B and G of the 80th Ohio became separated and did not cross the ravine with the other companies. Acting under orders from General Rosecrans, Major Lanning advanced the two

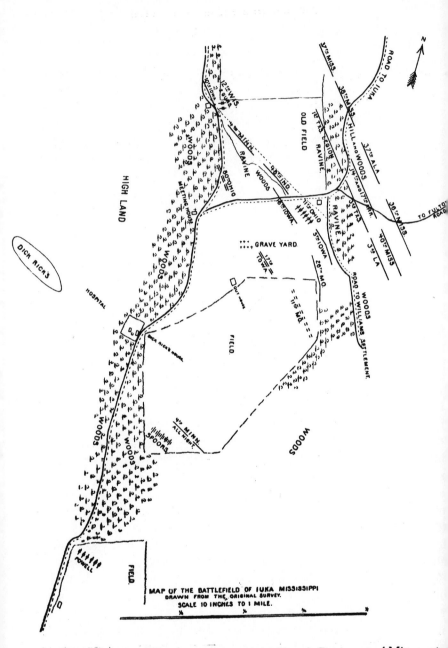

MAP OF THE BATTLEFIELD OF IUKA MISSISSIPPI
DRAWN FROM THE ORIGINAL SURVEY.
SCALE 10 INCHES TO 1 MILE.

From: Alonzo Brown's History of the Fourth Regiment of Minnesota Infantry Volunteers During the Great Rebellion, 1861-1865.

stray companies across the hollow and took a position so that the right rested in the ravine. They held this position for about one hour until Lanning was ordered to take a position on the old road leading to the Yow House.[39]

Meanwhile, on the right, the 17th Iowa was also having problems. When they were ordered forward, the regiment became divided near the center and Colonel Rankin took the right wing forward. Captain Young remained behind with a portion of the left wing. When they were fired on by the Confederates, the right wing panicked. Colonel Rankin had his horse shot from under him and he was thrown against a tree. This rendered him incapable of leading the regiment and the command passed to Captain John Young. He tried to rally the men and lead them back into battle but the troops could not be quieted and reformed until they had fallen back almost to the road near the old log church.[40]

Here, Captain Young succeeded in stopping the retreat and got a line partly formed and again marched them forward. By the time he got them to the former line, his command consisted of the right wing of his regiment and stragglers from several other units. The men remained there for about 45 minutes, when a soldier from the 5th Iowa reported that Young's unit was firing into them. Young advanced his men forward and into a tremendous volley from the direction of the Rebels. A Yankee soldier ran back saying that the firing was coming from another Federal regiment! The undergrowth and smoke were so dense, it was difficult to distinguish friend from foe. Captain Young, therefore, ordered his men to fall back to the original line, where the men were halted, about-faced, and ordered to kneel. Here they remained until the firing in their front became heavy again, causing the men to panic and run another 100 yards to the rear. The men stood there but for a short time when firing from the front and rear resumed, again causing a dreadful stampede among Young's men. He said they "all commenced firing in all directions without regard to where their guns were aimed." The indiscriminate firing continued but for a short time and Young again was able to rally the men and keep them in "pretty good line" until the retreat was sounded.[40]

General Sullivan, taking advantage of the stand of the 80th Ohio, rallied soldiers from the 4th Minnesota, 26th Missouri, 16th Iowa, and 18th Indiana regiments. General Hamilton ordered Sullivan to retake the abandoned battery of the 11th Ohio, which temporarily was held by He'bert's troopers. The Unionists gave three lusty cheers and rushed toward the greyclads defending the battery. The Texans were evidently taken by surprise and retreated off the ridge.[42]

The Texans quickly regrouped, however. Captain John T. Whitfield of Company D, 27th Texas, led Companies D, K, and M against General Sullivan's column. Attacking the Union left flank, the Confederates checked the Yankee counterattack. Sullivan's troops retreated, pursued by Whitfield's cheering Texans. General Sullivan was able to quickly regroup his men, however, and the Confederates were driven from the captured battery another time. But the success was short lived. Reinforced by the 14th and 17th Arkansas, Colonel Whitfield's dismounted Texas cavalrymen would soon chase the Federals from the battery for the last time.[43]

Confederate and Union officers at a meeting at Chancellorsville in 1884 near a stone marking the site where Stonewall Jackson fell. Standing left to right in back: General He'bert, General J. C. Robinson, General Roy Stone, General W. S. Rosecrans, Colonel G. C. Kniffin, General Longstreet, General H. L. Hunt. Confederate Private Warren Foster is standing in front of the tree. Seated left to right: Major Smith of Stonewall Jackson's staff, General J. Dickenson, Major Stein, V. Chancellor. Courtesy Massachusetts Commandery Military Order of the Loyal Legion and the U. S. Army Military History Institute.

COLLAPSE OF THE 11th OHIO
CHAPTER TWENTY-ONE

Surrounded on three sides and with only a handful of men left, the 11th Ohio Battery could not repel General He'bert's fifth and final charge. Four times before, the mutilated and weary Confederates had been checked but on the fifth attempt the guns were taken. During the fight, Lieutentant Sears was taken to the rear with a wound and Henry M. Neil assumed command. Second Lieutenant Alger, who fought the center section, was captured. Acting Second Lieutenant Bauer, the commander of the line of caissons, was killed.[1]

The first two Confederate units to reach the cannons of the 11th Ohio Battery were the 3rd Texas and the 1st Texas Legion. Lieutenant W. F. F. Wynn of the 1st Texas Legion was the first man to place his hand upon a Federal cannon and just as he did so, he fell pierced by a mortal wound.[2] A soldier in the Third Texas reported the carnage:

"We charged the battery, and with desperate fighting took nine (sic) pieces and one caisson. The horses hitched to the caisson tried to run off, but we shot them down and took it, the brave defenders standing nobly to their posts until they were nearly all shot down around their guns, -one poor fellow being found lying near his gun with his ramrod grasped in both hands, as if he were in the act of ramming down a cartridge when he was killed. The infantry fought stubbornly, but after we captured their guns we drove them back step by step . . . ."[3]

In the attack on the 11th Ohio Battery, the two Texas units lost one third of their men that were engaged. Both regimental commanders were wounded; Mabry in the ankle and Whitfield in the shoulder. The two officers refused to leave the field.[4] Lieutenant Colonel Gilmore, commanding the 3rd Louisiana, also displayed great bravery in the charge on the battery and was wounded.[5]

The ground in front of the battery was heaped with dead bodies. Within a radius of a hundred yards around the battery there were at least one hundred dead men. A large number of the slain Confederates met their death from the canister of the Eleventh. The brigade commander's report states that the battery fired "with great rapidity and extraordinary accuracy."[6]

General Rosecrans, in his statement of the facts and results of the Battle of Iuka, stated that the Eleventh Ohio Battery participated:

"Under circumstances of danger and exposure such as rarely, perhaps never, have fallen to the lot of one single battery during this war."[7]

The battery entered the fight with ninety-seven men and five officers, commissioned and acting. Of these, eighteen were killed and thirty-nine wounded, many mortally. A number of the wounded had been bayoneted at their guns. Of the cannoneers alone, forty-six were killed or wounded. Forty-six out of a total of fifty-four. More than five men out of every six![8]

One of the Confederates of the 3rd Louisiana Infantry Regiment gave this description of the fight for the battery:

" . . . gaining sight of a . . battery from Cincinnati, O., charged it with desperate fury notwithstanding it poured into their ranks a most destructive fire, the guns being heavily loaded with buck-shot. The fighting was of the most desperate character on both sides, the Confederates being opposed by the flower of Rosecran's army the early volunteers from the West, men accustomed to the use of arms, and of undoubted courage. For the third time during the war the Louisianians met the Fifth Iowa regiment, a stalwart body of men-heavy infantry. They were nearly cut to pieces in this battle. At times both lines would stand and pour destructive volleys into each other's ranks, then the Confederates would rush forward, with tremendous yells, invariably driving back the foe in their impetuous charge. The fight was mostly with small-arms. The battle continued until after dark, an incessant, prolonged roar of musketry. The captured guns were seized and run to the rear. The loss in officers by the regiment was fearful. It is unneccessary to state that the Louisiana regiment fully sustained its blood-earned reputation; and this was by far the hardest-fought battle they had yet participated in, and the number of killed and wounded fully attest the truth of the statement, and the part they took in the affair."[9]

In the fight for the cannons, the 5th Iowa lost 217 men, the 48th Indiana 100, the 16th Iowa 75 and the 26th Missouri 97.[10]

The statistics compiled by Colonel Fox in his "Regimental Losses in the American Civil War," show that the day's record in killed and mortally wounded equaled, within one, the total killed in any light battery during its entire term of service! This work also states that the losses of the Eleventh at Iuka were 22% greater than those sustained by any other light battery in any one engagement during the war![11]

Although the guns of the 11th Ohio was captured and recaptured several times before dark, only two members of the battery were taken prisoners. The brave Ohioans never abandoned the cannons voluntarily. One Confederate prisoner said later:

"Those battery boys had so much spunk that we took pity on the few who were left."[12]

It may have been this respect for the courage of the battery men that caused the Rebels to let the few survivors go. If the Confederates had only known, however, that only fourteen days later they would have to fight the same men with the same guns at Corinth, they would have made a special effort to capture all of the men while they had the chance.13

Of eighty horses in the 11th Ohio Battery, only three survived. In one mass lay eighteen dead horses. These three teams, instead of trying to escape had swung together and died together. The horse belonging to junior First Lieutenant Henry M. Neil, who assumed command of the battery when Lieutenant Sears was wounded, received seven wounds. Toward the close of the battle, he sank down and was left for dead. Some time during the night he revived and was found by an officer of Rosecrans' staff who rode him until daylight. The horse survived the war two years, then suddenly dropped dead in his stall. A bullet had finally worked its way into an artery.14

Of the other three surviving horses, one had an interesting history. He was a fine, strong bay who always worked as near leader. At the 11th Ohio's first battle, New Madrid, the horse's rider was literally cut in two by a thirty-two pound ball. The horse kept his place, covered with the blood of the rider, poor James Bibby. After this bloody baptism he seemed to bear a charmed life. At the end of the war, he was mustered out with the battery, still able to do full duty.15

First Lieutenant Cyrus Sears wrote from Pitt, Ohio, on November 6, 1884 about the part that the 11th Ohio played in the Battle of Iuka:

"The official report from the battery showed an expenditure of one hundred and sixteen rounds, mostly canister, and double canister at that- and pains were taken to make this report accurate. This battery went into the fight with about one hundred and five men and had sixteen killed on the field and thirty-nine wounded. Forty-six of these (killed and wounded) were of the gunners, of whom there were a total of fifty-four. Three out of four officers shared the same fate. Forty-two horses were killed upon the field and (a coincidence) forty-two were so disabled from wounds that they had to be turned over unfit for service."16

In an article on "The Chances of Being Hit in Battle", during the war, The Century Magazine for May, 1888 stated:

"The Eleventh Ohio Battery sustained the greatest loss in any one action. At the battle of Iuka it lost sixteen killed and thiry-nine wounded, the enemy capturing the battery, but the gunners, refusing to surrender, worked their pieces to the last and were shot down at the guns. The battery went into action with fifty-four gunners, forty-six of whom were killed or wounded, the remainder of the casualties occurring among the drivers or others."17

132

U. S. Brig. General John B. Sanborn. In the Battle of Iuka he was a colonel and commanded the 1st Brigade of General Hamilton's Division. Courtesy of Massachusetts Commandery Military Order of the Loyal Legion and the U. S. Army Military History Institute.

Just before Confederate General Little was killed, he had ordered Colonel John D. Martin to split his brigade, taking the 36th Mississippi and the 37th Alabama Regiments to support General He'bert's left wing and using the other two, the 37th and 38th Mississippi Regiments, to support the right of He'bert's line. Little was to take command of the right regiments and Colonel Martin the left. In obedience to orders, Colonel Martin moved the two regiments to the left of General He'bert's Brigade, extending the Rebel left to the skirts of an old field.[1]

Meanwhile, with General Hamilton's main line of defense continuing to fall back from General He'bert's powerful thrust, Generals Rosecrans and Hamilton decided that they had better commit more of their reserve troops before it was too late. General Stanley's Division had reached the vicinity of the battlefield and his closest brigade, Mower's or the Second Brigade, was ordered forward by General Rosecrans. This brigade was led by a dedicated and capable colonel, John Mower. He was a large man in stature, had been born in Vermont, raised in Massachusetts, and had fought in the Mexican War. His nickname was "Fighting Joe" because it was said that he was "all fight from head to foot." Colonel Mower would become one of the finest combat soldiers in the Union Army.[2]

The Second Brigade was also named the "Eagle Brigade" because it had "Old Abe" as its mascot (see Chapter 6). Colonel Mower, obeying orders, directed his men forward and after a short distance commanded the head of the column to halt. The colonel turned around and looked, only to discover that just one of his four regiments, the 11th Missouri, was following him (his other regiments were the 47th Illinois, the 26th Illinois, and the 8th Wisconsin). For some reason the other regiments had not moved forward.

Undaunted, the giant Mower ordered the 11th Missouri to advance. The Missourians cheered and, in double-quick step, hurried toward General Hamilton's line of battle. Major Weber, the regimental commander, heard heavy firing on the extreme right and hastened his men onward in that direction. Due to the density of the woods and undergrowth immediately to the right of Hamilton's line, Weber formed his bluecoats in the open field on the right and then moved forward in line of battle.

Meanwhile, Colonel Martin had been hurrying the Mississippians and Alabamans across a hollow. As the greyclads reached the top of the hill they came face to face with Mower's Missourians who had just entered the woods from the old field. The battle-lines were only about thirty paces apart. The Yankees immediately fired a volley into the Confederate line. The firepower was terrific but, owing to the cover of the hill, there were few fatalities. One of the confused Rebels ran toward Colonel Mower's line shouting, "For God's sake, stop firing into your own men; you are firing into the Thirty-seventh Mississippi."[3] The request was promptly answered by a cheer and a volley stronger than the first. The firing then became intense from both sides and the smoke from the guns became so dense that an object could not be seen fifteen feet ahead. The Rebels advanced slowly and the Missourians obstinately disputed every inch of the ground.[4]

One of the men of the 37th Alabama Infantry Regiment said that he fell down when the 5th Iowa fired their first volley, probably because of sheer fright. He also said that the orderly loading and firing that they had been taught and drilled did not materialize on the battlefield. He said:

"We was all aloadin an afiring as fast as we culd and they wernt no front rank ner rear rank."[5]

The deadly fighting between the 36th Mississippi and 37th Alabama Regiments on the Confederate side and the Missourians on the Union side lasted about forty-five minutes. On three tries, Martin's brave Confederates charged the 11th Missouri troops and three times they were repulsed. It began to grow dusky from the smoke and increasing twilight. Still the heavy firing and hand-to-hand combat continued, although the participants could not visualize their foe five paces away.

A Rebel participant remembered one of the Union volleys:

". . . the shots hit a lots of our boys and the grund, bushes and trees. It put me in mind of a summer hail storm." He also wrote that . . "Jim Galloway was hit in the stomik. Hit sound like he was hit with a switch."[6]

Major William F. Slayton had dismounted behind the 37th Alabama formation and was holding onto the reins of his horse. The thundering of the guns frightened the poor animal and he bolted and severely injured two bystanders, Captain Moses B. Green and Cpl. W. R. Kelly.[7]

At this time, Colonel Martin noticed that General He'bert's brigade had stopped firing. He went down to He'bert's line and requested Colonel Colbert to give one more volley to the front, to demonstrate that they were still there in force. With this, the Mississippians and Alabamans charged, with fixed bayonets and cheering, into the smoking Union line. Bayonets and pistols were used at close quarter by both sides and numerous prisoners were taken.

Major General William S. Rosecrans, Commander of the Union forces engaged in the Battle of Iuka. Courtesy of Massachusetts Commandery Military Order of the Loyal Legion and the U. S. Army Military History Institute.

A soldier of the 37th Alabama, Private Sam Singletary of Company A, recalled after Colonel Martin ordered a bayonet charge:

" . . We went right into their lines. A Yankee Major being the first to see our approach shot a man named Judkins through the arm with his pistol. By this time five or six of us had our muskets on him and were pressing our triggers when he said for God's sake men don't fire, which saved his life."[8]

Judkins was given the pistol and the privilege of escorting the Major to the rear of the Confederate line. Judkins was last seen sitting astride the Yankee officer under a tree punching him with the pistol and threatening to kill him.[9]

Finally, Colonel Mower issued orders for the Union troops to fall back. The Confederate soldiers of the 40th Mississippi Regiment had begun to infiltrate the woods between the 5th Iowa and the 11th Missouri and the ammunition for the Missourians' newly issued Enfield rifles had run out. Darkness was enveloping the battlefield. Many wounded Rebels and Yankees were crying desperately for help who would never see the light of morning. When the Missourians retreated, the Colonel Martin's troops did not pursue. Instead, Martin received an order from General He'bert to fetch the other two regiments of his command, the 37th and 38th Mississippi and to extend the line to the left. This he did and his brigade rested upon their arms until daylight.[10]

The 11th Missouri was the only regiment of Mower's Brigade (and, in fact, of all of Stanley's Division) that became heavily engaged during the Battle of Iuka. The 47th Illinois, Colonel Thrush commanding, formed on the left of the 11th Missouri. The 26th Illinois formed on the right and retired. The Eagle Regiment (the 8th Wisconsin) was held in reserve and did not see much action.[11]

One of the men in the 8th Wisconsin Regiment who was standing in the rear of the line, however, had a bullet come too close for comfort. He had the bough of a tree pulled down and was holding it in his mouth when it was cut off by a bullet. During some of the heaviest of the fighting the 8th Wisconsin was ordered to lie down on the ground and wait for an attack. As they did, bullets swarmed over their position.[12]

Fuller's Brigade (of Stanley's Division) was behind Mower's Brigade and had formed the rear of the Union column during the march to Iuka. They had moved in the following order: The 39th Ohio Infantry, Colonel Gilbert; Light Company F, Second U.S. Artillery, Captain Maurice; 27th Ohio Infantry, Major Spaulding; 63rd Ohio Infantry, Colonel Sprague; Battery M, First Missouri Light Artillery, Captain Powell; section of battery, 8th Wisconsin, Lieutenant McLean; and 43rd Ohio

Infantry, Colonel Smith. When the brigade was about three miles from Iuka, they were halted in the road south of the hospital (Rick's Place). The batteries were moved to the east of the road and placed in position near the edge of the woods and on a hill which overlooked the open field directly south of the cemetery. The regiments remained in that position until sunset, when Colonel Fuller received orders to advance immediately to the front. Fuller gave the order "Double-quick" and the infantry ran forward, swinging their hats and cheering lustily.[13]

Oscar L. Jackson, commanding one of the companies of the 63rd Ohio, was encouraged by the tremendous shouting he heard from the front. He turned to his company and commented, "Boys, things are going about right there now." A few moments later an officer dashed up to Colonel Sprague, the commander of the 63rd Ohio, and said, "Colonel bring your regiment up to the front as soon as you can. The enemy have captured Sand's battery, the only one we could get into action, and our men are giving back." Colonel Sprague turned in his saddle and yelled, "63rd, double-quick forward!"[14]

The men of Jackson's company had their entrenching tools with them; their axes, mattocks, and spades. When Colonel Sprague gave his command, Jackson called to his company, "Pioneers! drop your tools, march!" and away the men went toward the fighting, bullets dropping all around them."[15]

The light was fading, however, before any of the men of Fuller's Bridage reached the battleline and only one of the regiments, the 39th Ohio, got a chance to burn any powder. They fell into position to the left of the 47th Illinois. The men of the 39th thought that they saw the Confederates approaching and fired into the line. To their regret, it was a Union column that was retiring after an unsuccessful attempt to recover the cannons of the decimated Ohio battery. Only six casualties occured in the 39th and two in the 63rd Ohio. It was so dark that the men could not distinguish the blue from the grey uniforms.[16]

One of the soldiers of the 39th Ohio, Private George Cadman of Cincinnati, Ohio, received only a superficial chest wound in the battle. When he was hit, his first thought was that "if he lost his gun it would cost eighteen dollars," his second was to "grope about until he found it," and his third was to "get into his place as fast as possible."[17]

THE BATTLE ENDS
CHAPTER TWENTY-THREE

On the far eastern side of the battlefield, Captain Willcox's battalion of Michigan cavalry fought with some Rebel cavalrymen. This occured about one half mile east of the Jacinto Road. The Southerners were driven back and Willcox dismounted his men and placed them behind the crest of a commanding hill. From this position, Willcox's men were able to fire on the left flank of the Rebel battle line as they crossed in their front. Willcox was not attacked until after the 11th Ohio Battery was taken. After its capture, a combat patrol from the 3d Louisiana was forwarded to teach the Yankee cavalrymen a lesson. The Michiganders made good use of the terrain, however, and repulsed the attackers. They captured one of the Confederate lieutenants and a stand of colors.[1]

The fierce battle had almost ended when Gates' and Green's Brigades marched up "eager to avenge the death of their friend and commander " and reported to General Price. Following General Little's death on the battlefield, a staff officer had been sent to bring the two battle tested brigades to the front to reinforce and to relieve He'bert's and Martin's mutilated units. General Price ordered the two brigade commanders to report to General He'bert, who had assumed command of Little's Division.[2]

Darkness finally set in and the flashes of the Yankee and Rebel guns almost met. Prisoners were taken and retaken. It was difficult to distinguish friend from foe. Still the skirmishing continued. Major Russel almost lost his life by giving orders to a company of the enemy, mistaking them for one of his own. Sergeant White of the 3rd Louisiana captured a Union unit's flag. Scarcely had he done so, when he was captured, was again re-captured, and finally captured again. Like their Texas co-fighters, the 3rd Louisiana was engaged in the heaviest of the fighting. One of the Louisianas said that, "in less than three hours, out of two hundred and thirty-eight men (of the 3rd Louisiana) who went into the fight, one hundred and fifteen were killed and wounded."[3] Darkness put an end to the battle, and the men laid down their arms in the full expectation of renewing it early the next morning.

At the time, General Price's plans were for a morning renewal of the fighting and he told General He'bert to redeploy his division accordingly. He'bert decided to pull back his Second Brigade, which had forced the Yankees back step by step some 600 yards[4] and had suffered most of the casualties. As soon as Colonel Gates' troops (The First Brigade) had been moved to the front, He'bert's old brigade (The Second) was quietly withdrawn. Martin's Brigade (The Fourth), after being joined by the two regiments which had been at first sent to the right, was posted on Gate's left. Brigader's General Martin E. Green's Brigade was held in reserve. A regiment of infantry was sent to protect the St. Louis Battery, which had been deployed on the extreme left during the battle. General Maury's Division was pulled back from the position it occupied on the Burnsville Road. Maury massed his troops in town ready to march to He'bert's support the moment the battle started again.[5]

On the way to the front to relieve He'bert's Brigade, the men of Gates' Brigade met several detachments rolling down the captured Federal artillery. The cannons appeared to the Confederates to be the best, "as fine as is ever found upon the field; the pieces were entirely new and had never been in action before. ."[6] The captured artillery pieces were spiked, as the Confederates did not have any spare horses to pull them along with them. ("Spiking guns" means that round steel files or nails are driven into the touch-holes, giving the enemy the trouble of drilling these out before the guns can be of any value again.)[7]

At about 9:00 p.m. Gates Brigade proceeded to the front, where the toughest fighting had occured.[8] The Brigade formed and some of the men were thrown out at a short distance as pickets and skirmishers, covering the line of the deployed units. One of the detachment accidentally stepped upon a wounded Union soldier, who was lying on the ground. He spoke out, "Don't tread on me!" One of the Confederates asked,

"What regiment do you belong to?"

"The Thirty-ninth Ohio," the wounded Yankee answered.

"How many men has Rosecrans here?" he was asked again.

"Near forty-five thousand."

A little Irishman of the Confederate party curtly answered, "Our sixty-five thousand are enough for them!"[9]

The Confederates bivouacked upon the ground from which General Hamilton's men had been driven a few hours before. For several hours the Rebels were occupied with burying their dead and removing their wounded. The Union troops camped on the slope of the hill to the southeast.[10] The Rebels and Yankees lay on their arms, only one to two hundred yards apart. During the night, the guards of Gates' Brigade brought in several prisoners.[11]

In the Federal encampment, the 39th Ohio and the 47th Illinois held the front, slightly in the rear of the previous position of the advance regiments, which were withdrawn to replenish their ammunition. The 11th and 26th Missouri took position in a depression of the ground in the open field in rear of the woods in which the fight had occured. The 10th Iowa and the 80th Ohio held the Union left, on the road running north.[12]

U. S. Brig.-General Charles S. Hamilton, Commander of General
Rosecrans' Third Division in the Battle of Iuka. Courtesy of
Massachusetts Commandery Military Order of the Loyal Legion and the
U. S. Army Military History Institute.

During the night rations were brought up and distributed so that the men would not have to go into battle the next day with an empty stomach.

One of the Union night lines passed through the graveyard behind where the battery had been captured. Another line of battle was formed south of the hospital. These preparations, including placement of the artillery pieces, consumed nearly the entire night. Troops of Stanley's Division moved up, throughout the night, from where they had been stopped, some over a mile south of the battlefield. Positions were selected and the batteries planted on the high grounds south of the Rick House by Colonel J. L. Kirby Smith of the 43rd Ohio. All dispositions were made for a renewal of battle the following morning.[13]

The Confederates converted the Methodist Church into a hospital. Many of the Confederate and some of the Federal wounded were gathered up during the night and hauled into town where their wounds were attended to. Many of the private homes were also used to house and treat the sick and wounded. The Iuka Springs Hotel and Seminary buildings were utilized as hospitals.

The moon was nearly full the night after the battle and the thickly strewn corpses were easily visible in the strong light. The polished gun-barrels and bright sword bayonets of the enemy's guns were scattered over the battlefield and sparkled and shined in the moonlight. Everything bore evidence of the bloody afternoon just ended. The dead men were lying so thickly on the ground that one could have easily stepped about from one to another without touching the earth. Evidence of the terrible struggle was all around; bushes were twisted together, tangled up, and broken down in every conceivable manner.[14]

The carnage around the captured Union battery was grotesque. It did not look as if a single man or horse escaped. One of the caissons was turned upside down, having fallen back upon a couple of the horses, one of which was wounded and still struggling under it. Immediately behind was a pile of not less than fifteen men who had been killed defending the 11th Ohio Battery. They were all bluecoats and most of them artillery-men. Some of the limbers were standing with one wheel in the air. Bloody corpses were strewn thickly all around, intermingled with the bloody bodies of the badly wounded. One of the observers commented that he had been on many battlefields, but had never witnessed as many dead men in so small a space as there were lying immediately around the captured battery.[15]

Colonel Oscar Jackson of the 63rd Ohio Infantry Regiment later wrote: " . . . I counted forty dead bodies on one spot the size of four rods square."[16]

142

A Missouri soldier recalled his feelings:

"That night is well remembered as one marked by many conflicting emotions. Though already much hardened to the rough usages of war and the fearful events which inevitably accompany it—though somewhat accustomed to look upon the faces of the dead and fields of carnage as certain and natural results, yet the groans and cries of the wounded for help and water, the floundering of crippled horses in harness, and the calls of the infirmary corps, as it passed to and fro with litters in search of and bearing off the wounded, rendered the scene very gloomy, sad and impressive. As the night wind rose and fell, swelling with louder, wilder note, or sinking into a gentle, wailing breath, it seemed an invocation from the ghosts of the dead, and a requiem to the departing spirits of the dying.

There were few grey-coats among the dead around, and I gazed upon the blue ones with the feeling that they had come from afar and taken much pains to meet such a fate. It was but little akin to compassion, for war hardens men - especially when their country, their home and firesides are invaded and laid waste.

Only a few feet from me a groan escaped the lips of a dying man, and I stepped to his side to offer the slight relief that my situation could afford. He was lying almost upon his face, with a thick covering of the bruised bushes twisted over him. Putting them aside, I spoke to him, and turned him into a more comfortable position. He was unable to speak, but looked as though he wanted something, and I placed my canteen to his lips, from which he eagerly drank. After this an effort to speak was made: he could only murmur something inarticulate and unintelligible and at the same time a look of intense gratitude spread over his countenance. He was a Federal officer, as was easily perceived from his sword, dress and shoulder-straps. Some of the infirmary corps soon passed, and I asked them if they had any brandy or could do anything for him. Their answer was that he was too far gone to lose time with, and their brandy had given out. A few minutes after, he died.

A wounded soldier some distance off, hallooed at intervals until after midnight, repeatedly calling, "Caldwell guards!" -- the name of his company, which belonged to the Third Louisiana. The regiment had gone to the rear. I could not leave my post to go to his assistance, and his cries ceased after midnight. Whether he received attention in time or died unnoticed where he had fallen, I never knew."[17]

At some points, the distance from the Confederate to the Union picket line was less than seventy yards. During the night some of the Union men thought they would smoke but no sooner than a match was lit than a "Put

143

out that light!" would be ordered. One of the Confederates on the line struck a match to light his pipe. Immediately several shots were fired from the Union line, without effect, but reminding the soldier of the nearness of his enemies. One witness says that this was the only firing that occurred throughout the night but Dudley, in his account of the Battle, says:

"There was some firing between the pickets of the two armies during the night and a few men were killed and wounded."[19]

One of the soldiers on the Confederate line recalled:

"The horrors of war and battlefields are terrible. All night we could hear the cries, yells, and prayers of the wounded and dying around us, without the power of relieving their distresses, being just between the opposing lines."[20]

Another man from Missouri, a member of Gates' Brigade, wrote in his diary:

"The wounded was (sic) groaning until very late (some had not been taken off when we left . . .)"[21]

The cries for "Water, water; only a drop of water!" from the dying and wounded men fell upon the ears of compassionate soldiers but whenever one of them attempted to pass the canteen, the crack of musket fire quickly changed his mind and warned him to stay close.[22]

J. H. Greene of the 8th Wisconsin Regiment wrote that the night after the battle they had orders to remain perfectly quiet and under no circumstances could they build any fires. About midnight, some of the men of the 8th went to the rear and started a small fire to boil some coffee. Greene related that just as they did so, General Rosecrans happened along and said, "That's right! Kindle fires, call the fire of the enemy and get your d__d head blown off." Needless to say, the fire was quickly extinguished.[23]

Forty years after the terrible battle, Private Sam Singletary of Company A of the 37th Alabama Regiment recalled the pitiful cries of the wounded Yankees that lay behind the Confederate line. The odor of burnt leaves mixed with that of fresh human and equine wounds to produce a horrible smell. He wrote:

"We held the battle ground during the night and lay among the dead and dying Yankees. It was heart rending to hear them call for their doctor, captains call for their friends and as the night wore on they gradually ceased. Some dying, others being carried to the hospital. I never smelled bruised leaves but what my mind goes back to Iuka. The smell of the leaves, powder, and blood made me so sick till I had to vomit."[24]

An Ohioan recalled in his diary his feeling the morning after the carnage:

"A battle field is a strange, melancholy sight after the conflict is ended. As you walk over it, some strange curiosity impels you to examine the countenances of the fallen and the nature of their wounds. On an eminence perhaps the bodies of friend and foe lie mixed indiscriminately, showing where the struggle was warmest. A little farther on and you find them scattered and as you reach broken or wooded ground, you hunt for them as for strawberries in a meadow. Then the different postures of the dead. Some fall dead instantly. Others struggle into the dark region of the hereafter; whilst many, placing themselves in fantastic or grave positions, appear to leave life as if it all was a farce, or in calm meditation . . . . An old soldier here called my attention to a curious circumstance, and that was the peculiar expression on the faces of those killed by the bayonet. They have a contorted appearance, as if cramped, that enables them to be selected from among a pile of dead from those who were otherwise slain. There was only a case or two of this kind. They are very rare on any battle field."[25]

J. H. Greene of the 8th Wisconsin noted that "the underbrush was cut down by bullets as clean as if a party of axmen had gone through and chopped it down."[26]

Union Major Cromwell of the 47th Illinois Regiment went out the night after the battle to make a personal inspection of the pickets. Becoming lost in the darkness, he wandered into a Confederate picket and was made a prisoner. After his release he vowed that he would never again be taken alive. Later, in Jackson, Mississippi, a squadron of Captain McLane's Company of Wirt Adams Confederate Cavalry came dashing down a side street and came upon the daring young Colonel. Cromwell, true to his word, refused to surrender, and setting spurs deep in his horse's side, sprang ahead. A quick volley was fired by the Confederates and the heroic form of Cromwell fell rolling in the dust.[27]

During the early part of the night, General Price's troops made a lot of noise which sounded to the Federals like "chopping sounds" and "sounds of the construction of batteries." There was moving of troops and commands of halting and aligning, as if the Confederates were massing in the Union front. At midnight the Union troops heard Rebel wagon trains moving in a southeasterly direction.[28]

General Rosecrans was very disappointed at not hearing anything from the other Union forces and, not knowing whether he could expect any reinforcements, had to make plans on the assumption that he would have to fight the Confederates alone and unaided. He brought Stanley's three batteries forward and unlimbered them in the field south of the

Federal Hospital (The Rick's Place). Rosecrans and his staff reconnoitered and picked a line where the infantry should re-form in the event Price renewed the attack. Hamilton's Division, which had been involved in the heaviest of the fighting, was regrouped in a field south of where the artillerists had placed their cannons. Rosecrans intended to use Hamilton's troops to attack General Price's left flank. Hoping for, but not counting on, assistance from General Grant, Rosecrans sent his superior a message informing him that he had met the Confederates in force. Except for reporting the loss of several guns, Rosecrans' dispatch contained only a few details of the fighting.[29] It was sent at 10:30 p.m. from two miles south of Iuka:

"We met the enemy in force just above this point. The engagement lasted several hours. We have lost two or three pieces of artillery. firing was very heavy—You must attack in the morning and in force. The ground is horrid, unknown to us and no room for development. couldn't use our artillery at all, fired but few shots—Push in onto them until we can have time to do something. We will try to get a position on our right which will take Iuka"[30]

The courier bearing Rosecrans' message had to take a circuitous route, traveling west nearly to Jacinto before he found a road leading to Burnsville. Union Colonels Clark B. Lagow and T. Lyle Dickey, having been sent to General Rosecrans' battle station by General Grant to explain to Rosecrans the plan of operations, also decided to return to Burnsville to give General Grant a report of the battle. On September 21, Colonel Dickey wrote to his wife explaining the difficulties the two men encountered that night from Iuka to Burnsville:

". . . Col. Lagow & I were sent by Gen. Grant to visit Gen Rosecrans & explain to him the plan of operations—We went south ten or twelve miles & then turned north East & over-took Gen Rosecrans at a farm house 7½ miles from Iuka—His army was stretched along the road—some five miles—the head of the column being within 5 miles of Iuka & skirmishing with rebel Cavalry — We dined with Gen Rosecrans & then rode with him to the head of his column -- which (the column) was in mean time advancing — & about 1½ miles south west of Iuka -– the head of the column encountered the enemy in force an hour before sundown. Our troops came forward in double quick and the roar of canon & rattle of Muskety became loud rapid & general - on both sides. The shells burst around us - the bullets whisted through the air & it began to sound like some of the sharp passages at the battle of shiloh — Col Lagow & myself after witnessing the battle for half an hour — (our folks holding their ground firmly) set out for Gen Grants Head Quarters at Burnsville to

146

report the state of affairs & have Ords army push on in the Morning" -- As we rode back for three miles we met our troops pressing eagerly forward & heard the roar of battle till was quite dark - From this point our route lay through a deep forest — over steep hills & low bottoms — with a blind winding path — It soon became pitch dark — & although clear star-light night — in the woods it was very dark. In our progress we lost the road & traveled a mile by the north star our only guide through grapevines — briers & fallen trees brush piles &c — at length my horse which was ahead halted & putting his nose down refused to go forward — I told Col. Lagow that my horse refused to go — that we had no doubtless come to some obstruction — He said 'Let me try it' & spurred his horse past me & to his surprise plunged horse & man down a perpendicular bank five feet high into the bed of a creek — The horse fell flat on his side & caught Lagow's leg under him — They both grunted & got up again & found they were not seriously hurt — We could find no crossing & had to build a fire — tie our horses & lie down in the woods till daylight — At day-light we mounted & galloped seven miles to Burnsville."[31]

Luckily, the couriers sent by the longer route reached General Grant earlier, but it was still almost 3:30 a.m. on September 20th before Rosecran's telegram was handed to Grant. It was at this time that Grant first learned that the battle had taken place. He immediately notified General Ord of the fact and ordered him to attack Price "early in the morning."[32] General Grant (at Burnsville with nine hundred men from General Ord's command) and General Ord (between Burnsville and Iuka on the Burnsville road) had been listening for the sounds of guns in the south or southeast but the day of the battle the wind blew in the wrong direction to transmit sound to either Grant or Ord. General Grant later said:

"During the 19th the wind blew in the wrong direction to transmit sound, either toward the point where Ord was or to Burnsville where I remained . . . The wind was still blowing hard, and in the wrong direction to transmit sound toward either Ord or me. Neither he nor I nor any one in either command heard a gun that was fired upon the battlefield."[33]

General Ord supported Grant's statement, saying:

"The wind freshly blowing from us in the direction of Iuka during the whole of the 19th, prevented our hearing the guns and cooperating with General Rosecrans.[34]

However, Colonel Dubois, who was guarding the Union line from Jacinto to Rienzi, heard gunfire, fifteen miles away. And with the wind blowing away from their position, McArthur's men, guarding the railroad at Ord's extreme left, heard the noise of battle.[35]

Death of Gen. Little.

From Ephraim McD. Anderson's Memoirs.

General Ross' Division of Ord's command, however, saw a lot of smoke from the direction of Iuka. At the time they were about 7 miles from Iuka on the Burnsville Road. General Ord received this dispatch from General Ross about 6:00 p.m., two hours after Ord had been ordered by Grant to move his whole force forward to within 4 miles of Iuka:[36]

                                        September 19, 1862 -- 4 p.m.
Major-General Ord:
    For the last twenty minutes there has been a dense smoke arising from the direction of Iuka. I conclude that the enemy are evacuating and destroying the stores.

                                        L. F. Ross,
                                        Brigadier-General

At 11:30 P.M., the night after the battle, General Ord was at the head of his column four miles from Iuka on the Burnsville Road. Ord said, "Ducat, this is too bad." Ducat agreed with him and said,"Let us ride in and get permission to go forward at daylight." The two subsequently returned to Burnsville where General Grant was still headquartered at the depot. There they received Grant's permission.[37]

General Grant received a lot of criticism about the lack of communication between him and Rosecrans and because he did not learn of the battle until it was already over. It does seem incredible that some noise of the fighting was not heard at their positions, only a few miles away, since the artillery firing was so heavy. Grant was accused of being drunk and incompetent for command, but this has not been confirmed. General Ord would probably have advanced, even without specific orders, if he had been sure Rosecrans was attacking. To add credulence to Grant's story, Dudley wrote that he had been told by a Confederate soldier who was stationed on General Maury's right flank (and not more than four miles from the battlefield) that he and his comrades also failed to hear the sounds of the battle.[38]

As an example of the suspicions and criticisms that General Grant had to contend with following the Battle of Iuka, the letter of Franklin Dick of St. Louis, written on September 28, 1862, to Attorney General Edward Bates, is offered:

"Seeing it stated that the late attack by Rosecrans upon Price at Iuka failed, for want of co-operation by the Genl Grant, I consider it my duty to state, that General Grant was drunk in St. Louis on Friday the 26th instant. I did not see him myself, but Henry T. Blow met & talked with him, and stated to me, that the Genl was 'as tight as a brick' Believing, as I do, that much of our ill success results from drunken officers, I intend to do my duty in reporting such crime upon their part, so that the facts may reach those who have power to apply the remedy... I make this fact as to Grant known, because I have heard it denied that he now drinks—If drunk in St. Louis on the 26th, he may be drunk in command of his army a few days later."[39]

One day later, on September 29, the following article was printed in the Cincinnati Commerical:

"Great victory against Confederates, and appeared that they were beaten and surrounded. Union forces waited for morning to complete the job, but by that time the enemy had run off in the night.

The question among our troops then arose: how did the enemy get away? Why did not our forces on the Burnside(sic) Road engage them in the rear during the battle, and thus entirely capture them? You may slightly, but not fully imagine the bitter curses that went up from our subordinate officers and men when they learned that Hellish Whiskey was the whole cause. And yet, when we contemplated that "drunkness in high places" prevented us from capturing General Price with his twenty-three thousand men, which could have been easily done, the enthusiasm of victory was cooled very much indeed."[40]

Major William F. Slaton. The photograph on the right was taken after the war. Slaton's horse bolted with one of the first volleys at the Battle of Iuka and he was later captured at Lookout Mountain. (Courtesy of Mrs. A. Waldo Jones of Atlanta and Dr. Gerald Golden of Martinsburg, West Virginia.)

THE BURIAL OF GENERAL LITTLE
CHAPTER TWENTY-FOUR

After the close of the day's hostilities, a very saddened General Price returned to Iuka to his headquarters. He was drained of energy and almost in shock over the death of his "most trusted lieutenant". The loss of General Little was, in reality, a severe blow to Price's command. Captain Tom Snead, General Price's adjutant, rated Little as "the very best division commander" he encountered during the war.[1]

General Little's aide-de-camp, Frank Von Phul, sought General Price at his headquarters to determine the burial arrangements for Little's body. Their conversation, which appeared in the New Orleans Picayune, August 11, 1901, lends insight into the psychological turmoil that General Price experienced after the battle:

"Going to the headquarters of General Price a little later, I said: 'General, what shall I do with General Little's body?'"

"'My Little, my Little; I've lost my Little,'" was the reply, and the lines of sorrow were like furrows on his brow.

"'General,'" I said, after a moment's hesitation, 'what shall I do with General Little's body?'"

"'My Little; I've lost my Little, my only Little.'"

"I waited again, and once more tried: 'General Price, what shall I do with General Little's body?'"

"'My Little is gone; I've lost my Little.'"

"That was the only reply I could get from General Price. He was almost crazed with grief, and I don't believe he knew what I was asking him.

"Going down the steps, I met Colonel Tom Snead, the adjutant of General Price, and I asked him. He told me he would see Price and would come over to our headquarters after a while.

"It was about 10 o'clock at night when he came....................."
"The soldiers dug a grave in the little garden just to the rear of our headquarters, and a few minutes before midnight the saddest funeral train I ever witnessed in my life formed in line and moved to where the fresh earth had been rolled back."

"Each of us carried a lighted candle that flickered mournfully in the night air, and we gathered about the open grave as the rough coffin was lowered in the earth. Father Bannon, of St. Louis, the chaplain of the First Missouri brigade, stood at the head. Wright Schaumburg, came next. Then we were all grouped around the sacred spot, each man with a lighted candle. There were Colonel Thomas Snead, the adjutant to General Sterling Price; Lieutenant Peter Sangrain, of the army; John

Kelly, a civil engineer; Colonel John Reed (Reid), myself and General Little's orderly. There may have been some others whom I have forgotten."

"It was just midnight as the last spadefull of earth was placed upon the grave and patted into shape. Our candles still flickered in the darkness, sending out weird shadows. A plain piece of pine board was set at the head marked: "General Henry Little".[2]

The small cottage which served as General Little's headquarters is now the residence of Mr. and Mrs. Neil Davis and is named "Twin Magnolias" for the picturesque trees in the front yard. The structure is across Quitman Street (old Highway 72) from the old Tishomingo County Courthouse in Iuka. According to Dudley, General Little was buried on a lot (which in 1896 was being used as a garden) east of the residence and southeast of the courthouse.[3] In an addendum to General Little's Diary, Reverend Johnathan Bannon wrote that the body was buried in a lot on the ground owned by Mr. Convers of Iuka, Mississippi.[4]

General Little's remains were later removed to Green Mount Cemetery in Baltimore, Maryland.[5] One who recently has visited his gravesite describes it as follows: "It (is) situated in an old, once elegant section of that city now turned ghetto. Like a fortress, the cemetery is surrounded by an ancient stone and mortar fence about ten feet high. For more than a hundred years its wrought iron gates have maintained the privacy of those interred there. In a remote section beneath a huge Sycamore an ancient headstone reads B. Gen. Henry Little CSA."[6]

General Dabney H. Maury, in his account of the battle, had this to say of General Little:

"But one reflection saddened every heart. General Henry Little had fallen dead in the very execution of the advance which had won the bloody field. He was conversing with General Price when he was shot through the head, and fell from his horse without a word. He was buried that night by torchlight in Iuka. No more efficient soldier than Henry Little ever fought for a good cause. The magnificent Missouri brigade, the finest body of men I had then ever seen, or have ever since seen was the creation of his untiring devotion to duty and his remarkable qualities as a commander. In camp he was diligent in instructing his officers in their duty and providing for the comfort and efficiency of his men and on the battlefield he was as steady, cool and able a commander as I have ever seen. His eyes closed forever on the happiest spectacle he could behold, and the last throbs of his heart were amidst the victorious shouts of his charging brigade."[7]

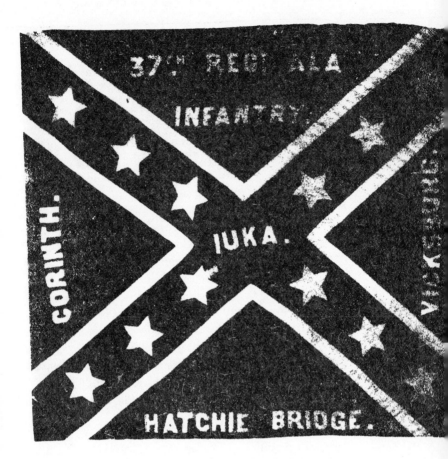

The battle flag of the 37th Alabama Infantry Regiment, afte restoration. (Courtesy of Dr. Gerald T. Golden of Martinsburg, Wes Virginia.)

RETREAT
CHAPTER TWENTY-FIVE

Although he was grieving deeply over the loss of General Henry Little, General Price was resolved to begin the battle again at daylight and was very confident of victory. He ordered General Maury to move his division from its position in front of General Ord to the front of General Rosecrans. Armstrong and Wirt Adams were directed to place their cavalry in position in front of Ord, so as to cover the movement of Maury's Division and also to hinder the advance of the Federals upon Price's right. General Price then went to the house of a friend, instead of to his own headquarters in the Colonel Moore House. He instructed his adjutant, Captain Snead, not to awaken him until one hour before daylight.₁

After burying General Little by torchlight, Captain Snead returned to the Colonel Moore House, determined to remain awake all night. Some time after midnight General He'bert, who had succeeded to the command of General Little's Division upon his death, arrived at the headquarters building. He'bert said that his brigade was so badly cut up and was so much disheartened by the death of General Little that he was apprehensive of the morrow. At about 2:00 a.m., while General He'bert was still there, General Maury also came in and said that he was convinced that General Grant would attack the following morning in overwhelming force, brush the Confederate cavalry out of his way, destroy the Rebel trains, and attack General Price's Army in the rear. Wirt Adams came in next and was in agreement with General Maury's views. All three men insisted upon seeing General Price. Captain Snead was hesitating, trying to decide what to do, when one of General Van Dorn's staff arrived with important dispatches from the General. He also asked to see General Price. Captain Snead did not hesitate any longer, but took the men to General Price's lodgings. It was nearly dawn when "Old Pap" was awakened and he thought that Captain Snead had come to awaken him for battle. He was greatly disappointed when he was told of the true cause of their coming. General Price tried to convince his subordinates that their apprehensions were groundless and that a victory was in the Confederates' grasp. The generals had already studied the situation, however, and were not convinced by General Price's attempted persuasions. Realizing that he could not fight a battle successfully when all of the chief officers were so fearful of it, he reluctantly directed the generals to carry out the orders which had already been issued the previous morning - for the withdrawal of the army to Baldwyn.[2] He refused, however, to agree to a further proposal that the wagon train, ladened with captured Union spoils, be burned.[3]

General Maury wrote later:

"The old man was hard to move. He had taken an active personal part in the battle that evening; his Missourians had behaved beautifully under his own direction, the enemy had been so freely driven back, that he could think of nothing but the complete victory he would gain over Rosecrantz(sic) in the morning. He seemed to take no account of Grant(Ord) at all. His only reply to our facts and our arguments, as he sat on the side of his bed in appropriate sleeping costume, was: "We'll wade through him, sir, in the morning; General, you ought to have seen how my boys fought this evening; we drove them a mile, sir."[4]

"But," General Maury protested, "Grant has come up since then; and since dark you have drawn me from before him. My brigades are lying in the streets, with their backs to Grant; and the whole wagon train is mixed up with us, so that we can't get into position promptly in the morning. As sure as we resume battle, placed as we are, we shall be beaten, and we shall lose every wagon. You can't procure another wagon train like this, not if you were to drain the State of Mississippi of all its teams. We have won the fight this evening. We decided on going back anyhow, in the morning, to Baldwin, and I don't see that anything that has happened since we published that decision should detain us here any longer."[5]

The others in attendance sustained General Maury's views. General Price finally admitted the prudence of a quick withdrawal instead of assuming the aggressive later that morning. Orders were issued for the wagon train to move. General Maury was instructed to send one of his brigades to escort the wagon train and to remain with the other two brigades as rear-guard for the retreating army.

General Price afterwards wrote in his Official Report:

"I had proposed to renew the battle in the morning and had made my dispositions accordingly, but having ascertained toward morning that the enemy had by means of the two railroads massed against me a greatly superior force, and knowing that my position was such that a battle would endanger the safety of my trains even if I should be victorious, of which I had but little doubt, I determined to adhere to my original purpose and to make the movement upon which I had already agreed with General Van Dorn. Orders were issued accordingly . . ."[6]

Shortly after 2:00 a.m., orders for the withdrawal were given and the wagon trains, which had already been loaded, were immediately put into motion down the unguarded Fulton Road. The wagon trains were the slowest and most vulnerable part of the column and General Price wanted them well on the way toward Bay Springs before the Federals knew that a withdrawal was being carried out. One of General Maury's brigades, Phifer's, accompanied the train. The other two brigades of Maury's Division (Cabell's and Barry's) were used to cover the retreating Confederates rear.[7] By daylight, these brigades had taken position on the heights east of town.[8]

In the meantime, General He'bert's troops, whose outposts were in contact with the Federal forces, kept up their demonstrations during the early part of the morning, making appearances of flanking the Federals to the right and left, pretending to establish batteries in front, halting, dressing up, etc. This kept the Yankees unaware of the withdrawal that was taking place.

"Not one wink of sleep visited my eyes," Rosecrans later wrote. Throughout the night he inspected the Union Army's front. In the darkness he could hear the Confederates "making great noises". They chopped, drove stakes. One voice cried: "Fall in there." Rosecrans suspected that the Rebel troops were taking new positions. At midnight, teamsters yelled and slapped leather on horses' rumps. "Gee-up!" -- and heavy wagons creaked in the night air. General Rosecrans thought that Price might be emplacing cannons along the height he hoped to occupy. He felt "great uneasiness," as he later said.[9]

By 4:00 a.m. it became obvious to General Rosecrans that a large movement was being carried out but the fastness of the Confederate position prevented him from finding out anything definite.[10] Just before daylight, He'bert's pickets were drawn in and the Confederate Army began southward down the Fulton Road behind the wagon train. Some of General He'bert's men who had stood the brunt of the battle the evening before, were put in front. To clear the road for the other troops, some of these men had to move at double-quick time for six miles.[11]

At daybreak, the Union skirmishers advanced and found that the Confederate position had been vacated. General Rosecrans ordered General Stanley to push ahead and occupy Iuka. With Fuller's Brigade in the lead, Stanley's column moved out. After reaching the open fields north of the scene of the previous afternoon's battle, Fuller formed his troops into line of battle. While the regiments were deploying, Captain Albert M. Powell had his cannoneers of Battery M, 1st Missouri Light Artillery unlimber their six guns. Opening fire, the bluecoats shelled some Confederates near the Fulton Road with case-shot, causing a hasty flight and confusion in their ranks.[12]

One of the Alabama soldiers later recalled:

"Just before day on the morning of the 20th we were called into line and began the retreat. Our route lay through Iuka and when we reached that place we were delayed for sometime, and the federal artillery appeared on a high hill south of us, unlimbered and the ominous puff of white smoke told us what was coming long before the shells passed over our heads. They fired three or four shots, but we did not remain a target for them, for somehow or other our legs got in double quick action and took us away from there.

In crossing the creek made by the Iuka Springs, I could see the bottom dry, about as often as otherwise, for the boys in their hurry to get away from the shells had about knocked all the water out of it."[13]

Gates' Brigade was used to screen the withdrawal of General He'bert's men. One of the troopers in this brigade later wrote:

"It was sun-rise some time before we reached the town. Our brigade brought up the rear, and our company deployed as skirmishers. The Federals advanced immediately after daylight, and their lines were in full view, as they debouched into a large field near the edge of town. A battery was hurried forward, and opened upon us as we marched through, but their shot passed over our heads without effect."[14]

Then the Union battery fired several shells into the town of Iuka, one of which crashed through the corner of the Iuka Springs Hotel. Another shell went through the roof of the Merrill House (now the Nelson House, across Quitman Street from Iuka High School) burning the rafters.[15]

With General Price's Army in full retreat down Fulton Road, General Maury rode up and put the 2nd Texas Regiment and Bledsoe's battery of four guns in the rear for protection. The 2nd Texas formed in line of battle on a ridge in the southern portion of the town and held there until the rest of the army had moved out. After waiting there for some time, they saw the enemy marching on the opposite side of town. Seeing this, Colonel Rogers rode in front of the regiment and said: "Men, again you are called to the post of danger, which is the post of honor. Do your duty like men." The men of the 2nd Texas were heartened by their beloved Colonel's words but were duly apprehensive as they watched the head of the Union column come to within a half mile of them and began placing their batteries and forming lines of battle. As the last of the Confederate Army pulled out, the 2nd Texas and Bledsoe's Battery were ordered to follow and began their retreat down Fulton Road on the southeastern part of Iuka. As one of the men of the 2nd Texas later wrote, they were "anxious for the enemy to come near enough for us to have a strike at them."[16]

Because the army's wagon train moved so slowly, it was 8:00 a.m. before[17] the last of the Confederate soldiers left Iuka. They had to reluctantly leave behind the captured cannons of the 11th Ohio Battery, because there were not enough horses to pull them. After drawing the

Federal guns from the battlesite by hand, the Texans and Mississippians had to sadly spike and abandon them.[18]

As the Federals advanced into town, Colonel John Fuller, who led Stanley's column, was met near the corporation line by a group of citizens, headed by Mr. Sam DeWoody, who was waving a sheet tied to a broom handle. In addition to saying that they wished to surrender Iuka, the entourage of elderly citizens asked "for the protection of private property."[19] Mr. DeWoody was well familiar with the suffering of war. His house at Eastport had already been burned by the Yankees and the DeWoody family had come to Iuka as refugees. All of Mr. DeWoody's papers, books, and other belongings had been destroyed in the Eastport fire.[20] The group of Iukans told the Union troops that the Confederates were all in the ditches that had been dug by the Federal Army.

Entering Iuka, the Federals learned that Price's Army had retreated by the way of the Fulton road, leaving behind their dead and seriously wounded. In addition to these, the Federals found a number of stragglers loitering in town, who could have easily escaped if they had tried. These were quickly rounded up by Rosecrans' Provost guards.[22]

As soon as he came into town, Rosecrans organized a pursuing force. General Stanley's Division was detailed to follow the Confederates down the Fulton Road. Hamilton was ordered to countermarch by the Jacinto Road to Barnett's. Colonel Mizner's command was divided. Colonel Hatch's 2nd Iowa, which had just reported to Mizner, was to cooperate with Stanley's force. Wilcox's 3rd Michigan was ordered to attempt to gain entrance to the Fulton Road some distance in front of Price's column and set up a roadblock in front of the wagon train. A courier was sent to Grant's headquarters with a message telling of the occupation of Iuka and the measures that General Rosecrans had placed in motion.[23]

HEADQUARTERS ARMY OF THE MISSISSIPPI,
Iuka, Miss., September 20, 1862—9:45 a.m.

Maj. Gen. U. S. GRANT, Commanding District:

GENERAL: Rebels left all their sick and wounded at this place; part of their little camp equipage. They are retreating with all possible speed. Stanley follows them directly and Hamilton endeavors to cut them off from the Bay Springs road. The men double-quick with great alacrity. General Little killed, General Whitfield wounded. The rebel loss estimated by themselves 400 to 500 killed and wounded; they have left many in the hospitals, many on the ground, which is covered with their dead—some fully three-fourths of a mile from where engagement took place. We shall bring our wounded into the town at once, Please order hospital stores and attendants for 500 sick and wounded. Why did you not attack this morning?

W. S. ROSECRANS,
Brigadier-General, U.S. Army, Commanding.

P.S.—Could you re-enforce if necessary at Barnett's. It is now said that he gave orders to the colonels of his regiments to cut their way at all hazards to a point 35 miles from Iuka. It is said he expected Tilghman, with a command of released prisoners of about 7,000 strong who were to have joined, but he sent word to them not to come up, as he was in "a tight place".

W. S. ROSECRANS,
Brigadier-General, U. S. Army, Commanding.24

The wind had blown heavily toward the south and east the day before and no sound of the battle had reached General Ord. During the night, however, he had received a report of the battle from some Negroes. So upon hearing the sounds of the first artillery fire, he ordered his troops toward Iuka. Ord suffered some delay because of General McArthur's unfamiliarity with the hill roads but, by 7:00 a.m., was within 3½ miles of Iuka.25 General Ord pushed forward before receiving the following dispatch from General Grant which was written at 8:35 a.m.:

BURNSVILLE, September 20, 1862-8:35 a.m.
General ORD:
Get your troops up and attack as soon as possible. Rosecrans had two hours' fighting last night and now this morning again, and unless you can create a diversion in his favor he may find his hands full. Hurry your troops all possible.

U. S. GRANT,
Major-General.26

By the time General Ord's vanguard reached Iuka, General Rosecrans' troops were already in command of the town. General Grant proceeded from his headquarters in Burnsville to Iuka where he found that "the Old Woodpecker Price" had retreated and Generals Stanley and Hamilton were in pursuit.

The Rebels, it was discovered, had carried almost everything with them except their wounded and the captured artillery pieces.27 The Union tents which had been left standing when Colonel Murphy hastily evacuated on the 14th were recaptured -- but were totally useless. Price's men had cut and ripped them with knives so that they were worthless. They had been too heavy and bulky for the already overloaded wagons.28

160

This was the first knowledge that General Grant had of the Fulton Road being left open for the Confederates' escape. He had assumed that it would be occupied so that General Price would have no choice of routes other than: 1. east, where he would have to cross the difficult Bear Creek Bottom or 2. northeast with the Tennessee River to cross or 3. to conquer his way out. A partial examination of the country afterward, however, convinced General Grant that if Rosecrans' troops had moved in separate columns up the Jacinto and Fulton Roads as planned, they could not have supported each other until they reached Iuka. In favor of his original proposal, however, was the fact that if one of the advancing columns had to retreat, General Ord's force could have been instrumental in protecting the rear.29

General Rosecrans, in defending his decision made at Barnett's to utilize only the Jacinto Road, later commented:

"I here ascertained that the Fulton Road crossed the Tuscumbia four and a half miles east of this point, and there were not cross-roads between it and that leading hence to Iuka, by which columns advancing on them separately could certainly and safely communicate with each other, and also that the enemy's strength was believed to be between 20,000 and 30,000 strong. I therefore determined that it would be unsafe to move Stanley's division up the Fulton Road, whereby I should divide my command, consisting of only four brigades, into two columns, not within supporting distance of each other."30

Adam Badeau, General Grant's biographer, says that Rosecrans' movement on the single road, his strength and the condition of his force, and the fact that the Fulton Road was left open, were betrayed to General Price on the afternoon of the fight by Dr. Burton, a Rebel assistant surgeon of Claiborne's regiment. The doctor had secured the confidence of General Rosecrans and had been employed by him as a scout and spy. Dr. Burton had remained with Rosecrans on the 19th until he saw the route that he pursued toward Iuka and had learned the condition of the Union troops. He then left the Federal Army and hurried into Iuka to give the information to General Price who utilized it in planning and executing the retreat.31

It was 9:00 a.m. when Colonel Hatch's Cavalry left Iuka by way of the Fulton Road. Behind the horsemen was Stanley's Division with Fuller's Brigade in the lead. The rear of Price's column was known to be about an hour's march to the south. However, because of the Confederates' large wagon train, their progress would be necessarily slow and the Union troops felt confident they could overtake them. Also, there was the possibility that Willcox's Cavalrymen might be able to block the road, thus delaying General Price's retreating column long enough for Stanley's men to overtake it. 32 General Rosecrans sent the following messages to General Grant, informing him of their pursuit:

HEADQUARTERS ARMY OF THE MISSISSIPPI,
Near Iuka, September 20, 1862.

GENERAL: The enemy, occupying a tongue of land between two roads skirted by woods, made great demonstrations of flanking us right and left; appeared to be establishing batteries in front, halting and dressing up. Meantime their train was moving to the rear, but could not tell in what direction. About 4 a.m. it began to be obvious that a movement of great magnitude to resist your or my attack was going on. I watched their movements all night, but the fastnesses of their position prevented my learning anything definite until daylight, when skirmishers were ordered forward and soon ascertained they were retreating. Stanley, with Thirty-ninth Ohio, section of artillery and Mizner's cavalry are pushing them rapidly. Mizner has ordered up cavalry on the Russellville Road while his main force is pushing in on an oblique road leading from battle-field to Fulton road. The sound of their trains had not died away when we began to move. What sort of a rear guard they have cannot say. Men are pushing forward as fast as excessive fatigue will admit.

W. S. ROSECRANS,
Brigadier-General, U.S. Army.33

HEADQUARTERS ARMY OF THE MISSISSIPPI,
One mile south of Iuka, September 20, 1862—8:45.
Maj. Gen. U. S. GRANT, Burnsville:
GENERAL: Dispatched you this morning at 7 o'clock to go by Iuka, but orderly said rebels were there; have sent it by courier line.

Night closed on us before we had more than six regiments engaged, some of them but slightly. The rebels were in a position on a high ridge running to a point at the forks of the roads, where we had to attack them, and commanding the only cross-road connecting Fulton and the Jacinto roads. The fight was sharp at the point where they captured the battery (reported now not to have been carried off, but left in the woods.) Our loss will probably amount to 400 killed and wounded. Rebels were obliged to leave many of their dead on the field. They made great noise of establishing batteries in the woods during the night and massing troops. It excited my suspicions. I watched the movements all night, but could do nothing until daylight, when skirmishers going out reported enemy retreating. Cavalry and infantry were promptly put in motion to pursue. Cavalry just report seeing rebel train and infantry on Fulton road moving south. General Stanley has reached Iuka, I believe, but having received no report from him I can give no orders. Should it prove so, I shall order Hamilton's division to face about and march to Barnett's; Stanley's to follow, and endeavor to cut off his retreat south and drive him into the defiles of Bear Creek. Iuka is deserted. Column retreating on Fulton toward Russellville road.

Have ordered Hamilton to go to Barnett's; will order Stanley to follow. Cavalry will go in advance, supported by a fresh regiment.

W. S. ROSECRANS,
Brigadier-General, U.S. Army, Commanding.[34]

Rosecrans waited for Grant in Iuka. At about noon, Rosecrans was "startled by the sound of music", and, looking up, saw the head of General Grant's column entering the town. Except for the visit by Lagow and Dickey, this was the first contact he had had with Grant in more than thirty hours. Grant assumed command and ordered a brigade to take charge of the captured stores and hospitals. He ordered Rosecrans to "pursue the enemy as far as you think pursuit will be likely to result in any benefit to us or injury to them." Grant rode with Rosecrans for several miles down the Fulton Road, then turned back and Rosecrans galloped ahead to join Stanley's infantry force.[35]

The retreating Rebels, however, urged on by the "wagon boss" General Price, were making fairly good time down the Fulton Road. Old Pap "would hurry up the teamsters," wrote one of the Confederate soldiers later, "and tell them he would have them hung if they didn't keep the wagons close up -- he kept them scared all the time in that way and they drove double quick."[36]

(Upper, from left to right) Union General E. O. C. Ord, General U. S. Grant, David McLain. McLain was Old Abe's eagle-bearer during the Battle of Iuka. (Lower) Old Abe and the Eighth Wisconsin color guard. This photograph was taken about ten months after the Iuka battle.

CARING FOR THE WOUNDED
CHAPTER TWENTY-SIX

As soon as it was ascertained that a clash was iminent, the Union medical director, Surgeon Archibald B. Campbell, established a field hospital one half mile in the rear of the battlefield for the Union soldiers. He located it alongside the Jacinto road, at the Rick Place, where there was a good source of water. Campbell said that he placed the hospital "at the only place within 2½ miles of the field where there was water to be obtained." Immediately after the firing began, the wounded began to arrive at the hospital. Most of the wounded were transported there by two carriers but those whose legs were nearly shot away were brought, in some instances, on blankets by six men. The details that had previously been ordered for that duty remained busy, quickly depositing those with injuries and returning to the battlefield for others. As the battle increased in intensity, large numbers of the Unionists were injured by the musket and cannon fire and later, in the fierce hand-to-hand combat. A steadily increasing stream of the seriously wounded kept the surgeons at the hospital busy, dressing and debriding wounds and amputating. Considering the number of injuries, everything worked smoothly and the surgeons performed their work admirably. Soon the hospital was overcrowded with the injured and dying and a second depot was established about a half mile in rear of the first (about a mile south of the battlefield). This second hospital was established under the supervision of Surgeon Thrall.[1]

The northerly wind that had blown during the afternoon and that had prevented Generals Grant and Ord from hearing the sounds of battle, subsided by nightfall and allowed the busy surgeons, nurses, and attendants to treat and dress the wounded by candlelight just as well as could have been done inside a house. By 11:00 p.m., all of the wounded that had been brought to the hospital had been attended to, although many more lay crying and moaning on the field of battle behind the Confederate lines.[2]

George E. Sly of Company A of the 4th Minnesota Regiment was one of the soldiers utilized in transporting injured Federals to the hospital (the Dick Rick House). Sly was only about 16 years old at the time and his story is amusing to read:

" . . The musicians were ordered to return to the hospital (an old log house) and bring up the litters. The bass drummer and I started out of the brush in the rear of the right of our regiment just as the rebels fired. We laid down on the side hill and the bullets cut the grass around us. The

Forty-eighth Indiana ran and I went back in the brush and lay down behind a log. When the regiment in rear fired into the Forty-eighth Indiana I was on the same side of the log and did not know which side was the safest. When the firing stopped I went back to the road and met a wounded orderly sergeant; thought it a good chance to get out of danger, took his things and we started back and met the cavalry guard, who commanded me to return to the front; I would not obey until compelled to by a pistol; found the regiment and concluded to stay with the sergeants; helped carry a wounded lieutenant Company E (Goodwin) to the hospital in a blanket; returned to the regiment and moved to the right after dark, and getting between the lines in the bush we were fired on by both lines; great confusion; officers shouting, 'Here Company A!' Here, Company B!' etc; helped carry a wounded man to the hospital; could not find my things; laid down on the bare ground under a tree and shivered all night."[3]

It was also a scary night for Mrs. Williams, an aged lady, and her daughter, Miss Nancy Williams. Because of Mrs. Williams infirmities, she could not be easily moved, and the two ladies spent the night in the top floor of the Rick's House while the Federals utilized the bottom floor as their hospital. Mr. Ricks was in the Army and his wife and children had fled to a place of safety. The Williams ladies were apparently unharmed by the Federals but had to endure the screams and pleas of the wounded and dying soldiers.[4]

Lamers describes Dr. Campbell's work:

"In the calm night, with no breath of air stirring, the candle flames scarcely wavered as Dr. Campbell, in blood-splattered apron, piled up a grisly stack of amputated arms and legs."[5]

On General Price's side of the battle, the medical personnel had also been extremely busy. The severely injured Rebels were transported north of the battlefield where they were deposited and treated in private homes, churches, the Seminary buildings, and the Iuka Springs Hotel next to the railroad track, which had previously served as the Union hospital. The citizens of Iuka, many of whom several months earlier had exhibited Union sentiments, now came forward with their Southern and compassionate spirit and generously gave of their homes, their possessions, and skills to care for and comfort those wounded Confederates being brought into their town in increasing numbers.

Expecting a renewal of the fighting the following morning, around 11:00 p.m. General Rosecrans ordered the Federal wounded to be moved further to the rear. With the aid of Captain Mott, acting commissary of subsistence, the ambulances were brought up to the hospital and loaded under the energetic supervision of Surgeon

Thornhill. The patients were received at the new depot, 2½ miles in the rear, by Surgeons Lynch and Hamm. All of the injured had reached the new depot by an hour after daylight and the last patients were about to be unloaded when Rosecrans' order was received to move them into Iuka. General Price had evacuated during the night and early morning, leaving his dead on the battlefield and his wounded in private homes and churches, the Seminary buildings, and the Iuka Springs Hotel. Two able and skillfull surgeons, Drs. B. G. Dysart and L. McDowell, were left behind to care for the severely injured and sick Confederates.

Surgeons Thrall and Hamm attended to the reloading of the patients, assisted by the other surgeons present. Upon reaching Iuka, the Union surgeons discovered that in their rapid retreat, the Confederates had left behind their dead and seriously wounded. Wounded Rebels were in the Seminary buildings and in the old Union hospital, the Iuka Springs Hotel. Many severely injured Rebels were left in the Methodist Church and behind the church, covered by tarpaulins, were several dozen bodies gathered for burial.6 General Rosecrans, in his report, stated that 342 Rebels were left in the hospitals when Price retreated.7 He also said:

"The rebels killed were far more than we thought yesterday; they had collected 162 dead for burial 200 yards in rear of their little hospital, where they were found yesterday covered with tarpaulins. Those 16 where Colonel Stanton was lying were collected by the rebels to be carried down to the same point. My count was 99. These with the 162 make 261 rebels killed. This, at the usual allowance, would make them 944 wounded. Our men found bloody rags, etc., along the line of their march."8

Upon consultation with Medical Director Holston, Director Campbell decided that the U.S. Medical Department would occupy the Iuka Springs Hotel and give the Seminary buildings to the Confederates for the care of their seriously wounded. There were ample Rebel hospital stewards and surgeons left behind for this purpose. At this time, the entire charge of the wounded was turned over to Surgeon Holston and Campbell reported back to Barnett's for duty.9

One of the seriously wounded Confederates left in Iuka was Captain Dunn of Company F of the Third Texas Cavalry Regiment. Dunn was from Athens, Texas and was a lawyer by profession. He was a very small man in stature, almost a dwarf, but a brave and gallant soldier. He was also a member of the Mormon Church and was a great lover of fun. It is said that he would "sacrifice comfort and convenience and risk his reputation in order to perpetrate a joke."10

Captain Dunn had the unfortunate experience of having one of his lower limbs fractured by a grape shot during the Iuka Battle. He was being cared for by some of the local Iuka ladies who had volunteered their services as nurses. During the course of their treatments, these ladies inquired of the injured Confederates whether or not they were married, if they were religious, and if so, what their denominational preference was. One of these Southern attendants put these questions to the jokester, Captain Dunn. He did not deny that he was married and acknowledged that he was a member of the Church of Latter Day Saints. The lady blurted out, "Why, you a Mormon!" and left. She soon told all of the other ladies that visited the hospital the astonishing information that one of the Texas soldiers was a Mormon! At first the other nurses did not believe it but finally some of them accepted it as the truth when the interviewer told them she had heard it with her own ears. Others thought that it certainly must be a joke or a mistake. To settle the question, a committee of discrete ladies was formed and they went directly to Captain Dunn and said: "Captain Dunn, we have heard that you are a Mormon and have come to you, as a committee, to learn the truth of the matter. Are you a Mormon?" Captain Dunn answered in the affirmative. Then they asked, "Have you more than one wife?" "Yes," he answered, "I have four wives." The nurses were astonished. They then asked, "Captain Dunn, don't you think it awful wrong? Don't you think it's monstrous to be a Mormon?" "No, madam," he replied, "that's my religion, the religion I was brought up in from childhood. All of my regiment are Mormons. All of them that are married have two or more wives. The colonel has six; some have four, and some five, just as they may feel able to take care of them." Following this conversation the Iuka ladies had a meeting and expressed their indignation and displeasure with Captain Dunn. They had given themselves, their time and their worldly goods so that these soldiers might better be cared for. They had donated their clothes so that the wounded might have bandages. Even prayers had been offered. For this! for a despicable Mormon with four wives!! They unanimously voted that their special services in his behalf would terminate immediately. From that point on, they continued to minister to the wants and needs of the wounded but would not look at or talk to Captain Dunn and did not treat him with the cups of cold water, soups, cakes, and pies they so unselfishly gave the other injured Confederates.[11]

Finally, the other soldiers noticed that Captain Dunn was being neglected and spurned by the Iuka nurses. They inquired into the reason for his being singled out for this punishment and interceded with the nurses in his behalf. They urged the ladies that whatever his faults were, he was a brave soldier and had been wounded trying to defend the ladies' homes. They convinced the nurses that he was a human being even if he was a Mormon and that he was suffering from his injuries and should not be allowed to die from neglect. The ladies reconsidered their position and it is said that Captain Dunn fared better than he had before the Mormon question had ever been raised.[12]

One day, one of the Iuka ladies asked Captain Dunn how he got his leg so badly crushed. He said to her with a straight face, "Well, madam, I am captain of a company, and when we got into the battle the Yankees began shooting cannonballs at us, and to protect my men I got out in front of them and would catch the cannonballs as they came and throw them back at the Yankees; but when the battle grew real hot they came so fast I couldn't catch all of them, and one of them broke my leg."[13]

As the wounded Confederates in Iuka recovered, they were paroled by the Yankees and allowed to go free. The paroles were filled out by a Federal officer and presented to the Confederate soldiers for their signatures. Most of the men did not read the form very carefully. They were only interested in obtaining their freedom until they could be exchanged. When one of the recovered Confederate officers, Colonel H. P. Mabry, received his parole, he read it very carefully. He was described as "H. P. Mabry, a colonel in the so-called Confederate States Army". Colonel Mabry refused to sign the form unless the "so-called" designation was removed. He was informed that it could not be deleted. "Then," stated the colonel, "I will not sign it." "In that case," the officer told him, "you will have to go to prison." "Well," the colonel replied, "I will go to prison and stay there until I rot before I will sign a parole with that 'so-called Confederate States' in it." Another officer, Captain Lee of the Third Texas had similar feelings and refused to sign the parole. Both of the men were sent to a Federal prison in Illinois where they remained until they were exchanged.[14]

When the Mormon, Captain Dunn, was paroled, he went to Texas for a rest until he thought he might be exchanged. On his return, he was traveling through Arkansas when a woman on a train inquired of him where he was going. The volunteer nurses of Iuka must not have harmed his sense of humor for he answered, "Madam, I am going to Richmond in the interest of the women of Texas. I am going to make an effort to induce the Confederate congress, in view of the great number of men that are being killed in the war, to pass a law providing that every man, after the war ends, shall have two wives."[15]

The Merrill House, one of the oldest homes in Iuka, was built in the 1850's. During the Battle of Iuka a shell went through the roof, burning the rafters. The house is across Quitman Street from Iuka High School. Mike Nelson (pictured) currently resides in the house which has been restored and remodeled by the Nelson family.

170

AMBUSH
CHAPTER TWENTY-SEVEN

Proceeding as rapidly as possible down Fulton Road with the 2nd Texas and Bledsoe's Battery in the rear, Price's Army was closely pursued by Rosecrans' Federals. The Rebels knew that an attack from the rear was imminent, as they had only an hour's start on the pursuers and the march was slowed because of the large wagon train. There was also the possibility that Willcox's Michiganders might move ahead and block the Fulton Road, delaying General Price's column long enough for the Federal infantry to overtake it.

General Maury's Division left Iuka about 8:00 a.m. About an hour later, at 9:00 a.m., the Union chase began, with Colonel Hatch's Iowans, followed by Stanley's Division, in pursuit. Pushing rapidly forward, Hatch soon established contact with Armstrong's Cavalry which was screening the rear of General Price's retreating forces. Several light clashes occured but Armstrong maneuvered his cavalrymen with skill and the Union horsemen could not secure an opening for a determined attack.1

Meanwhile, Willcox's Michigan cavalrymen were unable to obstruct Price's rapid retreat. On two occasions, the Union horsemen found roads connecting the Jacinto and the Fulton Road but they were unable to advance due to Armstrong's omnipresent cavalrymen. Consequently, Willcox's men could not slow, much less stop, General Price's movement.2

It was very difficult for General Price to keep the wagon train, loaded with the captured Federal supplies, traveling at an adequate speed down the narrow Fulton Road. One incident that occurred at this time is described by one of the Louisianans:

"General Price came riding up among the teamsters furious with anger. He was dressed in a many-colored shirt, well known by every soldier in the army as the dress he assumed when there was work to be done. A slouched hat covered his head and a sabre was buckled around his portly person. We never remember to have heard General Price swear, only on this occasion, and he was not choice in his language at this time. He ordered the teamsters to drive on, adding, "If one of you stops, I'll hang you, by G-d". The trains went out of Iuka at a full run, the teams being urged to their utmost speed. When the loads became too heavy, clothing, tents, blankets, and bundles were thrown out on the roadside. If a wagon broke down, the mules were unhitched and a torch applied to the useless vehicle. There was no time to stop or think of saving the contents of these disabled wagons."[3]

About seven miles from Iuka the Confederates found that they were being closely pursued. Colonel Rogers ordered a halt and formed the 2nd Texas in line facing the rear. Two guns of Bledsoe's Battery were placed in the center. The Confederates waited but the pursuing Yankees did not fall for the trap. Colonel Rogers then directed his men to resume their march.[4]

At about two o'clock p.m., when the rear of the column was about eight miles from Iuka, Maury's Division had to be halted because the road in front had become obstructed. While General Price was waiting for He'bert's troops to move on, General Armstrong and Colonel Wirt Adams approached him with an idea for another ambush. The plans were for the 2nd Texas Infantry and Bledsoe's Missouri Battery to hide in the dense woods on both sides of the Fulton Road. After unlimbering their guns, the Missourians would charge the Federals with canister. Colonel Robert McCulloch's 2nd Cavalry was to be massed on the road, behind a hill. The Federals were to be led into the trap by Wirt Adam's daring Mississippi cavalrymen, feigning a retreat. General Maury listened intently and agreed with the planned ambush. The Rebel units moved quickly into their designated battle stations.[5]

The 2nd Texas Regiment went into formation on a high ridge, overlooking a depression between it and another ridge over which they had just passed. The ground in between the ridges was densely covered with blackjack bushes. From the top of one ridge to the top of the other was about 200 yards on a straight line, while going down one and up the other would be at least 300 yards. The Rebels could plainly see a cemetery on a hill that they had just passed.[6]

As planned, Wirt Adams' Mississippi cavalry made contact with Colonel Hatch's Iowans and then retreated rapidly down Fulton Road. The bluecoats followed speedily after the Confederate cavalrymen. The quickness with which the greyclads retreated, however, raised suspicion that the Yankees might be entering a trap. Accordingly, General Hatch ordered his skirmishers to dismount. As men of the 2nd Texas watched, the Federal Cavalry dismounted on the hill containing the graveyard. They ran down the hill to a spot of about two acres that was more thickly set with brush than any other.

Captain Bledsoe, the Missourian commanding the battery, had two of his guns aimed directly at the thicket. Bledsoe was about six feet three inches tall, bony, swarthy, resolute, and seemingly did not know the meaning of the word "fear". He did not on that occassion leave the **handling** of the guns to his subordinates. He took personal command of

172

the two cannons. When he saw the men run for the thicket he double-shotted the two guns, putting about fifty pounds of buckshot in each, and aimed them at the thicket. Colonel Rogers ordered the infantrymen of the 2nd Texas to fire when Captain Bledsoe gave the command. Bledsoe waited quietly behind the cannons while dismounted cavalrymen assembled themselves in the brush. He withdrew a plug of tobacco from his pocket and filled his mouth by tearing off about half of it. He then returned the tobacco to his pocket, his eyes at all times fixed upon the movements of the cavalrymen. As soon as he was satisfied that they were within range of his guns, he commanded, "Fire!" At his command, the infantry being ready, a volley from the rifles of the infantry and a discharge from the two cannons simultaneously filled the air with noise and smoke. After firing their first volley, the men reloaded and stood ready. Colonel Rogers was in position where he could not see very well what was going on in the front but ordered, "Continue firing!" Some of the men told their captain, Capt. G. W. L. Fly, that they could see nothing to shoot at but he echoed, "Continue firing!"[7]

When the Confederates opened fire, General Hatch's dismounted Union cavalrymen dropped to the ground for safety. The minie balls and canister from the cannons whizzed over the Yankees' heads, not injuring a single man.[8]

The moment the firing ceased, Colonel Robert McCulloch's 2nd Missouri Cavalry charged the bluecoats. Hatch's men quickly jumped to their feet and fell back fighting in the timber until they joined the reserve of mounted men. The Iowans deployed behind a rail fence on both sides of Fulton Road. When the 2nd Missouri Cavalrymen came into view, Hatch's men fired at them with their Colt revolving rifles. The firing momentarily checked the Confederate advance. Then Bledsoe's gunners appeared with two of their cannons and began firing grape and canister. Upon seeing the guns, Hatch gave orders for his regiment to retire. The Confederates, realizing that Union reinforcements would be along shortly, decided to fall back toward Price's main body of retreating troops. General Maury recalled the cavalry and artillery and the division again headed south. Although only six of Hatch's men were wounded in this clash, the ambush served to curb the enthusiasm of the bluecoats' chase. The Union pursuit was abandoned and the Confederates, under General Price, marched toward Baldwyn without further interruption.[9] Colonel Hatch reported that he captured ten prisoners, 300 to 400 stand of arms, and a wagon and had only six men wounded and three horses killed.[10] General Maury said in his report that the Confederate loss was one killed and three wounded and that the Federals' loss was "of necessity much greater."[11]

One of the men of the Second Texas gave this overly optimistic description of the ambush:

"The enemy's loss must have been very heavy, for the woods were full of riderless horses and staggering men, and the little squadron of Confederate cavalry charged among them and captured some prisoners. This ambuscade taught the enemy a severe lesson, and they gave no further trouble."[12]

Another wishful member of the 2nd Texas, Captain G. W. L. Fly, who later commanded the regiment[13] and was actively engaged in the ambush, said this in later years:

" . . . . As a result of the fire of the infantry and Bledsoe's two guns, I was afterward informed that forty new graves were filled in the cemetery, with Yankees that were killed by that one volley. Having dismounted at the graveyard, when they advanced again to this place they buried their dead in the graveyard."[14]

Union General Hamilton said of the pursuit:

"The Fulton road being open, there was nothing to interfere with the enemy's escape. A pursuit was made . . . but a pursuit of a defeated enemy can amount to little in a country like that of northern Mississippi, heavily wooded, and with narrow roads, when the enemy has time enough to get his artillery and trains in front of his infantry. To make an effective pursuit, it must be so close on the heels of the battle that trains, artillery, and troops can be made to blockade the roads by being mixed in an indiscriminate mass."[15]

By the following day, September 21, the Union troops were back in their old encampments at Jacinto and Price's Army of the West had passed through Bay Springs. Two days later "Old Pap's" army was back in Baldwyn. One of the Missourians expressed the feelings of many of the Confederates in his diary entry of September 23rd:

"Our trip accomplished, and we are again in camp at Baldwin. But I am totally at a loss, as well as every body else, to know what we accomplished by it."[16]

A Rebel correspondant, traveling with General Price's retreating army, gave this account of the behavior of the Confederates in an article published in the Jackson <u>Mississippian</u>;

"During the entire retreat we lost but four or five wagons, which broke down on the road, and were left. Acts of vandalism, disgraceful to the army, were, however, perpetrated along the road, which made me blush to own such men as my countrymen. Cornfields were laid waste, potato-patches robbed, barn-yards and smoke-houses despoiled, hogs killed, and all kinds of outrages perpetrated in broad daylight and in full view of officers. I doubted, on the march up and down the retreat, whether I was in an army of brave men, fighting for their country, or merely following a band of armed marauders, who are as terrible to their friends as foes. I once thought General Bragg too severe in his discipline; but I am satisfied that none but the severest discipline will restrain men upon a march.

"The settlements through which we passed were made to pay a heavy tribute to the repacity of our soldiers; and I have no doubt that women and children will cry for the bread which has been taken from them, by those who should have protected and defended them. This plunder, too, was without excuse, for rations were regularly issued every night; and, though the men did not get their meals as punctually as when in camp, still there was no absolute suffering to justify such conduct, and it deserves the severest reprobation."[17]

The old Dr. Hodges' Home south of Iuka. The advancing Federal troops passed close to this house on their advance to Iuka prior to the battle. Standing in front of the house is the present owner, Paul Morris. Since this photograph was taken, Mr. Morris has done extensive reconstruction of the old home.

BURYING THE DEAD
CHAPTER TWENTY-EIGHT

The day after the battle, Federal troops searched the battlefield for the dead. Upon going forward to the ground on which the great fight had occurred, the men discovered the guns of the 11th Ohio Battery that had been captured by General Price's men at such great sacrifice. The cannons were standing in the road between the two lines of battle, about 100 yards in front of the position where they had been taken. Upon closer examination, the Yankees found that the retreating Rebels had spiked the guns with two-penny nails in their vents.[1]

The dead lay thickly scattered on the ridge that had been occupied by the 5th Iowa and the battery and also in the woods to the rear and northwest, where the Union troops had slaughtered so many of each other. In the low ground behind the battery, twelve horses belonging to two caissons had become tangled together and were piled up in a heap resembling a pyramid of horseflesh. Some below were wounded and others dead. On top of the heap with his hind feet entangled down among the dead and wounded beneath him, was a noble looking animal with head and ears erect, his right fore-leg bent over the neck of a horse beneath him, and his eyes wide open. Out of his nostrils there extended, like a great white beard, a foam fully a foot long and streaked with purple. He was dead. One of the Federals later said that it was the grandest and most awful spectacle of war that he had viewed during his entire four and a half years of service in the Civil War.[2]

The dead of the Union Army were collected and buried in large graves, laid side by side, with their blankets wrapped around them.[3] In Lyla McDonald's history of Iuka she said (in 1923) that they were buried "on the hills back of the school and boarding house" and that "After the war the Federal dead were taken up and carried in box cars to Corinth where they were interred in the National Cemetery".[4]

Rosecrans' men were not as careful about burying the Confederate dead. According to Colonel Oscar Jackson of the 63rd Ohio, "(They) were buried where they fell all over the field, at best in a careless manner."[5] Most of the Confederates that died in battle and subsequently died of their wounds or disease were interred in mass in the large trench in Shady Grove Cemetery.

Ten days after the battle, when Cyrus Boyd walked over the field of carnage, he discovered about forty men buried in one grave "besides numerous other graves scattered all through the woods . . . Saw many of the enemies'(sic) dead lying around not more than half covered. The ground in many places was white as snow with creeping worms. The darkness of the forest and the terrible mortality made it one of the most horrible places I was ever in."[6]

One of the men killed in the Iuka battle was W. P. Crawley of Company C of the Third Texas Cavalry Regiment. The Third Texas, a part of He'bert's Brigade, was involved in the thickest of the battle with a total of 96 wounded and killed out of 388 men in the regiment. Only about four or five of Crawley's friends knew it, but he carried a belt of gold around his waist beneath his clothes. Crawley, along with W. P. Bowers, Carter Caldwell, and W. T. Harris were the four men killed that were in Company C. Samuel B. Barron was one of the men that knew that Crawley carried the gold belt around his waist and said in his reminiscences after the war that he presumed that the gold belt was buried with Crawley in Iuka.[7]

After the dead were buried, General Rosecrans ordered Hamilton's and Stanley's Divisions to Barnett's. Colonel Jackson describes the march:

"After burying our own and the enemy's dead, we marched back on the road by which we had come, as far as Barnett's Cross Roads and encamped. We were very scarce of rations, many having lost their haversacks. I dropped mine during the battle and this morning I was glad to borrow a piece of pilot bread and to find a haversack containing a fine, large piece of mess pork. I had no scruples about eating of it and shared it among several grateful officers and men."[8]

Jackson recounted his feelings as he passed the ruins of Mrs. Moore's houseplace which had been burned by the Federals on the march to Iuka:

"When we moved foward everything was a blaze, and today as we returned, nothing remains but chimneys and blackened logs to mark the place where lived these double scound-rels, traitors and guerillas. This is the way to fight them and the men feel that they have a commander who fights rebels in earnest. It has been supposed by some that the burning buildings gave the enemy notice of our approach and caused them to come out and meet us, but this is not certain."[9]

Finally, the men were back at Barnett's again. Jackson recorded in his diary the following details of camp life:

"When we reached Barnets, we killed several fine beeves and I never relished anything better than I did this evening a piece of beef's liver, grained with salt and roasted on the end of a stick. To make coffee on the march, the boys provide themselves with an empty tin can with a wire stretched across the top for a bail. They put the coffee and water in this little can which they carry with them, and holding it on a stick in the flame

178

of a camp fire, soon have coffee boiling."[10]

Meanwhile in Iuka, a letter to Miss Annie Parks had been found in her yard on the eve of the battle. She never learned the fate of the writer:

HEADQUARTERS CAVALRY BRIGADE,
September 16, '62, 4 o'clock P.M.

"Miss Anna: The enemy are advancing in heavy force on both sides of our flanks. An engagement is almost inevitable. Before mixing in the 'horrid din and strife of the battlefield', I must return you my sincere thanks for your kindness to one who was a stranger in a strange land. If I do not live to thank you in person, I know that there is One above who never permits a kind action to go unrewarded. If I fall, please forward to St. Louis, to the following address, 'Mrs. Kate A. Bacon, St. Louis, Mo.,' what you can learn or hear concerning my end.

"If I do not fall, you will see me again. It may be foolish for me to talk of presentiments, but I feel different from what I ever have before on going into an engagement. But I have given myself to my country.

"God bless you! I have no time to write more. You may think this bold, but this is no time for ceremony. That God may protect you is the prayer of your admirer,

CHARLES E. BACON."[11]

Mr. Milton Scruggs of Iuka standing in front of the old Scruggs Home north of town. The house was built by Jobe H. Scruggs who migrated to Tishomingo County in the early 1800's. Union soldiers slept in the hall of the house during the War Between the States and fed their horses from Mr. Scrugg's crib. The children: Anthony, John, Joe, Phineas, Kate, Caroline, Julie, Etha, and Nan were all born in the house. Anthony later became Mayor of Iuka.

THE COURTMARTIAL TRIAL OF COLONEL MURPHY
CHAPTER TWENTY-NINE

Colonel Robert C. Murphy of the 8th Wisconsin Infantry was left in Iuka with a small rear guard of about 1500 men to guard and remove the large quantity of stores that were left there after the withdrawal of the majority of the Federal forces. When faced with the approach of General Price's Army, he had no choice but to retreat, which he did, causing a large amount of commissary stores to fall in the hands of the Confederates. These stores should have been destroyed but Colonel Armstrong had already cut the railroad and telegraph line between Burnsville and Iuka, and Colonel Murphy deemed it prudent to hastily retire to save his life and the lives of his men.

General Grant, in a letter of September 14th to General Rosecrans said:

"I was disgusted when news came of Col. Murphy having retreated to Farmington or near there."[1]

On September 14, Brig. General David S. Stanley arrested Colonel Murphy and, on the next day, filed charges against him of "Misbehaving himself in the presence of the Enemy," and "Shamefully abandoning a post which he had been commanded to defend." On September 23, Colonel Murphy sent to Major John A. Rawlins a lengthy defense of his conduct at Iuka. This letter was endorsed by General Rosecrans as follows:

" . . . I think extreme fright and want of judgement of Col. M so manifest as to need no comment. For example says that he formed line facing westward expecting a fight at Burnsville and when he learned that two cos of Sharp-shooters were there he still remained in order of battle one hour until Capt. Webster requested him to 'get out of his way' -- He never went to the telegraph office nor did anything to know if his retreat was not sufficient -- Nor did wait for further orders he got out of the way of Capt. Webster and got prosperously into Farmington--"[2]

On October 2, Major John Rawlins endorsed the letter:

"The Major General Command'g from a careful examination of within statement of Colonel Murphy in the absence of other evidence, is of the opinion that he was justified in his action in the evacuation of Iuka; but the opinions of the officers under whose immediate command he was at the time, being adverse, deems it for the good of the service as well as justice to Colonel Murphy, that the trial before Court Martial on the charges preferred should proceed."[3]

The courtmartial convened on September 30, 1862 pursuant to

general orders no. 130. Brigadier General J. McArthur was president of the court. The charges and specifications preferred against Colonel Murphy were as follows:

Charge 1st:

Misbehaving himself in the presence of the enemy.

Specification: In this that the said Colonel R. C. Murphy, 9th Wisconsin Volunteer Infantry at Iuka in the State of Mississippi on the 14th day of September 1862 when threatened with an attack by the enemy did omit and refuse to give the enemy battle, and did run away from the enemy and withdraw his troops from the town of Iuka, and hastily retreat with his troops before an inferior force of the enemy, and did continue to retreat with haste to the town of Farmington, without making a stand or attempting to check the pursuit of the enemy.

Charge 2nd:

Shamefully abandoning a post which he had been commanded to defend.

Specification: In this that he the said Colonel R. C. Murphy, 8th Wisconsin Volunteer Infantry, having been placed in command of the town of Iuka, Mississippi, then occupied by United States troops, as a military post by his commanding officer, Brigadier General W .S. Rosecrans, with orders to hold the same until the commissary and hospital stores had been removed, did disobey said orders and did shamefully abandon said post and withdraw the troops under his command from said post before said commissary and hospital stores had been removed, and did neglect to destroy said stores, this on 14th day of September 1862.[4]

During the course of the proceedings, many witnesses for the prosecution and the defense were brought forth and gave testimony. Colonel Murphy contended that the force at Iuka on the 13th of September did not determine to evacuate, but the knowledge that a superior force was coming. In this he was correct. He had not received an order to hold the post at all costs. With the telegraph wire cut by Armstrong's men, he was left to use his own judgement and the only prudent choice he had was a prompt evacuation.

For his failure to destroy the government stores, he justifiably deserved a great deal of the blame. Although he ordered Captain Simmons to destroy his stores and told the cavalry leader, Captain Webster, to assist Simmons in the destruction of them, it was his duty as commanding officer of the post to ensure that his orders were carried out. Although General Price's army was well on its way toward Iuka, there was ample time to oversee the burning of the commissary and other stores.

After much deliberation on the evidence that was presented, the court found Colonel Murphy not guilty of all of the charges. The court did therefore honorably acquit him of the offences in the alleged charges and specifications. His commanding general, Major General W. S. Rosecrans, however, still felt that he was guilty and issued the following statement after his acquittal:

"The General Commanding, with much regret, feels compelled to disapprove the findings and sentence of the Court. The evidence shows full the abandonment of the Post and public stores without pressure from the enemy. It shows a rapid retreating march, without the show of anything deserving the name of pursuit. The forming of a line of battle, faced to the rear, without a shadow to justify it. It shows a Colonel in command of a covering column, retreating without feeling of the enemy's advance, which had subsequently to be done; leaving to fall into the hands of the rebels, public stores, which he was bound by the first principles of military caution to have seen destroyed, and that he could have remained three hours later to accomplish without seeing a rebel infantry soldier to interfere with him. But when seven miles distant, and behind a defile, he forms a line of battle faced not toward, but from the defile, and presses forward to Farmington, some ten miles, leaving at Burnsville, without heed or notice, the telegraph operator and two companies of Sharpshooters, for a garrison to meet the enemy from whom he was retreating.

The General Commanding, having himself felt a high personal and official regard for Colonel Murphy, considers that to pass over such conduct with nothing but the announcement of an honorable acquital, would be to sanction that which would ruin the service.

Colonel Murphy is released from a rest, and will report to Brig. Gen'l Stanley for duty."[5]

General Grant disagreed with General Rosecrans and sided with Colonel Murphy at the time of his court-martial. He recognized that Colonel Murphy's command was small compared to that of General Price and felt that he had done well to get away without being captured. His leaving the large stores to fall into General Price's hands was regarded as an oversight and he excused it on the grounds of military inexperience. A couple of months later, however, General Grant realized that he had been wrong.

On the 20th of December, 1862 General Van Dorn appeared at Holly Springs, Grant's secondary base of supplies, and captured the garrison of 1,500 men commanded by Colonel Murphy. All of the Federals' munitions of war, food, and forage was destroyed. The capture was another disgrace to Colonel Murphy who had been warned of Van Dorn's approach but made no preparations to meet him. He did not even notify his command! Van Dorn claimed to have captured and paroled 1,800 men and 150 officers and to have taken 2 locomotives, 50 cars, and army supplies and cotton valued over $4,000,000.00. Van Dorn reported that he had only 50 men wounded.[6]

The order for Colonel Murphy's dismissal from the U. S. Army was written January 8, 1863 and read to the Army January 10, 1863. The date of dismissal was dated to December 20, 1862, the day of the surrender. Grant later said that the surrender at Holly Springs proved to him that General Rosecrans' judgement of Murphy's conduct at Iuka was correct. Grant said, "The surrender of Holly Springs was most reprehensible and showed either the disloyalty of Colonel Murphy to the cause which he professed to serve, or gross cowardice.[7]

Maj. General W. S. Rosecrans

This monument was erected in 1902 in Shady Grove Cemetery by the
United Daughters of the Confederacy to mark the graves of the
Confederates killed in the Battle of Iuka. It was later moved and now
rests on the west lawn of the old Iuka Courthouse.

APPENDIX
A. STATISTICS

As in more recent wars, it was not unusual for leaders of both Civil War armies to exaggerate the enemy's battle losses and to minimize their own. Such was the case in the Battle of Iuka. There is such a discrepancy in the Confederate and Union reports, especially as regards the Rebel losses, that it is impossible to arrive at precise statistics.

The 2nd Brigade and the 4th Brigade of General Little's Division were the only two Confederate brigades that were heavily engaged in the battle. The 2nd Brigade went into battle with 1,774 men and the Fourth with 1,405 men. The regiments which suffered the most in the 2nd Brigade were the 3rd Louisiana Infantry, the First Texas Legion (dismounted cavalry), and the Third Texas (dismounted cavalry). In the 4th Brigade, the 37th Alabama was the heaviest engaged. The following tabulation (microfilm, National Archives) gives the statistics of General He'bert's Brigade:

	Killed	Dangerously Wounded	Seriously Wounded	Slightly Wounded	Total Wounded	Total Killed & Wounded	Wounded Left Behind	Wounded Brought Along	Sick Men Left Behind
40th Mississippi Regiment	10	8	14	15	37	47	28	9	24
17th Arkansas Regiment	2	3	5	4	12	14	10	2	0
3rd Texas Cavalry Regiment	22	6	35	33	74	96	41	33	6
14th Arkansas Regiment	2	1	9	5	15	17	8	7	1
1st Texas Legion	18	9	32	39	80	98	65	15	4
3rd Louisiana Infantry	9	10	44	27	81	90	70	11	1
TOTALS	63	37	139	123	299	362	222	77	36

Similar (although slightly different) statistics are recorded in the Official Records:

Command	Killed	Wounded	Missing	Strength
40th Mississippi Regiment	10	39	21	314
17th Arkansas Regiment	2	12	3	109
3rd Texas Cavalry	22	74		388
14th Arkansas Regiment	2	15		116
1st Texas Legion	18	80	1	460
3rd Louisiana Infantry	9	81	15	264
Saint Louis Battery		1		52
Clark Battery		3		71
Total	63	305	40	1,774

[2]

The 4th Brigade, with the following number of men engaged in the battle,

37th Mississippi	453
36th Mississippi	326
38th Mississippi	322
37th Alabama	304
Total	1,405

[3]

had this number lost in killed and wounded:

Command	Killed	Wounded	Total
36th Mississippi Regiment	1	21	22
37th Mississippi Regiment	5	27	32
38th Mississippi Regiment	4	4	8
37th Alabama Regiment	12	43	55
Total	22	95	117

In General He'bert's official report, he gave the following list of casualties of the entire 1st Division.

Command	Killed	Wounded				Total killed and wounded	Left at Iuka		Left on the road	
		Dangerously	Severely	Slightly	Total	Total	Wounded	Sick	Wounded	Sick
General officers*	1									
First Brigade			2	8	10	10	1	15		11
Second Brigade	63	37	139	127	303	366	222	36		
Third Brigade								40		59
Fourth Brigade	22	12	35	48	95	117	63	38		
Total	86	49	176	183	408	493	286	129		70

* Brig. Gen. Henry Little

5

General Rosecrans' report of the Confederate casualties was much higher. A total of 265 dead Rebels were allegedly found by Rosecrans' men, including 162 that had been covered with tarpaulins and were lying about 200 yards behind the Methodist Church, which had been converted into a hospital. Rosecrans stated in his report:

"His (Price's) loss was: Killed, 265; died in hospital of wounds, 120; left in hospital, 342; estimated number of wounded removed, 350; prisoners, 361; Total, 1438. Among his killed were General Little and Colonel Stanton. How many other officers we do not know. Among his wounded were 26 commissioned officers."[6]

A. B. Campbell, Medical Director, Army of the Mississippi, said that from personal inspection and from what he considered reliable information, the Rebel loss amounted to "over 520 killed, 1300 wounded, and 181 prisoners, not including the wounded."[7]

Captain William M. Wiles, the Union Provost-Marshal, certified that 265 Rebels were found upon the field and buried by Union troops. 120 died of wounds following the battle. 342 wounded were found at Iuka and 361 non-wounded prisoners were captured. His estimate of the total loss of Confederates killed, wounded and prisoners (included estimated number of wounded carried off by Price) was 1,438.[8]

The following is General Rosecrans' final casualty report:

Command	Killed Officers	Killed Enlisted men	Wounded Officers	Wounded Enlisted men	Captured or missing Officers	Captured or missing Enlisted men	Aggregate
SECOND DIVISION Brig. Gen. DAVID S. STANLEY							
First Brigade COL. JOHN W. FULLER							
27th Ohio				6			6
39th Ohio							
43rd Ohio				2			2
63rd Ohio							
1st Missouri Light Artillery, Battery M							
Wisconsin Light Artillery, 8th Battery (section)							
2nd. U.S. Artillery, Battery F							
Total First Brigade				8			8
Second Brigade COL. JOSEPH A. MOWER							
26th Illinois			1	4			5
47th Illinois		1		5	1		7
11th Missouri		7	6	60		3	76
8th Wisconsin			1	1			2
Iowa Light Artillery, 2d Battery				3			3
Michigan Light Artillery, 3d Battery							
Total Second Brigade		8	8	73	1	3	93
Total Second Division		8	8	81	1	3	101
THIRD DIVISION Brig. Gen. CHARLES S. HAMILTON							
Staff			2				2
Escort							
5th Missouri Cavalry, Company C		1		2			3
First Brigade Col. JOHN B. SANBORN							
48th Indiana		37	4	52		7	100
5th Iowa	3	34	10	169		1	217
16th Iowa	1	13	4	44		13	75
4th Minnesota		2	1	40		2	45
26th Missouri		21	5	70		1	97
Ohio Light Artillery, 11th Battery		16	2	33		3	54
Total First Brigade	4	123	26	408		27	588

Command	Killed Officers	Killed Enlisted men	Wounded Officers	Wounded Enlisted men	Captured or missing Officers	Captured or missing Enlisted men	Aggregate
Second Brigade **Brig. Gen. JEREMIAH C. SULLIVAN**							
10th Iowa				6		1	7
17th Iowa	1	3	3	35		4	46
10th Missouri				13			13
24th Missouri, Company F				1			1
80th Ohio			2	13			15
Wisconsin Light Artillery, 12th Battery		1		3			4
Total Second Brigade	1	4	5	71		5	86
Total Third Division	5	128	35	479		32	679
CAVALRY DIVISION **Col. JOHN K. MIZNER**							
2d Iowa				6			6
7th Kansas, Companies B and E							
3d Michigan			1	2			3
Total Cavalry Division			1	8			9
UNATTACHED							
Illinois Cavalry, Jenk's Company					1		1
Total Army of the Mississippi	5	136	44	569	1	35	790

9

B. LETTERS PERTAINING TO THE BATTLE OF IUKA

I. LETTER FROM AN UNKNOWN REBEL SOLDIER.

"I wrote you a short communication from Iuka, announcing its peacable capture on the 4th, by the army under General Price. I believe I was a little congratulatory in my remarks, and spread out on the rich fruits of the bloodless capture. Indeed, it was a sight to gladden the heart of a poor soldier whose only diet for some time had been unsalted beef and white leather hoe-cake — the stacks of cheese, crackers, preserves, mackerel, coffee, and other good things that line the shelves of the sutlers' shops, and fill the commissary stores of the Yankee army. But, alas! The good things which should have been distributed to the brave men who won them were held in reserve for what purpose I know not, unless to sweeten the teeth of those higher in authority (whilst the men were fed on husks), and I suppose were were devoured by the flames on the day of our retreat. We held peaceable possession of Iuka one day, and on the next day were alarmed by the booming cannon, and called out to spend the evening in battle array in the woods. How on earth, with the woods full of our cavalry, they could have approached so near our lines, is a mystery! They had planted a battery sufficiently near to shell General Price's headquarters, and were cracking away at the Third Brigade in line of battle under General Herbert when our brigade (the Fourth) came up at a double quick and formed on their left. And then for two hours and fifteen minutes was kept up the most terrific fire of musketry that ever dinned my ears. There was one continuous roar of small arms, while grape and canister howled in fearful concert above our heads and through our ranks. General Little, our division commander, whose bravery and kindness had endeared him to the men under his command was shot through the head early in the action, and fell from his horse dead. He was sitting by General Price and conversing with him at the time. The Third Brigade was in the hottest of the fire. They charged and took the battery, which was doing so much damage, after a desperate struggle, piling the ground with dead. The Third Louisiana Regiment, of this brigade, entered the fight with two hundred and thirty-eight men, and lost one hundred and eight in killed and wounded. The Third Texas fared about as badly. The troops against which we were contending were Western men, the battery manned by Iowa troops, who fought bravely and well. I know this, that the events of that evening have considerably increased my appetite for peace, and if the Yankees will not shoot at us any more I shall be perfectly satisfied to let them alone. All night could be heard the groans of the wounded and dying of both armies, forming a sequel of horror and agony to the deadly struggle over which night had kindly thrown its mantle. Saddest of all, our dead were left unburied, and many of the wounded on the battlefield to be taken in charge by the enemy . . . During the entire retreat we lost but four or five wagons, which broke down on the road and were left. Acts of vandalism disgraceful to the army were, however, perpetrated along the road, which made me blush to own such men as my countrymen. Cornfields were laid waste; potato-patches robbed, barn-yards and smoke-houses despoiled, hogs killed and all kinds of outrages perpetrated in broad daylight and in full view of officers. I doubted, on the march up and on the retreat, whether I was in an army of brave men fighting for their country, or merely following a band of armed marauders who are as terrible to their friends as foes. The settlements through which we passed were made to pay heavy tribute to the rapacity of our soldiers. This plunder, too, was without excuse, for rations were regularly issued every night."[10]

II. LETTER FROM A WISCONSIN SOLDIER

Camp near Corinth Sept. 22nd/62

Dear Parents:

I have just got back to camp where I found a letter from home waiting for me to read. You had better believe I read it the first thing and now the second thing to do is to answer it.

I suppose you will have heard before this time that Price has been routed again at Iucah Ala. Our Reg't was part of the detachment that was sent out in search of him. The Detachment was sent out under the command of Brig-Gen'l McArthur. There was another detachment sent out under Gen Ross, and another under Gen Rosencrans, and another under Gen Davis. They were all sent out for the purpose of dispersing Gen Price's command.

We started from camp about five o'clock on Wednesday morning (the 17th inst.). It commenced to rain just about daylight, but that did not stop our going. We took an easterly direction from Corinth and traveled until after dark. We then camped and went to sleep as well as we could in the rain. It rained all night and part of the next day. It then cleared away and we had pleasant weather all the rest of the time. We were gone just five days and we marched all day every day and one night until midnight so you can guess what kind of a time we had.

The third day out our Reg't and the 18th were sent out on a scouting expedition. We marched until about 3 o'clock in the afternoon through creeks and swamps before we saw anything suspicious. We were through a kind of plantation with Co's "B" & "D" as skirmishers. All at once we heard firing in front and we went ahead on the double quick and formed in line of battle ready to give it to them. The 18th was formed in line on the right of us and at right angles with us. When we formed in line the 18th thought that we were rebels and fired a few shots at us but they did no damage. One of them went so close to Capt. Harrison that it singed his whiskers for him. As for the rebels they did not wait to fire the second round but they skedadled as fast as possible, leaving one man killed and five wounded, one fatally. Besides that we took five prisoners and about a dozen horses with all their equipments. The men were armed with doublebarreled shotguns and some with carbines.

After the skirmish we had to march until after dark to come up with our division. The next morning we heard heavy firing in the direction of Iucah and our Gen'l rec'd orders to march for that place as fast as possible to reinforce Gen'l Rosencrans. We reached that place about noon but the rebels did not wait for us. They retreated that morning about seven o'clock leaving their dead and wounded on the field. Our loss and theirs was about the same. One of the cavalry men told me that the union men and rebels lost about 300 men apiece in killed and wounded, whether it was high as that or not I dont know.

We did not go on the battlefield for we had only just got to the town when we got word that Price was working round in our rear to attack Corinth, so we had to make our way back as fast as possible. The news is now that Price thinks that the most of the men are out of Corinth scouting the country in search of him and he thinks that he can come right in here as easy as can be. I only hope he does think so for he will find us ready to receive him with all due honors. There is nearly 40 thousand men in Corinth now and I guess that is enough to whip him out . . .

With love to all the family I remain

Your affectionate Son
J. K. Newton[11]

III. LETTERS FROM ROBERT BANKS, CONFEDERATE SOLDIER

Iuka, Sept. 15th 1862
Co. B 43 Miss. Regt. 3rd Brig.
Monday Morning

Dear Parents (Lucretia and Dunston Banks),

After marching four days (most of the time without anything to eat except parched corn and fruit where it could be obtained) and a greater part of the nights we (Gen. Price's Army) arrived here last night. The country through which we passed was the poorest I ever saw—nothing but hills overgrown with sturdy oaks and tall pines. The first day we marched 16 ¾ miles and bivouaced, the next our Regt. was the guard for the wagon train, that day we made only two miles owing to the bad condition of the roads, — every wagon stalled ascending one big hill — marched during the night after the moon rose. The fourth day (yesterday) we came twenty two miles — reaching Iuka in the night. So from last Thursday morning up to last night I slept about six hours and then without covering — I stood the march better than four fifths of the Regiment though I acknowledge that I am very much fatigue and should be asleep now -- but prefer writing as it may be some time before I have another opportunity of sending you a letter — With the exception of fatigue and a blister on one foot I feel better than I have for a month.

I have come to the conclusion that I can march as far as most any man in the regiment. We captured a good many commissionary stores — the Yanks live like fighting cocks —

Enlcosed find a piece of an envelope with M.C. picture upon it I picked it up in the Yank camp. I have two papers (St. Louis) of the ninth of September. Will send them to you but doubt whether you get them—had a splendid piece of cheese for breakfast that a Mo. gave me.

I do not know how long we will remain here — would not be surprised if we were ordered tomorrow - The distance from here to Dunstown (?) is fifty miles - I did not mention the number of miles traveled at night. If you do not hear from me soon do not be uneasy — circumstances are such that I can't send you a letter often — you may hear from me in less than a week or perhaps 'twill be more than a month — no telling — The Federals had fortified this place, but we came upon them so unawares that 'twant much to whip them—they did not even have time to burn their stores — in fact our own men thought when we first started that we were only going to Baldwin — Coming along the road I saw a great many country residences that were burned by their cavalry — had no idea that they had devastated the country so much.

I do not know the amount (was large) of stores captured or the number of prisoners.

This is a beautiful town — This is the most hurriedly written letter I ever wrote — there is no connection in it but I have mentioned as many different items as I could to be in such haste — excuse mistakes.

In haste but affectionately

Your devoted son
Robert (W. Banks)

P. S. Don't fail to have my shoes or boots (either will do — get the cheapest) made — want them broad, thick, bottom sewed and soft uppers.

Latest news — Just heard that we captured 150 prisoners yesterday and this morning — also we took Burnsville — Yanks burned the place — We leave tomorrow — going toward Corinth so 'tis said — Breckinridge is above and we below the Yanks — they have a large force — we'll manage them however — Adieu — Affect —

Bob. (Robert W. Banks)

Iuka, Miss.
Thursday eve Sept. 18th 1862

Dear Mother (Lucretia Banks),

I have written several letters home in the last few days — one day before yesterday — that evening we were ordered out expecting an attack to be made upon the place, but the enemy finding us too many for them retreated, after firing a few guns. Our cavalry still continue to bring in prisoners, at the rate of sixty to seventy a day. I saw one shell fall near our regiment (nobody hurt)

We have just returned from the field having been out in the rain without covering from the weather for forty-eight hours. I have not spent a night in a tent or shelter of any kind since last night one week ago. Yesterday we captured a locomotive and train (of twenty cars) and forty prisoners. I think you will hear from this army togather with Breck. and Van Dorn in a short time. Caesar* is considered by all to be one of the best boys in the camp. He is very useful and attentive. Poor fellow had a chill this morning. If I can mother I will get him at a private house if possible and if he should continue to have them I will get him home at the first opportunity.

Affect. your son,
Robert (W. Banks)

Please send me an oil cloth to sleep upon and throw around me when it rains. I needed something of this sort last night . . .[12]

* Caesar was a young slave who Banks took with him early in the war. In a later letter (Sept. 28) he wrote that Caesar was still having chills and that he was sending him home.

IV. LETTER FROM DAVID R. GARRETT OF THE 6TH TEXAS CAVALRY

Sept 28th, 1862
Tupulo, Mississippi

Wm Gibbard Esq

My Dear Friend. Your favor dated the 18th of August is now before me for response. I was pleased to learn that all was well. I can say in reply that all of our boys are in retreating order, for I can assure you we have been making it in double quick time on retreat from Iuka about fifty miles from this place. We marched up to Iuka in double quick & made about 2000 Feds skedadle from there & we captured about half a million of Stores. When we thought we were in the enjoyment of ease & plenty good things the Feds came down from Corinth in force of forty thousand & then you ought to have seen about 12000 Confederates skedadling down south, but before we left the 3d Texas, 3d Louisiana, two Arkansas Regiments gave them a little fight. The loss was heavy on either side, our loss was near 500 killed & wounded, that of the Feds three times our loss, the fight lasted one hour. None of our Grove boys was hurt or missing except Ab Beck, he has not been seen or heard of since the fight. We lost only a few men on the retreat. Woodhouse & Tom Woods is yet behind. Tom Wood just got tired & said he would not travel any further, the Fed he said could take him & go to hell with him & that is the last we had of him. Woodhouse has the rheumatism very bad & could not keep up, but I think he will come up all right in a few days, some of our men fell behind & was taken prisoners & was paroled & when they came into camp their Col gave them two minutes to get out of camp, if not they would pull hemp. A good many of our boys think that if they fall behind & be taken prisoners & then paroled they will get to go home, but they find there is no honor in being paroled & I think that is right that there should be no honor in it. I was sent to the hospital today. I was taken sick the day we started on the retreat from Iuka. I objected to coming to the hospital. I wanted them to hawl me a day or two & then I could keep up with the trains, but the surgeons would not let me go & so I am at the hospital, but unless I relapse I will leave here in a few days. I am lost when away from my command & I shall join it as soon as I can get to it. Capt Jack came on to the hospital as I did, he has been quite sick, but he is improving very fast & I think he will be able to return to his command in a few days. The whole Army left Baldwin this morning on their way to Tennessee, but I do not know to what point. I understand they will form a junction with Van Dorn & Breckenridge at Bolivar, Tennessee, if so they will advance in the direction of Nashville. I hope we will soon have all the Fed out of the Confederacy. I am anxious to get up about Nashville, I want to see how many of my old acquaintants has turned traitors Andy Johnson like, if I had any that class, I shall tell them to leave the Confederacy & I shall drive them as I would any other Fed, but I hope I will find them all right. I must close as I feel quite bad, I would be pleased to hear from you all at any time. Direct your letters to Tupola, Missi. If you did not start my horse, I want you to sell him, you or F. A. Stone, as he will be of no service to me for sometime, for I have but little idea that I will see Texas until the war is closed. Tell all to write. My respects to all inquiring friends. My kindest regards to your lady & all the family. I remain as usual your friend.

D. R. Garrett   13

197

V. LETTER FROM N. F. GLOVER OF THE 37TH ALABAMA INFANTRY REGIMENT

Sept 25, '62

We layed in arms most all day speckin the Yank to atak. The Col. said we cud be at rest on the boys was alayin aroun but all was a little scared that we would soon be afitin. After diner Capt. Green come by a hollerin to get in fermachen quick which we done. Our Regt. and the Miss. Regts. marched double quick to the rear cause the Yanks was acomin from behind. They was a brigade of our boys formed in a Bottel line. As we fored up behind. The Col. rode up behind the brigade in front an was lookin where they wus shots fired but not a lots. The Capt. give a order to lode an we did an there we stood a waitin with guns loded. I was a thirstin bad but ascared to take a drink. They was abringin up our canons and asettin up a batery behind us. Then the Yanks opened up with theyr canons. The oficers comensed a hollerin on account of our boys looked alike. They was a goin to fire but they was our boys in front. The bridge in front fired at the Yanks and comenced firin and relodin firin and relodin. Col. Dowdel give a left turn an a rite flank when we was out for enuf an we lined up besid the brigad we was behind. About time we com on a lin with them Yanks poped up everwher in front an comensed afirin. We fired a volley and when we was relodin they shot back from scarce a thro. The shots hit alot of our boys an the bushes an trees. The raket put me inmind of a hail storm an was scared an fell down Jim Galoway was hit in the stomik and it sounded like he was hit with a switch.

Well we marched perty as parad to the lin of Battel but when Yanks fired the first volley they wusent not front rank ner bak rank ner order arms, we was all a loadin an a shootin as fas as we culd. Nobody run tho an everybody stay on line with the colors changin shot fer shot. By n By the Yanks comensed apullin bak an Maj. Slaten was a hollerin to git on a lin an give em steel. The boys give a good holler an charged but we was to tuckered to run far. We come bak a littel after dark and formed a lin an put out pickets.14

C. UNION AND CONFEDERATE REGIMENTS ENGAGED IN THE BATTLE OF IUKA

K - Killed   W - Wounded
MW - Mortally Wounded   M - Captured or Missing   C - Captured

THE UNION

ARMY OF THE MISSISSIPPI - Major-General William S. Rosecrans
SECOND DIVISION, Brig.-Gen. David S. Stanley.

First Brigade, Col. John W. Fuller: 27th Ohio, Major Zephaniah S.

Spaulding; 39th Ohio, Col. Alfred W. Gilbert; 43d Ohio, Col. J. L. Kirby Smith; 63d Ohio, Col. John W. Sprague; M, 1st Mo. Art'y, Capt. Albert M. Powell; 8th Wis. Battery (section), Lieut. John D. McLean; F, 2d U.S. Art'y, Capt. Thomas D. Maurice. Brigade loss: w, 8. Second Brigade, Col. Joseph A. Mower: 26th Ill., Major Robert A. Gillmore; 47th Ill., Lieut.-Col. William A. Thrush; 11th Mo., Major Andrew J. Weber; 8th Wis., Lieut.-Col. George W. Robbins; 2d Iowa Battery, Capt. Nelson T. Spoor; 3d Mich. Battery, Capt. Alex W. Dees. Brigade loss: k, 8; w, 81; m, 4 = 93. THIRD DIVISION, Brig.-Gen. C. S. Hamilton, Staff loss: w, 2. Escort: C, 5th Mo. Cav., Capt. Albert Borcherdt (w). Loss: k, 1; w, 2 = 3.

First Brigade, Col. John B. Sanborn: 48th Ind. Col. Norman Eddy (w), Lieut-Col. De Witt C. Rugg; 5th Iowa, Col. Charles L. Matthies; 16th Iowa, Col. Alexander Chambers (w), Lieut.-Col. Add. H. Sanders; 4th Minn., Capt. Ebenezer Le Gro; 26th Mo., Col. George B. Boomer (w); 11th Ohio Battery, Lieut. Cyrus Sears (w). Brigade loss: k, 127; w, 434; m, 27 = 588. Second Brigade, Brig.-Gen. Jeremiah C. Sullivan: 10th Iowa, Col. Nicholas Perczel; 17th Iowa, Col. John W. Rankin (injured), Capt. Samson M. Archer (w), Capt. John L. Young: 10th Mo., Col. Samuel A. Holmes; E 24th Mo., Capt. Lafayette M. Rice; 80th Ohio, Lieut.-Col. Matthias H. Bartilson (w), Major Richard Lanning; 12th Wis. Battery, Lieut. Lorenzo D. Immell. Brigade loss: k, 5; w, 76; m, 5 = 86.

CAVALRY DIVISION, Col. John K. Mizner: 2d Iowa, Col. Edward Hatch; B and E, 7th Kans., Capt. Frederick Swoyer; 3d Mich., Capt. Lyman G. Willcox. Division loss: w, 9. Unattached: Jenk's Co., Ill. Cav., Capt. Albert Jenks. Loss: w, 1.

THE CONFEDERATE FORCES
ARMY OF THE WEST - Major-General Sterling Price

FIRST DIVISION, Brig.-Gen. Henry Little (k)

First Brigade, Col. Elijah Gates; 16th Ark. _____ ; 2d. Mo., Col. Francis M. Cockrell; 3d Mo., Col. James A. Pritchard; 5th Mo., _____; 1st Mo. (dismounted cavalry), Lieut.-Col. W. D. Mauplin; Mo. Battery, Capt. William Wade. Brigade loss: w, 10. Second Brigade, Brig.-Gen. Louis He'bert; 14th Ark.,_____; 17th Ark., Lieut.-Col. John Griffith: 3rd La., Lieut.-Col. J. B. Gilmore (w); 40th Miss., Col. W. Bruce Colbert: 1st Texas Legion (dismounted cavalry), Col. John W. Whitfield (w), Lieut.-Col. E. R. Hawkins; 3d Tex. (dismounted cavalry), Col. H. P. Mabry (w); St. Louis (Mo.) Battery, Capt William E. Dawson; Clark (Mo.) Battery, Lieut. J. L. Faris. Brigade loss: k, 63; w, 305; m, 40 = 408. Thrid Brigade, Brig.-Gen. Martin E. Green; 7th Miss. Battalion,

Lieut.-Col. J. S. Terral; 43d Miss., Col. W. H. Moore; 4th Mo., Col. A. MacFarlane; 6th Mo., Col. Eugene Erwin; 3d Mo., (dismounted cavalry), _____ ; Mo. Battery, Capt. Henry Guibor; Mo. Battery, Capt. John C. Landis. Fourth Brigade, Col. John D. Martin; 37th Ala., Col. James F. Dowdell (w); 36th Miss., Col. W. W. Witherspoon; 37th Miss., Col. Robert McLain; 38th Miss., Col. F. W. Adams. Brigade loss: k, 22; w, 95 = 117.

CAVALRY, Brig.-Gen. Frank C. Armstrong; Miss. regiment, Col. Wirt Adams; 2d Ark., Col. W. F. Slemons; 2d Mo., Col. Robert McCulloch; 1st Miss., Partisan Rangers, Col. W. C. Falkner. Loss not reported. 15

Brigadier-General Henry Little, C.S.A, killed at Iuka on September 19th, 1862.

CHAPTER NOTES
CHAPTER ONE

1. William M. Lamers, The Edge of Glory, p. 91.
2. William Watson, Life in the Confederate Army, p. 381.
3. Official Records, Series I, Vol. XVII, Part II, p. 645.
4. Alonzo L. Brown, History of the Fourth Regiment of Minnesota Infantry Volunteers During the Great Rebellion, 1861-1865, p. 58.
5. Official Records, Series I, Vol. XVII, Part II, p. 9.
6. William M. Lamers, The Edge of Glory, p. 91.
7. Albert Castel, "The Diary of General Henry Little, C.S.A.," p. 42.
8. Rickey H. Bullard, "Civil War Medical Treatment", p. 1.
9. Alonzo L. Brown, History of the Fourth Regiment of Minnesota Infantry Volunteers During the Great Rebellion, 1861-1865, p. 62.
10. Gunn, Jack W., "The Battle of Iuka", p. 142.
11. Ibid.
12. Ibid. p. 143.
13. Ibid., 143-144.
14. Official Records, Series I, Vol. XVII, Part II, p. 654.
15. Ibid., pp. 683-684.
16. Robert E. Shalhope, Sterling Price, Portrait of a Southerner, pp. 1-16.
17. Albert Castel, General Sterling Price and the Civil War in the West, p. 3.
18. Ibid.
19. Robert E. Shalhope, Sterling Price, Portrait of a Southerner, pp. 16-76.
20. Albert Castel, General Sterling Price and the Civil War in the West, p. 5.
21. Robert E. Shalhope, Sterling Price, Portrait of a Southerner, p. 172.
22. The Liberty Weekly Tribune, Liberty Missouri, January 25, 1866.
23. Albert Castel, General Sterling Price and the Civil War in the West, p. 11.
24. Robert E. Shalhope, Sterling Price, Portrait of a Southerner, p. 171.
25. Albert Castel, General Sterling Price and the Civil War in the West, p. 35.
26. Ibid., p. 82.
27. Ibid., p. 85.
28. Official Records, Series I, Vol. XVII, Part II, pp. 645-646.
29. Albert Castel, "The Diary of General Henry Little, C.S.A.," p. 42.
30. Capt. G.W.L. Fly, "Before, During, and After the Battle of Iuka."

31. Samuel B. Barron, <u>The Lone Star Defenders,</u> pp. 98-99.
32. Alonzo L. Brown, <u>History of the Fourth Regiment of Minnesota Volunteers During the Great Rebellion, 1861-1865</u>. p. 60.
33. <u>Ibid.</u>, pp. 60-61.
34. William M. Lamers, <u>The Edge of Glory</u>, p. 97.
35. <u>Ibid.</u>, pp. 13.
36. Ezra J. Warner, <u>Generals in Blue, Lives of the Union Commanders,</u> p. 410.
37. Robert G. Hartje, <u>Van Dorn, the Life and Times of a Confederate General</u>, p. 208.
38. <u>Ibid.</u>
39. William Watson, <u>Life in the Confederate Army</u>, p. 381.
40. <u>Ibid.</u>
41. <u>Official Records</u>, Series I, Vol. XVII, Part II, p. 168.
42. <u>Ibid.</u>, p. 173.
43. <u>Ibid.</u>, p. 177.
44. William and Ophia Smith (Eds.) <u>Colonel A. W. Gilbert, Citizen-Soldier of Cincinnati</u>, p. 105.
45. <u>Ibid.</u>, pp. 105-106.
46. <u>Ibid.</u>, p.106.
47. <u>Ibid.</u>
48. Ibid.
49. <u>Ibid.</u>
50. Carrol H. Quenzel, "Johnny Bull - Billy Yank," pp. 121-125.
51. William and Ophia Smith (Eds.), <u>Colonel A.W. Gilbert, Citizen-Soldier of Cincinnati</u>, p. 106.
52. <u>Ibid.</u>, pp. 106-107.
53. <u>Ibid.</u>, p. 107.
54. <u>Official Records</u>, Series I, Vol. XVII, Part II, p. 190.
55. <u>Ibid.</u>, p. 191.
56. <u>Ibid.</u>
57. <u>Ibid.</u>, p. 193.
58. William and Ophia Smith (Eds.), <u>Colonel A. W. Gilbert, Citizen-Soldier of Cincinnati</u>, p. 107.
59. Carrol H. Quenzel, "Johnny Bull - Billy Yank," p. 125.
60. <u>Ibid.</u>, p. 126.

CHAPTER TWO

1. <u>Official Records</u>, Series I, Vol. XVII, Part II, p. 665.
2. <u>Ibid.</u>

3. Thomas L. Snead, "With Price East of the Mississippi," pp. 726-727.
4. Official Records, Series I, Vol. XVII, Part II, pp. 663-664.
5. Ibid., pp.675-676.
6. Ibid., p. 676.
7. Ibid., p. 677.
8. Ibid.
9. Ibid.
10. Jack W. Gunn, "The Battle of Iuka," Journal of Mississippi History, Vol. XXIV (1962) p. 148.
11. Official Records, Series I, Vol. XVII, Part II, p. 682.
12. Ibid., p. 685.
13. Ibid., p. 687.
14. Ibid., p. 690.
15. Ibid.
16. Albert Castel, General Sterling Price and the Civil War in the West, pp. 96-97.
17. Official Records, Series I, Vol. XVII, Part II, p. 691.
18. Ibid., p. 693.
19. Ibid., p. 695.
20. Ibid., p. 697.
21. Archer Jones, Confederate Strategy from Shiloh to Vicksburg, p. 77.
22. Ibid., p. 78.
23. Official Records, Series I, Vol. XVII, Part II, p. 698.

CHAPTER THREE

1. Albert Castel (Ed.), "The Diary of General Henry Little, C.S.A.", p. 45.
2. Ephraim M. Anderson, Memoirs: Historical and Personal, p. 114.
3. Albert Castel (Ed.), "The Diary of General Henry Little, C.S.A.," p. 45.
4. Edwin C. Bearss, Decision in Mississippi, pp. 7-8.
5. Lieut. Col. Finley L. Hubbell, The Land We Love, Diary of Lieut. Col. Hubbel, of 3rd Regiment Missouri Infantry, C.S.A., p. 7.
6. General C. Osborn, (Ed), "The Civil War Letters of Robert W. Banks," Journal of Mississippi History, Vol. V.
7. Samuel B. Brown, The Lone Star Defenders, pp. 104-105.
8. Albert Castell (Ed.), "The Diary of General Henry Little, C.S.A," Civil War Times Illustrated, p. 45.

9. General Lewis Henry Little, "Diary of Lewis Henry Little," Civil War Times Illustrated Collection

CHAPTER FOUR

1. William M. Lamers, The Edge of Glory, p.98.
2. Alonzo L. Brown, History of the Fourth Regiment of Minnesota Infantry Volunteers During the Great Rebellion, 1861-1865, p. 74.
3. Ibid,
4. Edwin C. Bearss, Decision in Mississippi, pp. 9-15.
5. William and Ophia Smith (Eds.), Colonel A. W. Gilbert, Citizen-Soldier of Cincinnati, p. 107.
6. Ibid.
7. Ibid., pp. 107-108.
8. Ibid., pp. 108.
9. Ibid.
10. Ibid.
11. Ibid.
12. Ibid., pp. 108-109.
13. Ibid., pp. 109.
14. Edwin C. Bearss, Decision in Mississippi, pp. 9-15.
15. Diary of David McKinney, Civil War Times Illustrated Collection

CHAPTER FIVE

1. George C. Osborn (Ed.), "The Civil War Letters of Robert W. Banks," Journal of Mississippi History, Vol. V.
2. Edwin C. Bearss, Decision in Mississippi, p. 8
3. Albert Castel, "The Diary of General Henry Little, C.S.A.," Civil War Times Illustrated, p. 45.
4. Ibid.
5. Ibid.
6. Willie H. Tunnard, A Southern Record, pp. 181-182.
7. Ephraim McD. Anderson, Memoirs: Historical and Personal; Including the Campaigns of the First Missouri Confederate Brigade, p. 217.
8. William M. Lamers, The Edge of Glory, p. 100.
9. Ephraim McD. Anderson, Memoirs: Historical and Personal: Including the Campaigns of the First Missouri Confederate Brigade, p. 217.
10. Confederate Veteran, Vol. 1, 1893

CHAPTER SIX

1. J. Stanley Dietz, The Story of Old Abe the War Eagle, pp. 1-3.
2. C. P. Nelson, Abe, The War Eagle, p. 9.
3. J. Stanley Dietz, The Story of Old Abe the War Eagle, p. 5.
4. C. P. Nelson, Abe the War Eagle
5. F. A. F., Old Abe, the Eighth Wisconsin War Eagle, p. 25.
6. Richard H. Zeitlin, Old Abe the War Eagle, p. 5.
7. Court-Martial Case File KK 303 Robert C. Murphy, National Archives
8. Ibid.
9. Ibid.
10. Ibid.
11. Ibid.
12. Ibid.
13. Ibid.
14. Ibid.
15. Ibid.

CHAPTER SEVEN

1. Albert Castel (Ed.), "The Diary of General Henry Little, C.S.A.," p.
2. Ezra J. Warner, Generals in Gray, pp. 12-13.
3. Court-Martial Case File KK 303 Robert C. Murphy, National Archives
4. Ibid.
5. Ibid.
6. Ibid.
7. Ibid.
8. Ibid.
9. Ibid.

CHAPTER EIGHT

1. Court-Martial Case File KK 303 Robert C. Murphy, National Archives
2. Ibid.
3. Ibid.
4. Ibid.

5. Ibid.
6. Ibid.
7. Ibid.
8. Ibid.
9. Ibid.
10. Ibid.
11. Ibid.
12. Ibid.
13. Ibid.
14. Ibid.

CHAPTER NINE

1. Court-Martial Case File KK 303 Robert C. Murphy, National Archives
2. Ibid.
3. Ibid.
4. Ibid.
5. Ibid.
6. Ibid.
7. Ibid.
8. Ibid.
9. Ibid.

CHAPTER TEN

1. Edwin C. Bearss, Decision in Mississippi, p. 18.
2. Albert Castel (Ed.), "The Diary of General Henry Little, C.S.A.", p. 46.
3. Homer L. Kerr, Fighting with Ross' Texas Cavalry Brigade C.S.A., p. 42.
4. Samual B. Barron, The Lone Star Defenders, p. 105.
5. Edwin C. Bearss, Decision in Mississippi, p. 20.
6. Ibid., p. 21.
7. Dudley G. Wooten (Ed.), A Comprehensive History of Texas, 1685 to 1897, Vol. II, p. 584.
8. Homer L. Calkin, Elk Horn to Vicksburg, p. 30.
9. Albert Castel (Ed.), "The Diary of General Henry Little, C.S.A.," p. 46.
10. Joseph E. Chance, The Second Texas Infantry, From Shiloh to Vicksburg, p. 56.

11. Court-Martial Case File KK 303 Robert C. Murphy, National Archives
12. Ibid.
13. Samuel B. Barron, The Lone Star Defenders, p. 105.
14. Court-Martial Case File KK 303 Robert C. Murphy, National Archives
15. Homer L. Calkin, Elk Horn to Vicksburg, p. 30.
16. John S. C. Abbott, The History of the Civil War in America, Vol. II, p. 350.
17. Emphraim McD. Anderson, Memoirs: Historical and Personal, p. 218.
18. Official Records, Series I, Vol. XVII, Part I, p. 137.
19. Diary of A. W. Simpson.
20. Willie H. Tunnard, A Southern Record, The Story of the 3rd Louisiana Infantry, p. 182.
21. Homer L. Calkin, Elk Horn to Vicksburg, p. 30.
22. Emphraim McD. Anderson, Memoirs: Historical and Personal, p. 219.
23. Homer L. Calkin, Elk Horn to Vicksburg, p. 30.
24. Dudley G. Wooten (Ed.), A Comprehensive History of Texas, 1685-1897, Vol. II, p. 584.
25. Homer L. Kerr, (Ed.), Fighting with Ross' Texas Cavalry Brigade C.S.A., p. 12.
26. Finley L. Hubbell, The Land We Love, p. 98.
27. Albert Castel (Ed.), "The Diary of General Henry Little, C.S.A.," p. 46.
28. William Lamers, The Edge of Glory, pp. 97-98.
29. Albert Castel (Ed.), "The Diary of General Henry Little, C.S.A.," p. 46.
30. Albert Castel, General Sterling Price and the Civil War in the West, p. 98.
31. Official Records, Series I, Vol. XVII, Part I, p. 121.
32. Capt. G.W.L. Fly, "Before, During, and After the Battle of Iuka"
33. Emphraim McD. Anderson, Memoirs: Historical and Personal, p. 219.
34. J. V. Frederick (Ed.), "War Diary of W. C. Porter," p. 302.
35. Homer L. Calkin, Elk Horn to Vicksburg, p. 30.
36. Finley L. Hubbell, The Land We Love, p. 98.
37. Ibid.

CHAPTER ELEVEN

1. Samuel B. Barron, The Lone Star Defenders, pp. 105-106.
2. Homer L. Calkin, "James H. Fauntleroy's Diary for the Year 1862," p. 30.
3. Homer L. Kerr (Ed.), Fighting with Ross' Texas Cavalry Brigade, C.S.A., p. 42.
4. Finley L. Hubbell, "Diary of Lieut. Col. Hubbell," p. 98.
5. Albert Castel (Ed.), "The Diary of General Henry Little, C.S.A.," p. 46.
6. Edwin C. Bearss, Decision in Mississippi, pp. 23-24.
7. Ibid.
8. Ibid.
9. John Y. Simon (Ed.), The Papers of Ulysses S. Grant, Vol. VI, p. 46.
10. Albert Castel (Ed.), "The Diary of General Henry Little, C.S.A.," p. 46.
11. Edwin C. Bearss, Decision in Mississippi, pp. 24-25.
12. Ibid.
13. Ephraim McD. Anderson, Memoirs: Historical and Personal, p. 220.
14. Edwin C. Bearss, Decision in Mississippi, pp. 25-26.
15. Official Records, Series I, Vol. XVII, Part I, p. 61.
16. Edwin C. Bearss, Decision in Mississippi, p. 25-26.
17. Official Records, Series I, Vol. XVII, Part I, p. 61.
18. Homer L. Kerr (Ed.), Fighting with Ross' Texas Cavalry Brigade, C.S.A., p. 42.
19. Official Records, Series I, Vol. XVII, Part I, p. 61.
20. Ibid., p. 136.
21. Joseph E. Chance, The Second Texas Infantry, From Shiloh to Vicksburg, p. 58.
22. Albert Castel (Ed.), "The Diary of General Henry Little, C.S.A.," p. 46.
23. Edwin C. Bearss, Decision in Mississippi, pp. 26-28.
24. Homer L. Kerr (Ed.), Fighting with Ross' Texas Cavalry Brigade, C.S.A., p. 42.
25. Homer L. Calkin (Ed.), "James H. Fauntleroy's Diary for the Year 1862," p. 31.
26. Albert Castel (Ed.), "The Diary of General Henry Little, C.S.A.," p. 46.
27. Edwin C. Bearss, Decision in Mississippi, p. 28.
28. Diary of Lewis Henry Little
29. Albert Castel (Ed.), "The Diary of General Henry Little, C.S.A.", p. 46.

30. J. V. Frederick (Ed.), "War Diary of W.C. Porter," p. 302.

CHAPTER TWELVE

1. Official Records, Series I, Volume XVII, Part I, p. 65.
2. Edwin C. Bearss, Decision in Mississippi, pp. 29-30.
3. Ibid.
4. Albert Castel (Ed.), "The Diary of General Henry Little, C.S.A.," p. 46.
5. Homer L. Kerr (Ed.), Fighting with Ross' Texas Cavalry Brigade, C.S.A., p. 42.
6. Homer L. Calkin (Ed.), "James H. Fauntleroy's Diary for the Year 1862," p. 31.
7. Albert Castel (Ed.), "The Diary of General Henry Little, C.S.A.," p. 46.
8. Ephraim McD. Anderson, Memoirs: Historical and Personal, pp. 220-221.
9. Ibid.
10. Albert Castel, General Sterling Price and the Civil War in the West, p. 100.
11. Official Records, Series I, Volume XVII, Part II p. 708.
12. Ibid., p. 707.
13. Ibid.
14. John Y. Simon (Ed.), The Papers of Ulysses S. Grant, Vol. 6, p. 66.
15. Albert Castel, General Sterling Price and the Civil War in the West, pp. 100-101.
16. R.S. Bevier, History of the First and Second Missouri Confederate Brigades, 1861-1865, p. 129.
17. Albert Castel, "The Diary of General Henry Little, C.S.A.," p. 46.

CHAPTER THIRTEEN

1. Shelby Foote, The Civil War, A Narrative, Fort Sumter to Perryville, p. 716.
2. Ibid., pp. 117-118.
3. Edwin C. Bearss, Decision in Mississippi, p. 29.
4. Official Records, Series I, Volume XVII, Part I, p. 66.
5. Ibid.
6. U. S. Grant, Personal Memoirs of U. S. Grant, p. 212.
7. Ibid.
8. Edwin C. Bearss, Decision in Mississippi, pp. 29-30.

9. <u>Official Records</u>, Series I, Volume XVII, Part I, p. 67.
10. John Y. Simon (Ed.), <u>The Papers of Ulysses S. Grant</u>, pp. 172-173.
11. C. S. Hamilton, "The Battle of Iuka," p. 734.
12. <u>Official Records</u>, Series I, Volume XVII, Part I, p. 72.
13. John Y. Simon (Ed.), <u>The Papers of Ulysses S. Grant</u>, p. 69.
14. Edwin C. Bearss, <u>Decision in Mississippi</u>, p. 32.
15. <u>Ibid</u>.
16. <u>Official Records</u>, Series I, Volume XVII, Part I, p. 118.
17. <u>Ibid</u>.
18. Bernarr Cresap, <u>Appomattox Commander</u>, p. 85.

CHAPTER FOURTEEN

1. <u>Official Records</u>, Series I, Volume XVII, Part I, p. 116.
2. Alonzo L. Brown, <u>History of the Fourth Regiment of Minnesota Infantry Volunteers During the Great Rebellion, 1861-1865</u>, p. 80.
3. <u>Ibid</u>., p. 35.
4. Edwin C. Bearss, <u>Decision in Mississippi</u>, p. 34.
5. <u>Ibid</u>., p. 35.
6. John Y. Simon (Ed.), <u>The Papers of Ulysses S. Grant</u>, pp. 172-173.
7. <u>Official Records</u>, Series I, Volume XVII, Part I, p. 119.

CHAPTER FIFTEEN

1. <u>Official Records</u>, Series I, Volume XVII, Part I, p. 116.
2. Oscar L. Jackson, <u>The Colonel's Diary</u>, p. 65.
3. <u>Ibid</u>.
4. <u>Official Records</u>, Series I, Volume XVII, Part I, p. 116.
5. John Y. Simon (Ed.), <u>The Papers of Ulysses S. Grant</u>, Vol. 6, p. 72.
6. Ezra J. Warner, <u>Generals in Blue</u>, p. 199.
7. Edwin C. Bearss, <u>Decision in Mississippi</u>, p. 36.
8. W. Dudley, <u>The Battle of Iuka</u>, p. 4.
9. Alonzo L. Brown, <u>History of the Fourth Regiment of Minnesota Infantry Volunteers During the Great Rebellion 1861-1865</u>, p. 81.

CHAPTER SIXTEEN

1. Alonzo L. Brown, <u>History of the Fourth Regiment of Minnesota Infantry During the Great Rebellion, 1861-1865</u>, p. 82.
2. W. Dudley, <u>The Battle of Iuka</u>, p. 6.
3. <u>Ibid</u>., p. 5.

4. Alonzo L. Brown, History of the Fourth Regiment of Minnesota Infantry Volunteers During the Great Rebellion,1861-1865, p. 82·

5. Ibid., p. 83·

6. Ibid.

7. Edwin C. Bearss, Decision in Mississippi, p. 37·

CHAPTER SEVENTEEN

1. W. Dudley, The Battle of Iuka, p. 3·

2. Autrey W. Mangum, Down Memory Lane, p. 160·

3. Ephraim McD. Anderson, Memoirs: Historical and Personal, p. 221.

4. Willie H. Tunnard, A Southern Record, p. 182·

5. Samuel B. Barron, The Lone Star Defenders, p. 106·

6. Ibid., p. 101-102·

7. Edwin C. Bearss, Decision in Mississippi, pp. 40-41.

8. W. Dudley, The Battle of Iuka, p. 4-5.

9. Ibid., p. 5·

10. The Iuka Vidette, May 20,1909.

11. S. M. Singletary, "37th Alabama in Battle of Iuka,"Weekly Enterprise, May 8, 1902.

12. C. S. Hamilton, "The Battle of Iuka," pp. 734-736.

13. Edwin C. Bearss, Decision in Mississippi, p. 41·

14. Victor M. Rose, Ross' Texas Brigade, p. 70·

15. Samuel B. Barron, The Lone Star Defenders, p. 26-27·

16. Alonzo L. Brown, History of the Fourth Regiment of Minnesota Infantry Volunteers During the Great Rebellion,1861-1865, p. 86·

17. Willie H. Tunnard, A Southern Record, pp. 184-185·

18. Ibid.

19. Edwin C. Bearss, Decision in Mississippi, p. 41·

20. Alonzo L. Brown, History of the Fourth Regiment of Minnesota Infantry Volunteers During the Great Rebellion, 1861-1865, p. 82·

21. Official Records, Series I, Volume XVII, Part I, p. 90·

22. Ibid., p.94.

23. S.M. Singletary, "37th Alabama in Battle of Iuka," Weekly Enterprise, May 8, 1902.

24. Henry M. Neil, A Battery at Close Quarters, pp. 6-7·

25. Edwin C. Bearss, Decision in Mississippi, p. 42·

26. Ibid.

27. Henry M. Neil, A Battery at Close Quarters, pp. 8-15·

28. Official Records, Series I, Volume XVII, Part I, pp. 94-95·

29. Ibid.
30. William M. Lamers, The Edge of Glory, p. 111.
31. Henry M. Neil, A Battery at Close Quarters, pp. 7-8.
32. William M. Lamers, The Edge of Glory, p. 110.
33. Confederate Veteran, Vol. 19, 1911
34. Ibid.
35. William M. Lamers, The Edge of Glory, p. 111.
36. Official Records, Series I, Volume XVII, Part I, p. 73.
37. Willie H. Tunnard, A Southern Record, p. 447.
38. Official Records, Series I, Volume XVII, Part I, p. 73.
39. Alonzo L. Brown, History of the Fourth Regiment of Minnesota Infantry Volunteers During the Great Rebellion, 1861-1865, p. 99.
40. Ibid.
41. Ibid., pp. 99-100.

CHAPTER EIGHTEEN

1. Willie H. Tunnard, A Southern Record, pp. 184-185.
2. Henry M. Neil, A Battery at Close Quarters, p. 8.
3. Victor M. Rose, Ross' Texas Brigade, p. 70.
4. Samuel B. Barron, The Lone Star Defenders, p. 107.
5. Edwin C. Bearss, Decision in Mississippi, p. 43.
6. Victor M. Rose, Ross' Texas Brigade, p. 71.
7. Willie H. Tunnard, A Southern Record, pp. 184-185.
8. Ibid.
9. Confederate Veteran, Vol. 19, 1911
10. C. S. Hamilton, "The Battle of Iuka," p. 735.

CHAPTER NINETEEN

1. Albert Castel (Ed.), "The Diary of General Henry Little, C.S.A.," p. 5
2. Ezra J. Warner, Generals in Gray, pp. 188-189.
3. Thomas L. Snead, "With Price East of the Mississippi", p. 733.
4. Official Records, Series I, Vol. XVII, Part II, p. 684.
5. Victor M. Rose, Ross' Texas Brigade, p. 70.
6. Picayune, New Orleans, Louisiana, August 11, 1901
7. Albert Castel (Ed.), "The Diary of General Henry Little, C.S.A.", p. 46.
8. Picayune, New Orleans, Louisiana, August 11, 1901
9. Victor M. Rose, Ross' Texas Brigade, p. 70.

10. W. Dudley, <u>The Battle of Iuka</u>, pp. 6-7.
11. Albert Castel, <u>General Sterling Price and the Civil War in the West</u>, p. 102.
12. Victor M. Rose, <u>Ross' Texas Brigade</u>, p. 70.
13. Albert Castel, <u>General Sterling Price and the Civil War in the West</u>, p. 102.
14. Albert Castel (Ed.), "The Diary of General Henry Little, C.S.A," p. 46.
15. <u>Official Records</u>, Series I, Volume XVII, Part I, p. 125.
16. <u>Ibid.</u>, pp. 123-124.
17. R. S. Bevier, <u>History of the First and Second Missouri Confederate Brigades</u>, 1861-1865, p. 136.

CHAPTER TWENTY

1. Alonzo L. Brown, <u>History of the Fourth Regiment of Minnesota Infantry Volunteers During the Great Rebellion, 1861-1865</u>, p. 85.
2. <u>Official Records</u>, Series I, Volume XVII, Part I, p. 97.
3. Alonzo L. Brown, <u>History of the Fourth Regiment of Minnesota Infantry Volunteers During the Great Rebellion, 1861-1865</u>, pp. 87-89.
4. Edwin C. Bearss, <u>Decision in Mississippi</u>, pp. 44-45.
5. <u>Official Records</u>, Series I, Volume XVII, Part I, p. 98.
6. Alonzo L. Brown, <u>History of the Fourth Regiment of Minnesota Infantry Volunteers During the Great Rebellion, 1861-1865</u>, p. 89.
7. Edwin C. Bearss, <u>Decision in Mississippi</u>, pp. 44-45.
8. <u>Ibid.</u>
9. Alonzo L. Brown, <u>History of the Fourth Regiment of Minnesota Infantry Volunteers During the Great Rebellion, 1861-1865</u>, p.88.
10. C.S. Hamilton, "The Battle of Iuka", p. 735.
11. Edwin C. Bearss, <u>Decision in Mississippi</u>, p.46.
12. Henry M. Neil, <u>A Battery at Close Quarters</u>, pp. 9-11.
13. <u>Official Records</u>, Series I, Volume XVII, Part I, p. 99.
14. <u>Ibid.</u>
15. <u>Ibid.</u>, pp. 102-103.
16. Edwin C. Bearss, Decision in Mississippi, p. 46.
17. <u>Ibid.</u>
18. W. Dudley, The Battle of Iuka, pp. 15-16.
19. M. Amelia Stone, <u>Memoir of George Boardman Boomer</u>, pp. 236-237.

20. <u>Official Records,</u> Series I, Volume XVII, Part I, p. 108.
21. <u>Ibid.</u>, p. 134.
22. <u>Ibid.</u>, p. 108.
23. <u>Ibid.</u>, p. 109.
24. <u>Ibid.</u>, p. 135.
25. <u>Ibid.</u>, p. 109.
26. Alonzo L. Brown, <u>History of the Fourth Regiment of Minnesota Infantry Volunteers During the Great Rebellion,</u>1861-1865, p. 95.
27. <u>Official Records</u>, Series I, Volume XVII, Part I, pp. 100-101.
28. Alonzo L. Brown, <u>History of the Fourth Regiment of Minnesota Infantry Volunteers During the Great Rebellion,</u>1861-1865, pp. 85-88.
29. <u>Ibid.</u>, p. 87.
30. <u>Ibid.</u>
31. <u>Ibid.</u>, p. 90.
32. <u>Ibid.</u>, pp. 90-91.
33. <u>Ibid.</u>, p. 93.
34. <u>Ibid.</u>, pp. 93-94.
35. <u>Ibid.</u>, p. 95.
36. <u>Ibid.</u>
37. Edwin C. Bearss, <u>Decision in Mississippi,</u> pp. 49-50.
38. <u>Official Records</u>, Series I, Volume XVII, Part I, p. 112.
39. <u>Ibid.</u>, pp. 112-113.
40. <u>Official Records</u>, Series I, Volume XVII, Part I, pp. 109-110.
41. <u>Ibid.</u>, p. 110.
42. Edwin C. Bearss, <u>Decision in Mississippi,</u> pp. 49-50.
43. <u>Ibid.</u>

CHAPTER TWENTY-ONE

1. Henry M. Neil, <u>A Battery at Close Quarters</u>, pp. 8-9.
2. W. Dudley, <u>The Battle of Iuka</u>, p. 9.
3. Samuel B. Barron, <u>The Lone Star Defenders</u>, p. 107.
4. Edwin C. Bearss, <u>Decision in Mississippi</u>, p.48.
5. W. Dudley, <u>The Battle of Iuka</u>, p. 16.
6. Henry M. Neil, <u>A Battery at Close Quarters</u>, p. 12.
7. <u>Ibid.</u>, p. 10.
8. <u>Ibid.</u>, p. 12.
9. Willie H. Tunnard, <u>A Southern Record</u>, pp. 183-185.
10. Edwin C. Bearss, <u>Decision in Mississippi</u>, p. 48.
11. Henry M. Neil, <u>A Battery at Close Quarters</u>, p. 12.

12. Ibid., p. 13.
13. Ibid., pp. 13-14.
14. Ibid.
15. Ibid., pp. 14-15.
16. Alonzo L. Brown, History of the Fourth Regiment of Minnesota Infantry Volunteers During the Great Rebellion, 1861-1865, p. 100.
17. Ibid., pp. 100-101.

CHAPTER TWENTY-TWO

1. Official Records, Series I, Volume XVII, Part I, p. 132.
2. Richard H. Zeitlin, Old Abe the War Eagle, p. 20.
3. Official Records, Series I, Volume XVII, Part I, p. 88. (This is probably an error. The soldier probably said, "You are firing into the Thirty-sixth Mississippi!"
4. Ibid., p. 132.
5. Gerald T. Golden, "Friends of the 37th Alabama Infantry," November 8, 1986, p. 2.
6. Ibid.
7. Ibid.
8. Ibid.
9. Ibid.
10. Official Records, Series I, Volume XVII, Part I, p. 132.
11. Ibid., pp. 81-82.
12. J. H. Greene, Reminiscences of the War, p. 29.
13. Official Records, Series I, Volume XVII, Part I, pp. 82-83.
14. Oscar L. Jackson, The Colonel's Diary, p. 63.
15. Ibid.
16. Edwin C. Bearss, Decision in Mississippi, pp. 52-54.
17. Carrol H. Quenzel, "Johnny Bull-Billy Yank," p. 124.

CHAPTER TWENTY-THREE

1. Edwin C. Bearss, Decision in Mississippi, pp. 53-54.
2. Ibid., p. 54.
3. Willie H. Tunnard, A Southern Record, pp. 183-185.
4. Official Records, Series I, Volume XVII, Part I, p. 125.
5. Edwin C. Bearss, Decision in Mississippi, p. 54.
6. Ephraim McD. Anderson, Memoirs: Historical and Personal, p. 223.
7. Samuel B. Barron, The Lone Star Defenders, p. 108.
8. Finley L. Hubbell, "Diary of Lieut. Col. Hubbell," p. 99.

9. Ephraim McD. Anderson, Memoirs: Historical and Personal, pp. 223-224

10. C. S. Hamilton, "The Battle of Iuka," p. 735.

11. Finley L. Hubbell, "Diary of Lieut. Col. Hubbell," p. 99.

12. Official Records, Series I, Volume XVII, Part I, p. 74.

13. Alonzo L. Brown, History of the Fourth Regiment of Minnesota Infantry Volunteers During the Great Rebellion, 1861-1865, pp. 95-96.

14. Ephraim McD. Anderson, Memoirs: Historical and Personal, pp. 223-224.

15. Ibid.

16. Oscar L. Jackson, The Colonel's Diary, p. 64.

17. Ephraim McD. Anderson, Memoirs: Historical and Personal, pp. 224-225.

18. Ibid.

19. W. Dudley, The Battle of Iuka, p. 12.

20. Finley L. Hubbell, "Diary of Lieut. Col. Hubbell," p. 99.

21. Homer L. Calkin (Ed.), "James H. Fauntleroy's Diary for the Year 1862," p. 31.

22. Confederate Veteran, Vol. 19, 1911

23. J. H. Greene, Reminiscences of the War, p. 30.

24. S. M. Singletary, "37th Alabama in Battle of Iuka", Weekly Enterprise, May 8, 1902

25. Oscar L. Jackson, The Colonel's Diary, pp. 64-65.

26. J. H. Greene, Reminiscences of the War, p. 29.

27. Cloyd Bryner, Bugle Echoes, The Story of the Illinois 47th, pp. 81-82.

28. Official Records, Series I, Volume XVII, Part I, p. 74.

29. Edwin C. Bearss, Decision in Mississippi, pp. 56-57.

30. John Y. Simon (Ed.), The Papers of Ulysses S. Grant, Vol. 6, p. 69.

31. Rossiter Johnson, Campfires and Battlegrounds, pp. 177-178.

32. Ibid., p. 205.

33. Ibid.

34. William M. Lamers, The Edge of Glory, p. 119.

35. Ibid.

36. Official Records, Series I, Volume XVII, Part I, p. 119.

37. William M. Lamers, The Edge of Glory, pp. 119-120.

38. W. Dudley, The Battle of Iuka, p. 11.

39. John Y. Simon (Ed.), The Papers of Ulysses S. Grant, Vol. 6, p. 87.

40. William M. Lamers, The Edge of Glory, pp. 120-121.

CHAPTER TWENTY-FOUR

1. Thomas L. Snead, "With Price East of the Mississippi," p. 733.
2. Picayune, New Orleans, Louisiana, August 11, 1901.
3. W. Dudley, The Battle of Iuka, p. 16.
4. Albert Castel (Ed.), "The Diary of General Henry Little," p. 46.
5. Ezra J. Warner, Generals in Gray, p. 189.
6. Gerald T. Golden, "Friends of the 37th Alabama Infantry," November 8, 1986
7. Thomas Yoseloff, Confederate Military History, Vol. IX, p. 89.

CHAPTER TWENTY-FIVE

1. Thomas L. Snead, "With Price East of the Mississippi," p. 733.
2. Ibid.
3. Albert Castel, General Sterling Price and the Civil War in the West, p. 103.
4. Ibid.
5. R. S. Bevier, History of the First and Second Missouri Confederate Brigades, 1861-1865, p. 132.
6. Official Records, Series I, Volume XVII, Part I, p. 122.
7. Edwin C. Bearss, Decision in Mississippi, p. 55.
8. Ibid., p. 137
9. William M. Lamers, The Edge of Glory, pp. 113-114.
10. John Y. Simon (Ed.), The Papers of Ulysses S. Grant, Vol. 6, p. 72.
11. Samuel B. Barron, The Lone Star Defenders, p.109.
12. Official Records, Series I, Volume XVII, Part I, p. 81.
13. S. M. Singletary, "37th Alabama in Battle of Iuka," Weekly Enterprise, May 8, 1902
14. Ephraim McD. Anderson, Memoirs: Historical and Personal, p. 225.
15. Autery W. Mangum, Down Memory Lane, A History of Iuka, Mississippi, 1915-1983, p. 161.
16. Joseph E. Chance, The Second Texas Texas Infantry, From Shiloh to Vicksburg, p. 60.
17. Official Records, Series I, Volume XVII, Part I, p. 137.
18. Edwin C. Bearss, Decision in Mississippi, p. 55.
19. Lyla M. McDonald, Iuka's History, p. 19.
20. Irene Barnes, Eastport, Echoes of the Past, p. 79.

21. Official Records, Series I, Volume XVII, Part I, p. 83.
22. Edwin C. Bearss, Decision in Mississippi, p. 57.
23. Ibid., p. 58.
24. Official Records, Series I, Volume XVII, Part I, p. 70.
25. Ibid.
26. Ibid., p. 67.
27. Edwin C. Bearss, Decision in Mississippi, p. 58.
28. J. H. Greene, Reminiscences of the War, p. 30.
29. Official Reports, Series I, Volume XVII, Part I, p. 68.
30. William M. Lamers, The Edge of Glory, p. 110.
31. Adam Badeau, Military History of Ulysses S. Grant, Vol. I, pp. 114-115.
32. Edwin C. Bearss, Decision in Mississippi, p. 58.
33. Official Records, Series I, Volume XVII, Part I, pp. 70-71.
34. Ibid., p. 71.
35. William M. Lamers, The Edge of Glory, pp. 115-116.
36. Albert Castel, General Sterling Price and the Civil War in the West, p. 103.

CHAPTER TWENTY-SIX

1. Official Records, Series I, Volume XVII, Part I, p. 79.
2. Ibid
3. Alonzo L. Brown, History of the Fourth Regiment of Minnesota Infantry Volunteers During the Great Rebellion 1861-1865, pg. 98.
4. W. Dudley, The Battle of Iuka, p. 15.
5. William M. Lamers, The Edge of Glory, p. 113.
6. Albert Castel, General Sterling Price and the Civil War in the West, pp. 103-104.
7. Official Records, Series I, Volume XVII, Part I, p. 74.
8. Ibid., p. 72.
9. Ibid., p. 79.
10. Samuel B. Barron, The Lone Star Defenders, pp. 111-113.
11. Ibid., pp. 111-113.
12. Ibid.
13. Ibid., pp. 113-114.
14. Ibid., pp. 114-115.
15. Ibid.

CHAPTER TWENTY-SEVEN

1. Edwin C. Bearss, Decision in Mississippi, p. 58.

2. Ibid.
3. Willie H. Tunnard, A Southern Record, pp. 187-188.
4. Jospeh E. Chance, The Second Texas Infantry, From Shiloh to Vicksburg, p. 60.
5. Edwin C. Bearss, Decision in Mississippi, p. 59.
6. Joseph C. Chance, The Second Texas Infantry, From Shiloh to Vicksburg, p. 60.
7. Ibid.
8. Edwin C. Bearss, Decision in Mississippi, p. 59.
9. Ibid.
10. Official Reports, Series I, Volume XVII, Part I, p. 140.
11. Ibid., p. 137.
12. Dudley G. Wooten (Ed.), A Comprehensive History of Texas, 1685-1897, Vol. II, p. 585.
13. Harold Simpson and Marcus Wright, Texas in the War, 1861-1865, p. 99.
14. Jospeh C. Chance, The Second Texas Infantry, From Shiloh to Vicksburg, p. 62.
15. C. S. Hamilton, "The Battle of Iuka" p. 736.
16. Finley L. Hubbell, "Diary of Lieut. Col. Hubbell", p. 99.
17. John S. C. Abbott, The History of the Civil War in America, Vol. II, pp. 351-352.

CHAPTER TWENTY-EIGHT

1. Alonzo L. Brown, History of the Fourth Regiment of Minnesota Infantry Volunteers During the Great Rebellion, 1861-1865, p. 96
2. Ibid., pp. 96-97.
3. Oscar Lawrence Jackson, The Colonel's Diary, p. 65.
4. Lyla M. McDonald, Iuka's History, p. 21.
5. Oscar Lawrence Jackson, The Colonel's Diary, p. 65.
6. Cyrus Boyd, The Civil War Diary of Cyrus Boyd, p. 106.
7. Samuel B. Barron, The Lone Star Defenders, p. 108.
8. Oscar Lawrence Jackson, The Colonel's Diary, p. 65.
9. Ibid., p. 66.
10. Ibid., p. 65.
11. Confederate Veteran, Vol. II, 1903.

CHAPTER TWENTY-NINE

1. John Y. Simon, <u>The Papers of Ulysses S. Grant</u>, Vol. 6, p. 38
2. <u>Ibid.</u>, p. 177
3. <u>Ibid.</u>
4. Court-Martial Case File KK 303 Robert C. Murphy, National Archives
5. <u>Ibid.</u>
6. John M. Williams, <u>The Eagle Regiment, 8th Wisconsin Infantry Volunteers</u>, pp. 103-104
7. <u>Ibid.</u>

APPENDIX

1. Consolidated Report of Casualties on the 19th at Iuka in the 2nd Brigade, 1st Division, Army of the West , Confederates States Army Casualties, Lists and Narrative Reports, 1861-1865, National Archives (microfilm)
2. Official Records, Series I, Volume XVII, Part I, p. 127.
3. Ibid., p. 133.
4. Ibid.
5. Ibid., p.126.
6. Ibid., p. 74 .
7. Ibid., p. 80,
8. Ibid.
9. Ibid., p. 77-78.
10. Rossiter Johnson, Campfires and Battlefields, A Pictorial Narrative of the Civil War, pp. 205-206.
11. Stephen E. Ambrose (Ed.), A Wisconsin Boy in Dixie, The Selected Letters of James K. Newton, pp. 33-35.
12. George C. Osborn (Ed.), "The Civil War Letters of Robert W. Banks", Journal of Mississippi History, Vol. V, pp. 143-145.
13. Max Lale and Hobart Key, Jr. (Eds.), The Civil War Letters of David R. Garrett, pp. 65-66.
14. Glover, N. F. , An unpublished letter probably written from Baldwyn, Mississippi possessed by Dr. Gerald T. Golden, 202 Foxcroft Avenue, Martinsburg, West Virginia.
15. C. S. Hamilton, "The Battle of Iuka", p. 736.

BIBLIOGRAPHY
BOOKS

1. Abbott, John S. C., The History of the Civil War in America, Gurdon Bill, Springfield, Mass., 1866.
2. Ambrose, Stephen E. (Ed.), A Wisconsin Boy in Dixie, The Selected Letters of James K. Newton, The Univ. of Wisconsin Press, Madison, 1961.
3. Anderson, Ephraim McD., Memoirs: Historical and Personal; Including the Campaigns of the First Missouri Confederate Brigade, St. Louis, 1868.
4. Barnes, Irene, Eastport, Echoes of the Past, Iuka, Mississippi, 1983
5. Barrett, J. O. , Old Abe, The Live War-Eagle of Wisconsin, Atwood and Culver, Madison, Wisconsin, 1876.
6. Barron, Samuel B., The Lone Star Defenders, Zenger Publishing

Co., Washington, D. C., 1908.

7. Bearss, Edwin C., <u>Decision in Mississippi, Mississippi's Important Role in the War Between the States</u>, Mississippi Commission on the War Between the States, Jackson, Mississippi, 1962

8. Bevier, R. S., <u>History of the First and Second Missouri Confederate Brigades, 1861-1865</u>, **Bryan,** Brand and Company, St. Louis, 1879

9. <u>Biographical and Historical Memoirs of Mississippi</u>, The Goodspeed Publishing Company, 1891.

10. Boyd, Cyrus, <u>The Civil War Diary of Cyrus Boyd</u> (Ed. by Mildred Throne), Iowa City, Iowa, 1953

11. Brown, Alonzo L., <u>History of the Fourth Regiment of Minnesota Infantry Volunteers During the Great Rebellion, 1861-1865</u>, The Prisoner Press Co., St. Paul, Minnesota, 1892

12. Bryner, Cloyd, <u>Bugle Echoes, The Story of the Illinois 47th</u>, Phillips Bros., Springfield, Ill., 1905

13. Castel, Albert, General <u>Sterling Price and the Civil War in the West</u>, Louisiana State University Press, Baton Rouge, 1968

14. Chance, Joseph E., <u>The Second Texas Infantry, From Shiloh to Vicksburg</u>, Eakin Press, Austin, Texas, 1984

15. Cresap, Bernarr, <u>Appomattox Commander, The Story of General E. O. C. Ord</u>, A. S. Barnes & Company, Inc., San Diego, 1981

16. Dietz, J. Stanley, <u>The Story of Old Abe the War Eagle</u>, Madison, Wisconsin, 1946

17. Dudley, W., <u>The Battle of Iuka</u>, Iuka, Miss., 1896

18. F. A. F., <u>Old Abe, the Eighth Wisconsin War Eagle</u>, Curran and Bowen, Madison, Wis., 1885

19. Foote, Shelby, <u>The Civil War, A Narrative, Fort Sumter to Perryville</u>, Random House, N.Y., 1958

20. Gentry, Claude, <u>The Battle of Corinth</u>, Magnolia Publishers, Baldwyn, Mississippi, 1976

21. Grant, U. S., <u>Personal Memoirs of U. S. Grant</u>, The World Publishing Company, Cleveland and New York, 1952

22. Greene, J. H., <u>Reminiscences of the War, Bivouacs, Marches, Skirmishes and Battles</u>, Gazette Print, Medina, Ohio, 1886

23. Hamilton, C. S., "The Battle of Iuka," <u>Battles and Leaders of the Civil War</u>, Volume II, The Century Company, N.Y., 1884

24. Hartje, Robert G., <u>Van Dorn, The Life and Times of a Confederate General</u>, Vanderbilt University Press, 1967

25. Johnson, Rossiter, <u>Campfires and Battlefields, A Pictorial Narrative of the Civil War</u>, The Civil War Press, N.Y. 1967.

26. Kerr, Homer L. (Ed.), Fighting with Ross' Texas Cavalry Brigade C.S.A., The Diary of George L. Griscom, Adjutant, 9th Texas Cavalry Regiment, Hill Jr. College Press, Hillsboro, Texas, 1976.

27. Kitchens, Ben E., Gunboats and Cavalry, A History of Eastport, Mississippi, Thornwood Book Publishers, Florence, Alabama, 1985

28. Jackson, Oscar Lawrence, The Colonel's Diary, Sharon, Penn., 1922

29. Jones, Archer, Confederate Strategy from Shiloh to Vicksburg, Louisiana State University Press, Baton Rouge, 1961

30. Lamers, William M., The Edge of Glory, A Biography of General William S. Rosecrans, U.S.A., Harcourt, Brace & World Inc., New York, 1961

31. Lane, Max S. and Key, Hobart Jr. (Eds.), The Civil War Letters of David R. Garrett, Detailing the Adventures of the 6th Texas Cavalry, 1861-1865, Port Caddo Press, Marshall, Texas, 1963

32. McDonald, Lyla M., Iuka's History, Corinth, Mississippi, 1923

33. Mangum, Autery William, Down Memory Lane, A History of Iuka, Mississippi, 1915-1983, Iuka 1983

34. Neil, Henry M., A Battery at Close Quarters, Columbus, Ohio, 1909

35. Nelson, C. P., Abe, The War Eagle, Lynn, Mass., 1903

36. Rose, Victor M., Ross' Texas Brigade, Louisville, Ky., 1881

37. Shalhope, Robert E., Sterling Price, Portrait of a Southerner, University of Missouri Press, Columbia, Missouri, 1971

38. Simon, John Y. (Ed.), The Papers of Ulysses S. Grant, Southern Illinois University Press, Carbondale and Edwardsville, 1977

39. Simpson, Harold B. and Wright, Marcus J., Texas in the War, 1861-1865, The Hill Junior College Press, Hillsboro, Texas, 1965

40. Smith, William E. and Smith, Ophia D., Colonel A. W. Gilbert, Citizen-Soldier of Cincinnati, Historical and Philosophical Society of Ohio, Cincinnati, 1934

41. Snead, Thomas L., "With Price East of the Mississippi", Battles and Leaders of the Civil War, Volume II, The Century Company, N.Y., 1884

42. Stone, M. Amelia, Memoir of George Boardman Boomer, Rand and Avery, Boston, 1864

43. Tunnard, Willie H., A Southern Record, The Story of the 3rd Louisiana Infantry, Baton Rouge, La., 1866

44. Warner, Ezra J., Generals in Blue, Lives of the Union Commanders, Louisiana State University Press, Baton Rouge, 1964

45. Warner, Ezra J., <u>Generals in Gray, Lives of the Confederate Commanders</u>, Louisiana State University Press, Baton Rouge, 1959

46. Watson, William, <u>Life in the Confederate Army</u>, Chapman and Hall, London, 1887

47. Wooten, Dudley G. (Ed.), <u>A Comprehensive History of Texas, 1685-1897</u>, William G. Scarff, Dallas, 1898

48. Yoseloff, Thomas, <u>Confederate Military History</u>, Thomas Yoseloff Publishers, New York, 1962

49. Young, Patrick, <u>Old Abe the Eagle Hero</u>, Prentice, Hall, Inc., Englewood Cliffs, N.J., 1965

50. Zeitlin, Richard H., <u>Old Abe the War Eagle, A True Story of the Civil War and Reconstruction</u>, The State Historical Society of Wisconsin, Madison, 1986

NEWSPAPERS

1. <u>Badger Bulletin</u>, Iuka, Mississippi, June 14, 1862
2. <u>Commerical</u>, Cincinnati, Ohio, September 29, 1862
3. <u>Picayune</u>, New Orleans, Louisiana, August 11, 1901
4. <u>The Commerical Appeal</u>, Memphis, Tennessee, July 7, 1953
5. <u>The Iuka Vidette</u>, Iuka, Mississippi, May 20, 1909
6. <u>The Liberty Weekly Tribune</u>, Liberty Missouri, January 25, 1866
7. <u>The New York Tribune</u>, New York, September 26 & 27, 1862
8. <u>Weekly Enterprise</u>, Enterprise, Alabama, May 8, 1902

PERIODICALS

1. Calkin, Homer L. (Ed.), "James H. Fauntleroy's Diary for the Year 1862", <u>Civil War History</u>, Vol. II, (1956)

2. Castel, Albert (Ed.), "The Diary of General Henry Little, C.S.A.", <u>Civil War Times Illustrated</u>, October, 1972

3. Confederate Veteran, Vols. 1, 11, & 19

4. Frederick, J. V. (Ed.), "War Diary of W. C. Porter," <u>Arkansas Historical Quarterly</u>, Vol. XI

5. Golden, Gerald T., "Friends of the 37th Alabama Infantry", Martinsburg, West Virginia, November 8, 1986

6. Gunn, Jack W., "The Battle of Iuka", <u>Journal of Mississippi History</u>, Vol. XXIV (1962) pp. 142-157

7. Hubbell, Finley L., "Diary of Lieut. Col. Hubbell, of 3rd Regiment Missouri Infantry, C.S.A.," <u>Land We Love</u>, Vol. VI, Charlotte, N.C., 1868

8. Osborn, George C. (Ed.), "The Civil War Letters of Robert W. Banks", Journal of Mississippi History, Vol. V, Jackson, Mississippi, 1943

9. Quenzel, Carrol H., "Johnny Bull-Billy Yank", Tennessee Historical Quarterly, XIV (1955) 124

UNPUBLISHED SOURCES

1. Bullard, Rickey H., "Civil War Medical Treatment," Tupelo, Mississippi (unpublished article)

2. Consolidated Report of Casualties on the 19th at Iuka in the 2nd Brigade, 1st Division, Army of the West, Confederate States Army Casualties, Lists and Narrative Reports, 1861-1865, National Archives (microfilm)

3. Court-Martial Case File KK 303 Robert C. Murphy, National Archives (microfilm)

4. Diary of A. W. Simpson, Sentinel Prairie, Polk County, Missouri, Mississippi Department of Archives and History, Jackson, Mississippi

5. Diary of Lewis Henry Little, Civil War Times Illustrated Collection. These papers are in the Archives, U.S. Army Military History Institute, Carlisle Barracks, Pennsylvania

6. Fly, Capt. G.W.L., "Before, During and After the Battle of Iuka," Unpublished manuscript in possession of his grandson, Dr. W. Lamer Fly of Cuero, Texas

7. Glover, N. F., Letter to William Glover, September 25, 1862. This letter is possessed by Dr. Gerald T. Golden, 202 Foxcroft Avenue, Martinsburg, West Virginia

8. McKinney, David, "Diary of David McKinney," Civil War Times Illustrated Collection. These papers are in the Archives, U.S. Army Military History Institute, Carlisle Barracks, Pennsylvania

9. Smith, Ohira V., "Personal Memoirs of O. V. Smith", April, 1902, Joint Collection University of Missouri Western Historical Manuscript Collection - Columbia and State Historical Society of Missouri Manuscripts

ADDENDUM TO BIBLIOGRAPHY

1. Burdette, Robert J., <u>The Drums of the 47th</u>, The Bobbs-Merrill Company, Indianapolis, 1914.
2. Byers, Major S. H. M., <u>With Fire and Sword</u>. The Neale Publishing Company, New York, 1911.
3. Smith Albert E., "A Few Days with the Eighth Regiment, Wisconsin Volunteers at Iuka and Corinth, " <u>Mollus-Wisconsin</u> IV, pp. 61-67
4. Williams, John M., <u>The Eagle Regiment, 8th Wisconsin Infantry Volunteers</u>, Recorder Print, Belleville, Wisconsin, 1890

INDEX

231